Melanesian Pidgin and the Oceanic Substrate

 Melanesian Pidgin and the
Oceanic Substrate

ROGER M. KEESING

STANFORD UNIVERSITY PRESS
Stanford, California

Stanford University Press
© 1988 by the Board of Trustees of the
Leland Stanford Junior University

Printed in the United States of America

Published with the assistance of
The Australian National University

CIP data appear at the end of the book

Preface

This is a book no one could write. With the proliferation of linguistic and psycholinguistic theories regarding pidgins and creoles, the increasing engagement of formal syntactic theory with pidginization and creolization, and the expanding view of universal linguistic structures, constraints, and faculties, one would at least have to be a first-rate formal linguist to walk confidently down the path I have followed. Being an anthropologist, and not a linguist at all, I was perhaps led to wander down this path because of my innocence of such specialized knowledge. But being a high-powered linguist would not in itself be enough: I argue that one would also have to be a specialist in the comparative grammar of a particular set of Oceanic Austronesian languages to see some of the patterns I will set out in this work. Indeed, high-powered linguists who have looked at Melanesian Pidgin from afar have in my view sometimes erred precisely because they did not know enough about Oceanic Austronesian languages, most of which are spoken across a vast zone hundreds of miles from New Guinea (the main center of Melanesian Pidgin in terms of the number of speakers and the centrality of that language in contemporary national life).

One would also, I suggest, ideally be fluent in one or several of these Oceanic Austronesian languages, in an area where a dialect of Melanesian Pidgin is spoken (i.e., in Vanuatu or the Solomon Islands), have studied in some detail how speakers of Oceanic Austronesian languages actually use Melanesian Pidgin, and have collected texts showing syntactic repertoires and discourse strategies.

Moreover, to write this book properly, one would have to have a specialist's knowledge of the history and the linguistic structures of dozens of pidgins and creoles, widely scattered in time and space, and of the historical connections between areas of pidgin and creole use in the seventeenth, eighteenth, and nineteenth centuries—that is, to be a comparative specialist on pidgins and creoles, both linguistically and historically.

Finally, to write this book, a scholar would have to have spent years combing archives around the world, seeking scraps of linguistic and sociolinguistic evidence on Pacific pidgin and piecing together the record of connections, both linguistic and social, between communities not only in the Pacific proper but around its rim (Aboriginal Australia, China, South America).

I meet very few of these qualifications. This is a book written by an amateur linguist who is an equally amateur historian. I have been able to spend only a year or two doing piecemeal research on the vast and scattered relevant historical evidence. The book is unlikely to succeed in a total and sweeping way, but it is not intended to. Rather, I seek to highlight the pieces of a vast and complex puzzle I see most clearly (and others have often missed), as a partial and preliminary synthesis and as a catalyst to further study and counterinterpretation. Others—Mühlhäusler, Baker, Clark, Goulden—are covering similar territory in their ongoing research, and doubtless will reach conclusions rather different from mine. We will doubtless find different bits of evidence, and interpret the same evidence in different ways. But despite the inevitable limitations and biases of the argument I set out, that argument, and the evidence I offer in support of it—including my own field data from the Solomons—will have to be confronted by others covering the same ground in the future. In the field of pidgin and creole studies, where theory and data are expanding so rapidly, there seems no virtue in trying to do a final and definitive study, or waiting until all the relevant evidence is in.

The connections of Pacific pidgin to the pidgins and creoles of the China coast, Indian Ocean, and Atlantic, and to Australian Aboriginal forms of jargon and pidgin, would take two or three books to trace. These connections have now begun to be seriously explored, although much remains to be done. I have left these important connections almost completely unexamined, so as to delimit a partly manageable area for study; but the reader should not surmise that I regard them as unimportant.

Virtually all the writers who have treated the history of English-based pidgin(s) in the Pacific have given labels to successive stages or different points in the history of the language(s): we have various labels for a jargon stage, for the sandalwood period, and for the Labor Trade (and different plantation areas), with terms like Beach-la-Mar having different meanings for different writers. In my judgment, such a division into stages

and the labeling of corresponding forms of jargon or pidgin impose a spurious note of certainty and of discrete periodization, historically and linguistically. In the chapters to follow, although I break the historical account for the sake of convenience into time periods, I avoid treating them
as if they were sequential, discrete stages in a process; and in particular, I
avoid naming the developing lingua franca at different stages in its history. In this regard, I think, deliberate imprecision and circumlocution
are less misleading than to hypothesize periodization and allow the false
sense of certainty that can come when we give labels to languages.

Unlike Mühlhäusler (1985, 1986), I also see no grounds for distinguishing and naming as separate dialects local variants of a developing
Pacific pidgin spoken in different island groups or geographical areas (in
Samoa, in Papua, in Queensland, in Micronesia), where there is no compelling linguistic evidence for doing so (other than, predictably, local
lexical content). We err if we introduce those assumptions about dialect
diversification appropriate to terrestrially based, geographically separated
speech communities to an interlingual linguistic medium based at least as
much on ship as on shore, whose speakers (European and Islander) moved
widely through the entire region.

I am grateful to many scholars for assistance in the detective work and
linguistic analysis that gave rise to this book, including Ron Adams,
Derek Bickerton, Ann Chowning, Ross Clark, Tom Dutton, Talmy
Givón, Jacques Guy, David Hanlon, John Haviland, Francis Hezel, Alan
Howard, Christine Jourdan, Robert Langdon, Don Laycock, Frank Lichtenberk, Peter Mühlhäusler, Mary E. O'Neail, Michel Panoff, Andrew
Pawley, Saul Riesenberg, Malcolm Ross, Gillian Sankoff, Dorothy Shineberg, Anna Shnukal, Jeff Siegel, Linda and Gary Simons, Wolfgang
Sperlich, and Darrell Tryon. Peter Mühlhäusler has been especially gen-
erous in sharing his ideas and unpublished papers, even though my interpretations and his are often at variance: we have agreed to disagree.

The Research School of Pacific Studies of the Institute of Advanced
Studies, The Australian National University, provides a unique setting
within which an interdisciplinary project of this kind, with a focus on the
Pacific, can be pursued. As always, I am grateful for the opportunities
the School makes available for sustained research. I am also grateful to
the Centre National de la Recherche Scientifique for support during the
period in which revision of the original manuscript was undertaken.

I owe special thanks to Judith Wilson and Paula Harris of the Depart-
ment of Anthropology, The Australian National University, for assist-
ing in many ways in documentary research on nineteenth- and early-

twentieth-century Pacific pidgin, particularly in the period when I was revising the book in Paris and was dependent on them for archival sources.

To Christine Jourdan I owe special debts. My exploration of Pacific Pidgin has been shared with her in many ways; we have shared our data and our thoughts, in fieldwork, archival research, and the process of writing. She has listened to more about pronouns than she ever wanted to know, and felt anxieties about my invading her territory. It is our book in many ways, the product of a shared life and work and love.

R.M.K.

Contents

Melanesian Pidgin and the
Oceanic Substrate

Grammatical Abbreviations

ADJ	adjective or particle marking attributive adjectives	IRR	irrealis marker
ART	article	LOC	locative
ASP	aspect marker	MOD	modal
AUX	auxiliary	NEG	negative
CAUS	causative marker	NP	noun phrase
COMP	aspect marker of completion	NUM	number marker
CON	conjunction	PLU	plural marker
CONN	discourse connective	POSS	possessive particle or genitive marker
DEI	deictic	PRES	present tense marker
DEM	demonstrative	PRF	perfect marker
E	exclusive (3d-person pronoun)	PST	past tense marker
FP	focal pronoun	RED	reduplication
FUT	future tense or nonaccomplished mode marker	REL	relative marker
Incl.	inclusive (3d-person pronoun)	RHET	rhetorical
INF	infinitive marker	SRP	subject-referencing pronoun
		TNS	tense marker
		TOP	topicalization marker
		TTS	transitive suffix
		VP	verb phrase

CHAPTER I

Introduction

A BOOK I had not expected to write, an intellectual journey I had not planned to take—and one that has led me far from my own discipline—can well begin with the retracing of some first steps. This will introduce the questions to which this book provides partial and provisional answers.

Sitting on a Solomon Islands mountain in 1977, reading Derek Bickerton's review article on "Pidgin and Creole Studies" (1976), I was led to think more seriously than I ever had about the history and structure of Solomon Islands Pidgin.* I had earlier been struck, when I had learned Solomons Pidgin in the 1960s through the medium of Kwaio, an indigenous language I already spoke fluently, that this learning task mainly required learning Pidgin equivalents of Kwaio morphemes.† The syntax of Solomons Pidgin was essentially the same as the syntax of Kwaio, although somewhat simpler and lacking some of the surface marking; in most constructions, there was a virtual morpheme-by-morpheme correspondence between Kwaio and Pidgin. (This was not just an odd local process of calquing: the Pidgin I was learning in terms of Kwaio was spoken with only minor variations throughout the southeastern and cen-

---

*As an ethnographer, I had acquired the prejudices of my profession, which accorded low status to the use of pidgin in fieldwork, and I had set about immediately to learn the vernacular (in which I had acquired conversational fluency long before survey research in other parts of the Solomons forced me to acquire an adequate command of Solomons Pidgin).

†In the chapters to follow, where Pidgin is capitalized, it refers to the name of a language (usually Solomons Pidgin); where it is used in lower case, it refers to a category of languages.

tral Solomons, although it was everywhere adapted to local phonologies.)
Although most of the Pidgin lexical forms were ultimately derived from
English, I found this largely irrelevant to my language-learning task. The
semantic categories they labeled corresponded to Kwaio ones, not English
ones; grammatical morphemes corresponded to Kwaio ones, not English
ones. Thus semantically Pidgin *dae* corresponded directly to Kwaio *mae*
'be dead, die, be comatose, be extinguished,' not to English "die." Pidgin
baebae corresponded to the Kwaio marker of future/nonaccomplished
mode, *ta-*, not to English "by and by."

For me in 1964, this had been more of a practical language-learning
task than an intellectual puzzle. But Bickerton's paper led me to ponder
how it could have come to be, historically, that the structure of Solomons
Pidgin was so close to the structure of Kwaio and the other languages of
Malaita. I corresponded with him from the field, suggesting that the numerical preponderance of Malaitans in Queensland in the latter nineteenth century had led to a Malaitaization of Queensland Plantation Pidgin. As will be seen, Bickerton had other ideas, which at the time I
dismissed, although I now believe them to have been much closer to the
mark than mine.

I knew that the Bichelamar of what was then the New Hebrides was
quite similar to the Solomons dialect,* and that added a further dimension to the puzzle. Two years later, I read William Camden's detailed
comparison (1979) of Bislama and Tangoan, a northern New Hebridean
language, in which he made an argument similar to the one I was starting
to frame for the Malaita languages. The possibility of showing a close correspondence between indigenous languages and Melanesian Pidgin both
in the Solomons and in the New Hebrides did not necessarily invalidate
the argument. It has been known since Codrington's time (Codrington
1885) that the northern New Hebridean languages and southeastern Solomons languages were closely related and grammatically quite similar; and
I knew that speakers of these two sets of languages had together constituted the bulk of the Queensland labor force from 1880 onward.

I took the first steps down the path that led to this book, then, as a
matter of curiosity, as an anthropologist with a somewhat more than ama-

---

*There are unavoidable difficulties in referring to Pacific pidgins at various time peri-
ods. Thus what was referred to as "Beach-la-Mar" in the nineteenth century had become
"Bichelamar" in the colonial New Hebrides; and is now being referred to as "Bislama" in
postcolonial Vanuatu. The independence and renaming of what had been the New Hebrides poses similar problems. I use New Hebrides in most contexts, not only because most of
the events I am concerned with occurred long before independence, but because this usage
enables me to refer to the New Hebrides archipelago proper, in contrast to the Banks and
Torres Islands, included politically in the new nation of Vanuatu.

teur interest in linguistics—and impelled by my practical experience and intuitions and my from-the-ground-up (rather than from-the-theories-down) perspective to what Bickerton (1977: 61) has characterized as "substratomania." I remain a partially cured substratomaniac.

In the decade since, pidgin and creole studies have exploded into prominence in linguistic theory. Melanesian Pidgin (particularly the Papua New Guinea dialect, Tok Pisin) has had an important place in the theoretical arguments. Tok Pisin challenges specialist study: it is spoken by a large population, it is incorporated ideologically, politically, and practically into the machinery of a postcolonial state, and it is changing rapidly and creolizing in urban contexts, although it is still used as a plantation lingua franca. Linguistically, Tok Pisin constitutes an important case—representing a stable and expanded pidgin with a long, partly documented history, very different from the unstable transitional forms on which Bickerton (1981, 1984) has focused.

Although on historical, linguistic, political, demographic, and practical grounds Tok Pisin certainly merits the attention it has received, in some respects it is unfortunate that this dialect—particularly in the absence of detailed studies of the Solomons and Vanuatu dialects—has been taken as the canonical dialect of Melanesian Pidgin. Nothing in the now-voluminous literature on Tok Pisin clarifies the puzzle that intrigued me a decade ago; and much of it, from the vantage point of Solomons Pidgin and an Oceanic Austronesian language, seems to have missed essential patterns.

In the chapters to follow, I will argue that many of the most important developments in the expansion and stabilization of pidgin took place *prior to* the separation of the regional dialects of Melanesian Pidgin about a century ago, and hence these dialects have a fundamentally common grammar and lexicon. These include most of the elaborations that distinguish Melanesian Pidgin from what Bickerton calls "true pidgins," and from Atlantic and Indian Ocean creoles.

My reading of the historical and linguistic evidence is that Mühl-häusler (1977, 1985a, 1986) and before him Salisbury (1967) have radically overestimated the separateness of the New Guinea Pidgin lineage from the pidgin of Queensland and the recruiting areas of the southwestern Pacific. I read the evidence as indicating that the pidgin spoken both on the German plantations in Samoa and in some parts of the Bismarck Archipelago as of the first half of the 1880s was essentially the same as that spoken in Queensland, the New Hebrides, and the Solomons: these areas were part of a single, dispersed speech community. Only in the latter 1880s—and only after Pacific pidgin had acquired a striking degree of expansion and stability—did New Guinea Pidgin undergo the special developments, including relexification from Bismarcks languages, that distinguish Tok Pisin from other daughter dialects of Pacific pidgin.

Moreover, these developments not only took place earlier than most specialists have believed; most of them emerged in an area hundreds of miles from New Guinea. The initial developments of a distinctive Pacific pidgin, I shall suggest, took place in the central Pacific, in a zone where pidgin has not been used for many decades; and (counter to prevailing wisdom in pidgin studies) they took place in shipboard settings and trading enclaves, not on plantations. Only at a later stage of expansion did Pacific pidgin become a vehicle of labor recruitment and plantation communication.

Because this distinctive Pacific pidgin, growing out of a worldwide nautical pidgin, was primarily a medium of communication among ships crews of mixed-island origin, it was used across a vast expanse of ocean on which the islands are tiny, scattered dots. Morris Goodman (1985: 119) is correct in inferring that in this early period there was a "Pacific-wide nautical pidgin," which, although not yet fully stable, was relatively uniform across this entire area. If we take 1845 (relatively arbitrarily) as a historical baseline, he would also be substantially correct in inferring that this developing pidgin "became fairly homogeneous and stable within less than three decades" (p. 119)—that is, by the time the Labor Trade of the southwestern Pacific was in full swing, in the mid-1870s.

Local dialects of this pidgin began to emerge in the 1870s, when plantations replaced ships and trading enclaves as the main venues for the expansion of the developing regional pidgin. French, German, and indigenous languages of Queensland, Samoa, Fiji, and the Bismarck Archipelago added locally distinctive lexical content to a common lexicon derived from nautical pidgin (and such specific regional forms as the pidgin of the China coast) and directly from English. But I believe these local lexical innovations were, until the end of the 1880s, only minor elaborations and modifications of a common regional pidgin, variations quickly learned by the substantial numbers of Islanders who moved from one plantation area to another as recruiters, foremen, interpreters, cultural brokers, and multiple-term laborers.

Although Goodman is right about a single early dialect of Pacific pidgin spoken across a vast stretch of ocean, he is wrong in characterizing this as "a very heterogeneous linguistic milieu both genetically and typologically" (1985: 119). S. S. Mufwene (1986: 145) is closer to the mark when he observes that the Oceanic situation was different from that in West Africa in that "the Oceanic substrate languages are already typologically related." We will see that there are more than "typological" relationships between the significant substrate languages. Both in the critical phase prior to the onset of the Labor Trade and in the subsequent plantation period, most of the Islanders using this developing pidgin and contributing to its expansion and stabilization were native speakers of Oceanic Austronesian languages. Indeed, most of them were speakers of languages within a single putative subgroup of Oceanic, languages marked by grammatical conservatism in preserving structures deriving from Proto-Oceanic despite lexical diversification. I shall argue that crucial elements in the grammatical structure common to the regional dialects of Melanesian Pidgin represent "substrate influence" of a special kind: the excavation, as it were, by speakers of mutually unintelligible Oceanic Austronesian languages, of grammatical patterns common (at a fairly abstract level of underlying structure) to their native languages.

This then raises crucial questions about theories of "substrate influence" in pidgin and creole linguistics, and about the distinctiveness of Melanesian Pidgin in the worldwide spectrum of pidgins and creoles.

In the light of recent syntactic theory, no analysis of the genesis of a pidgin can uncritically invoke the importance of substrate models or ignore the centrality of universal grammatical patterns and faculties of language simplification and language learning in the process of pidgin formation. Nor can the common superstrate of English-based pidgins and creoles be ignored. In my view, the process of pidgin (and creole) formation and expansion provides a crucial and most demanding challenge for linguistic theory. The models we will ultimately need will draw on formal syntactic theory, psycholinguistics, and sociolinguistics; and each historical case will turn out to be different and demanding. In arguing the importance of substrate models in the formation of Pacific pidgin(s), I am underlining one of the central elements in a highly complex process. Substrates, superstrates, and bioprograms (Bickerton 1984) were all passengers on Pacific waters.

The general position of those Bickerton has referred to as "substratophiles" (1984: 186) has been considerably eroded, although there are signs (particularly in the papers in Muysken and Smith 1986) that substratophiles are on the march once more, and are regrouping for a counteroffensive. Bickerton (1981, 1984), in his broadside attack on "substratophile" claims, argues that the diversity of substrate languages militates against such interpretations, as in the West African case:

> The homogeneity of the African substratum has been much exaggerated. The claim by Alleyne [1980] that creole tense aspect can be accounted for in terms of a "generalized West African system" can hardly be sustained. . . .
> Over the whole range of creole languages, perhaps as many as a thousand ty-

pologically diverse substratum languages went into the making of the antecedent pidgins. . . . If substratum influence was at all significant in creolization, how could such diversity lead to the uniformity described? (1984: 184)

Bickerton goes on to note how a tightly structured universal-grammar-based model of creole formation accounts in a formally powerful and general way for syntactic patterns that have been interpreted in an ad hoc and unsystematic way in substratum-based explanations:

The finding that typical creole structures, including verb serialization and other forms often taken as indicative of African influence, can be derived from a single common grammar further weakens the substratophile position. Substratophiles have never attempted to compare whole systems, but have picked out and compared isolated rules and features from creole and substratum languages. . . . Yet all we have learned about languages supports the view that they constitute tightly knit wholes in which a few major choices define a wide range of superficially varied phenomena (1984: 184).

Melanesian Pidgin is in a curious position in relation to the lively arguments about substrate influence stirred to a boil by Bickerton's recent work. First, numerous writers from Schuchardt ([1883] 1980, [1889] 1980) and Churchill (1911) onward have pointed out some obvious parallels between Melanesian Pidgin and Oceanic languages, such as the inclusive/ exclusive distinction for first-person nonsingular pronouns. Several detailed comparisons between dialects of Melanesian Pidgin and particular Oceanic languages have been published, notably Ulrike Mosel's (1980) comparison of Tok Pisin and Kuanua and Camden's (1979) comparison of the Bislama of Vanuatu and Tangoan. Yet the putative parallels between Melanesian Pidgin dialects and substrate languages leave us uncomfortable, since these arguments seem to be possible whatever indigenous language is chosen for comparison. Moreover, some elements of Melanesian Pidgin that have been claimed to reflect substratal influences occur in other pidgins and creoles far from Melanesia.

Tok Pisin, as the best-known and (assumed) canonical dialect of Melanesian Pidgin, has also provided material for universalist arguments, particularly as it has undergone grammatical and lexical elaboration, standardization, and finally nativization. Thus Gillian Sankoff has analyzed what she takes to be the transformation of a temporal adverb (*baibai*) into a preverbal aspect marker (Sankoff and Laberge 1973), the "cliticization" of the predicate marker *i* (Sankoff 1977), and the embedding of relative clauses (Sankoff and Brown 1976) as exemplifying general patterns of syntactic elaboration. Mühlhäusler has argued in similar terms (1980), claiming that even speakers of pidgin who learned it as adults have had access to universal linguistic faculties in contributing to its expansion.

The relevance of these phenomena for universalist syntactic theory has been noted by Bernard Comrie (1981: 223):

In some dialects of New Guinea Pidgin . . . a plural marker *ol* (deriving etymologically from English all) is beginning to be used obligatorily for certain classes of nouns. Since pronouns already have a number distinction, it is not surprising, given the universal that plural distinction is more likely higher up the animacy hierarchy, to learn that this marker is first made obligatorily with human nouns [Mühlhäusler 1981]—even though there is no apparent motivation for this particular split in the indigenous languages of the area.

Yet Comrie goes on to comment that Tok Pisin is problematic as a source of evidence on universal linguistic processes, in comparison with documented instances of "nascent language." He questions the appropriateness of "inclusion of New Guinea Pidgin" as a case of "the development of pidgins," noting that "New Guinea Pidgin is a fully developed pidgin with a generally stable structure, so that the acquisition of New Guinea Pidgin by speakers of other languages is more in the nature of second language acquisition than spontaneous creation of a new language" (p. 223).

Bickerton (1984: 187) makes a similar argument, adding a historical dimension and specifically exempting Tok Pisin from his broadside critique of substratophile arguments: he comments that "the circumstances that gave rise to Tok Pisin were quite different from those that gave rise to true creoles. The several generations during which it existed as a nonnative language, and the degree of complexity it attained prior to nativization, render it immune to . . . arguments against substratal influence."

Bickerton introduces these remarks by noting that Tok Pisin provides the only recorded exceptions to a number of universal-grammar-based general propositions he advances regarding creoles. In creoles, Bickerton argues (1984: 187), "distinctions such as gender, agency, or transitivity, which are grammaticalized across a wide range of languages, are never overtly marked. . . . Grammatical gender is entirely absent: agency and transitivity are adequately indicated by the simple presence of a noun-phrase following the verb. [But] Tok Pisin has a transitivizing suffix *-im*."

Because Tok Pisin was complex and stable prior to "nativization," having developed as a pidgin for "several generations," we can expect to find extensive substratal influences (Bickerton 1984: 187): "indeed, precisely those features that differentiate it [Tok Pisin] from true creoles, such as the *ia* . . . *ia* relative clause bracketing discussed by Sankoff and Brown [1976], are the ones that reflect the indigenous languages of New Guinea [citing Bradshaw 1979]."

All this raises a series of questions. What time span does Bickerton have in mind for the "several generations" in the genesis of Tok

Pisin? Are they generations since the establishment of Tok Pisin in German New Guinea by way of Samoa (Mühlhäusler 1976, 1978a, 1985a)?
And if so, how can we account for the occurrence of such features as the
"transitivizing suffix *-im*" and third-person plural pronouns as plural markers in other Melanesian Pidgin dialects—Bislama, Solomons Pidgin,
Torres Strait Creole—supposed to have been separated from Tok Pisin
since the 1870s?

Does Bickerton suppose that "the indigenous languages of New
Guinea," in which he surmises we may find substrate models for Tok Pisin
grammatical patterns, are less diverse than those of West Africa? Does he
mean the dozens of distantly related Austronesian languages spoken in
the Bismarck Archipelago, the Massim, and coastal New Guinea, or the
hundreds of radically diverse Papuan languages, only problematically
lumped into ancient "phyla"?

All this is not to deny the possibility of substrate influences from New
Guinea languages, both Papuan and Austronesian, on the development
of Tok Pisin since the late 1880s. The impact of Kuanua (Tolai) in particular is well documented. But we must recognize that this is not the
place to look for the sources of grammatical patterns common to Tok
Pisin and the Vanuatu and Solomons dialects; the pidgin that developed
in New Guinea was transplanted into alien linguistic soil, very different
from that in which it first grew and flowered.

Bickerton characterizes the contrast between Melanesian Pidgin and
other pidgins (and creoles) in terms clearly congruent with the argument
I advance in the chapters to follow: but in this, too, he mistakenly sought
a supposedly (somewhat) homogeneous substrate in New Guinea, not in
the islands far from New Guinea where Pacific pidgin acquired much of its
distinctive grammatical shape:

> If (as in New Guinea) all substrates have strong genetic and/or areal resem-
> blances, superstrate models are rare and relatively inaccessible, and the period of
> use is sufficiently long, there may develop a language that is (for at least a large
> core of speakers) "effable," that is noticeably more homogeneous than Hawaiian
> pidgin, yet that is not (or at least was not, until relatively recently) the native
> tongue of any of its speakers (1977: 56).

Mufwene (1986: 145) comments in a similar vein that "part of Bickerton's language bioprogram may be rendered superfluous if the substrate
group, which is the main user of the pidgin or creole, fits into one single
linguistic type."

It is the congruence of Pidgin grammar and Oceanic Austronesian
grammar—what Bickerton curiously describes as the "effability" of Pacific
pidgin to the Islanders who have used and changed it, through the dec-

ades—and its historical and linguistic roots, that the chapters to follow will explore. The processes involved, I will suggest, are as important and as challenging to linguistic theory as the emergence of a creole under conditions of radical linguistic diversity.

In Chapter 2, I examine in sketchy fashion the evidence on the development of an English-based pidgin in the Pacific prior to 1850. I suggest that in this early period, the central Pacific (eastern Carolines, Rotuma, Fiji, Gilberts*) became the key area for the development of a Pacific lingua franca, and that beachcomber/deserter and trading communities, and ships with mixed Islander and English-speaking crews, were the main settings for this linguistic development.

In Chapter 3, I continue the account through the 1850s and 1860s, the period of sandalwood trade in the southwestern Pacific. I show that many of the linguistic developments usually supposed to have taken place during the later Labor Trade were firmly established by the 1860s; and I suggest that in this period again, ships with mixed Island crews provided a crucial setting for the development and dissemination of an expanding pidgin. I consider the possibility that a generation of children growing up in such a setting, and acquiring pidgin natively, may have contributed to its expansion and stabilization, as well as its later dissemination in the Labor Trade.

In Chapter 4, I examine briefly the evidence (mainly the linguistic evidence) on the pidgin in the Labor Trade, showing that most of the syntactic patterns common to contemporary dialects of Melanesian Pidgin were established by the early 1880s, and in many cases considerably earlier.

In Chapter 5, I examine Mühlhäusler's contention that Tok Pisin, the pidgin of New Guinea, had a substantially separate history from the pidgin dialects of the New Hebrides and Solomons, deriving from an early "Samoan Plantation Pidgin" through German plantations in the Bismarck Archipelago and other parts of New Guinea. I argue that the plantation communities of the central and southwestern Pacific remained closely interconnected until the late 1880s, and that before that time a single Pacific pidgin, with minor local dialectal variants and loan words, prevailed.

In Chapter 6, I examine the Oceanic Austronesian languages and their internal relationships. I focus in particular on the putative Eastern Oceanic subgroup, languages whose speakers were centrally involved in the development of a Pacific pidgin throughout the nineteenth century. I examine the "core" syntactic patterns of Oceanic (especially Eastern Oce-

---

*I use geographical terms rather than modern political labels (Kiribati, etc.) in referring to the nineteenth-century development of Pacific pidgin.

anic) languages, particularly the marking of agent-object relations with pronouns within the verb phrase, and transitive suffixes.

In Chapter 7, I begin to consider the theoretical problems, and the linguistic processes, involved in the dialectical process whereby pidgin was created and expanded in the nineteenth century. I examine the probable place of substrate and superstrate models, hypothesizing that speakers of Oceanic languages and English bent prevailing forms of pidgin to their own ends, and interpreted it in their own grammatical frameworks; and I consider in initial fashion how universal linguistic faculties, hierarchies of markedness and naturalness, and pathways of simplification contributed to this dialectical process. My argument is that, as Goodman (1985) and Mühlhäusler (1986) have suggested, we need to see the interaction of all three forces—substrate influence, superstrate influence, and universals—in shaping a developing pidgin, and need to search for what Mühlhäusler calls "developmental conspiracies" that open pathways for linguistic innovation and development. Considering recent views of second language learning and pidginization, I suggest that from the mid-nineteenth century onward Pacific Islanders have been the fluent speakers of Pacific pidgin whose speech served as a target language.

In Chapter 8, I develop these themes further, with reference to more-concrete evidence about the grammatical structures of a developing pidgin. I begin to show the costs, in terms of linguistic understanding, of treating the New Guinea pidgin lineage as separate from other dialects of Melanesian Pidgin, a theme that recurs in the chapters that follow. Focusing on the "core" syntax of Oceanic Austronesian languages and Pacific pidgin, I argue that these "core" patterns are directly represented in Melanesian Pidgin—and that this is a major source of its distinctiveness, in relation to other pidgins and creoles. At the same time, I show that these Oceanic patterns are highly conducive to "developmental conspiracies," in relation to both superstrate and universal patterns.

In Chapters 9 and 10, I narrow my focus to the pronominal system of Melanesian Pidgin, in historical perspective, arguing that it parallels the Oceanic pronominal system syntactically, as well as semantically. This, in turn, sheds light, both historically and syntactically, on the so-called "predicate marker" that has so exercised the analytical ingenuity of grammarians of Melanesian Pidgin.

In Chapters 11–13, I examine the development of Solomons Pidgin. In Chapter 11, I examine several ways in which—after the separation of New Hebrides and Solomons plantation communities at the turn of the twentieth century—speakers of Solomons (and especially Southeast Solomonic) languages continued to bend Pidgin grammar in the direction of substrate languages. In Chapter 12, I continue the argument, focusing on the Solomons Pidgin pronominal system, and showing that the Pidgin system has been analyzed by Solomon Islanders in ways congruent with their native languages. In Chapter 13, comparing the Kwaio language of Malaita with Pidgin as produced by Kwaio speakers, and drawing on data from speakers of other Malaita languages, I hypothesize that the historical processes I have set out have produced patterns in Pidgin that allow speakers of Eastern Oceanic languages to calque pervasively on their native languages in using (a local dialect of) Melanesian Pidgin. In paying close attention to discourse patterns in Solomons Pidgin, using substantial sequences of text, I contribute in small measure to closing a gap recently noted by Karen Watson-Gegeo (1986: 151), who comments that "one weakness of published pidgin/creole studies in the Pacific . . . is the emphasis on speech community and code at the expense of fine-grained examination of actual discourse."

Finally, in a brief concluding chapter, I sum up how and why the evidence I have presented challenges accepted views, and how and why Pacific pidgin has so pervasively acquired an Oceanic structure. In the end, the historical and linguistic scenario I portray is not so different from that envisioned by Bickerton in his 1977 comments about "effability" or by Goodman in his 1985 observation that Melanesian Pidgin dialects "can be traced back to a . . . Pacific-wide nautical pidgin, which took definite shape during the 1860s and 1870s [and became] relatively stable, homogeneous and structurally elaborated without the participation of native speakers, . . . probably within two or three decades after its inception" (p. 119). I seek in these chapters to give historical and linguistic substance to these characterizations, which taken together come closer to the mark than much of what has been written by Melanesian Pidgin specialists.

I will argue that an adequate model of substrate influence, in circumstances where dozens of mutually unintelligible but grammatically similar languages are involved, represents a considerable challenge to linguistic theory. The interplay between substrate and superstrate models, between universal faculties of language simplification and the excavation of shared grammatical structures underlying surface diversity among genetically related languages, and the massive lexification from the superstrate language to label substrate categories all seem to me to demand linguistic and sociolinguistic theory as powerful as that called for in the contexts of radical interlingual confrontation Bickerton takes as his focus. The possibilities of such a rapprochement between substrate and universalist analyses have been strongly argued and persuasively illustrated by Goodman

(1985), who notes that the selection of patterns from available substrate and superstrate models follows paths channeled both by innate language facilities and by strategies of second language acquisition. This view has been echoed by Mufwene, in his plea that "the universalist and substrate hypotheses complement one another" (1986: 129), that they are not "mutually exclusive" but "complement one another in accounting for the genesis of different pidgins and creoles around the world" (p. 144). Substratophiles and universalists can, I will suggest, live together happily in Melanesia. We need, in fact, to be both at once.

We need to look for substrate models in the right places. An archaeology of linguistic substrates in the Pacific must excavate carefully, in time and space. And it must place their influence in historically and sociologically plausible contexts, asking theoretically informed questions based on adequate data and appropriate local knowledge.

To begin to place the emergence of Melanesian Pidgin more clearly in time and space, and to begin asking strategic questions about substrate models, we need to go back in time before the beginning of the Labor Trade; and we need to shift our focus from New Guinea and the southwestern Pacific out into the central Pacific.

CHAPTER 2

Interlingual Contact in the Pacific to the Mid-Nineteenth Century

SINCE PREVAILING wisdom places the emergence of Melanesian Pidgin out of a fragmentary and understandardized jargon English as having taken place in the 1870s and 1880s, in contexts of plantation labor, any attempt to push back in time this first phase of elaboration and standardization may be greeted with skepticism. This view has not been dispelled, as perhaps it should have been, by Ross Clark's (1979) examination of the early history of Pacific jargons and pidgins. I suspect this is because Clark himself, despite the impressive textual evidence he assembles on early Pacific forms, is excessively conservative in interpreting his own data. I read the same evidence—and I am forced to rely on most of the same texts that he used—as indicating a greater grammatical richness and stability than he concedes to the developing lingua franca in its early stages. (In my view he also radically underestimates the importance of substrate grammars in shaping the emerging pidgin—a question to which we shall return.)

It is worth quoting at the outset what Bickerton wrote to me, in 1977 correspondence:

It occurs to me that if, somewhere in the South Pacific around 1850 or thereabouts, there had been a plantation settled over a period long enough for children to grow up and acquire and stabilize the language, that language could have been *repidginized* . . . and retained its structure as it was disseminated through the Pacific, taking on substratal undertones (or overtones!) in the various places it took root. . . . Such a development might have occurred . . . somewhere that's no longer pidgin-speaking [such as] one of the Micronesian islands.

As I noted in Chapter 1, at the time I dismissed his suggestions, accepting the received notion that a developed and stable pidgin had emerged in Queensland. I now believe that Bickerton was right about the geographical setting and time period, although *plantations* did not provide a setting for a developing Pacific pidgin until much later (on this, Bickerton himself was misled by received wisdom). The time period may turn out to have been slightly earlier than Bickerton surmised.

Whether nativization played a substantial part in the elaboration of a Pacific pidgin in this early period is an open question. There is a strong possibility that by the 1850s there was a substantial number of Islanders who had learned this pidgin as fluent childhood speakers; for almost all of them, however, it would not have been a first language. Indeed, Bickerton himself has revised his thoughts on the importance of nativization in the development of a Pacific pidgin: "The case for early creolization is, as you point out, still open, and I'm inclined to be less enthusiastic about it than I was, apparently, in 1977" (personal communication, June 20, 1986).

Scattered documentary evidence shows that some Pacific islanders, notably Tahitians and Hawaiians, had acquired some smattering of a jargonized English by the late 1700s and early 1800s. Thus Bligh complained in 1792 about the degeneration of Tahitian culture, under the influence of white sailors, since his earlier visits: "Our friends here have benefited little from their intercourse with Europeans. Our countrymen have taught them such vile expressions as are in the mouth of every Otaheitan. . . . Little of the ancient customs of the Otaheitans remain—all that was left aside. It is difficult to get them to speak their own language without mixing a jargon of English with it" (Lee 1920: 74, 78–79).

O'Connell (1972: 86) writes of his 1822 stay in Sydney that "the Kanakas [South Sea Islanders] discharged from American and English whalers, at Sydney, supply the Sydney whalers with half their crews. In the *Cape Packet*, out of sixteen hands, seven at least were Kanakas."

Richard Henry Dana's encounters with Hawaiians in San Diego in 1835 (Dana 1840) yield some interesting examples of an early jargon English interspersed with pidginized Hawaiian; the English-based segments include some elements pervasive in later Pacific pidgin:

Ay, me know that. By-em-by money *pau* [Anglo-Hawaiian 'finished']—all gone, them Kanaka work plenty.

New Zealand Kanaka eat white man—Sandwich Island Kanaka—no. Sandwich Island Kanaka *ua like pu na haole*—all 'e same a you!

No! We all 'e same a' you! Suppose one got money, all got money. You—suppose one got money—lock him up in chest. No good! Kanaka all 'e same a' one.

In this early period, jargon English continued to be used, and to develop, in the Polynesian islands that were fairly regular ports of call for European vessels. Thus in 1825 Lt. Hiram Paulding ([1831] 1970: 66), on the USS *Dolphin*, encountered a Marquesan who, on finding a piece of bread had been thrown onto his head, uttered with horror: "'Who put dat dare? Me Taboo here!' (putting his hand on his head) 'Tomorrow me sick, me die!'" Paulding comments: "I tried to find out from him what was meant by his being tabooed, but he spoke English so badly . . . that I was not much the wiser for his explanation."

I believe, on the basis of the fragmentary evidence available, that a crucial phase in the formation of a Pacific jargon from which pidgin emerged took place in the 1840s as whaling and trading ships began to frequent the islands of the central Pacific.

The most likely settings for this first stage in the expansion of a developing Pacific lingua franca appear on the basis of my own research to date to have been a series of interlinked island groups, principally Pohnpei (Ponape) and Kosrae (Kusaie) in the Carolines, the Gilbert Islands, and Rotuma, which were favored venues for whalers, traders, beachcombers, and deserters.* These were centers where Islanders quickly became skilled dealers in produce, water, wood, turtle shell, bêche-de-mer, and sex, and enthusiastic consumers of liquor, tobacco, and trade goods. From these islands (along with Hawaii, Tahiti, and other Polynesian islands) emanated a steady stream of crew members for the whaling and trading vessels.

Although little linguistic evidence is available for Pohnpei, the ingredients for the development of a precursor of a distinctive Pacific pidgin were all there:

Ship traffic at Ponape [increased] dramatically during the early 1840s as American whaling activities in the Pacific expanded. . . . As ship traffic at Ponape increased, so did the number of desertions and the size of the resident white population. Enticed by the "temporary fascinations of women" and the promise of a life

---

*A number of islands in the Pacific have been renamed in the postcolonial period. In some cases the new labels represent corrections of earlier European misrenderings (as in the case of "Ponape" and "Kusaie," now renamed Pohnpei and Kosrae) or replacement of a less locally appropriate name with an indigenous one (as in the case of "Aoba" in the New Hebrides, renamed "Ambae" in postcolonial Vanuatu). As previously noted, countries have been renamed as well, although the new labels have often had to be created (Vanuatu) or adopted from European labels (Kiribati, the Gilbertese orthographic rendering of Gilbert). I use the new labels for islands, but give the long-established ones in parentheses at the first occurrence to aid readers; I use established geographical rather than political labels for island groups except where reference to modern states is appropriate (although even here the texts often require clarification: the Gilbert Islands were at first called the Kingsmills).

of leisure, seamen continued to leave their ships and take up living ashore; the white population grew to fifty or sixty in 1840, and to one hundred fifty a decade later. Besides the veteran Englishmen on the island, the foreign colony was composed of Americans and Portuguese, largely from New England whaleships, and natives of other Pacific islands: Rotumans, Gilbertese, Maoris, and Tahitians (Hezel 1983: 122–24).

David Hanlon (n.d.) gives further glimpses of this diverse "colony" of Europeans and other Islanders. While "the greater number of Pohnpei's foreign residents were common seamen who had deserted from the whale-ships that began reaching the island in the mid-1830s," and most were English, the beachcombers included "a creole from the Seychelles" who arrived in 1836 and three Black Americans. Hanlon adds:

> Other Pacific Islanders also found themselves carried by circumstance to Pohnpei. Some deserted from whaling ships while others, brought to collect bêche-de-mer, . . . were abandoned by their white employers. In the middle decades of the nineteenth century, men from the East Indies, the Loyalty Islands, Belau [Palau], the Gilberts, Hawaii, Rotuma and Mangareva all struggled for survival on the island. . . . Exiles from the harsh life aboard a whaling ship, five Maoris . . . had established themselves at Rohnkiti [where they had taken] Pohnpeian wives. . . .
>
> By 1850, deserters from whaleships had raised the number of foreign residents on Pohnpei to approximately 150. Americans replaced Englishmen as the dominant nationality among the beachcomber community. Fishermen from the Azores and Cape Verde Islands . . . also reached the island aboard American whaling ships.

Hezel (1983: 122–24, 141) describes how the whaling ships responded to the desertions:

> Meanwhile, ships masters who found themselves short-handed due to desertions began to sign on Ponapeans as foremast hands. The *Honduras*, after most of its company was wiped out in the fight at Kosrae, took on practically an entire Ponapean crew before continuing its voyage to Honolulu. . . . As desertions continued, more and more of the islanders left Ponape for a few years to see the world from the fo'c'sle of a trading brig or whaling bark.
>
>   · · ·
>
> A growing number of islanders were acquiring their knowledge of the outside world by seeing it firsthand. Whaling captains, hard pressed to replace deserters, were offering more and more berths to islanders. . . . Those who were fortunate enough to return after a couple of years at sea came back with stories enough for a lifetime, even if they may sometimes have lost the fluency to tell them in their own language.

Saul Riesenberg, another expert on the early history of Pohnpei, notes (1972: 18) that "already in 1835 Ponapeans had signed on as members of the crews of visiting ships and had been to Hawaii and Sydney." An observer writing in the 1860s described the ubiquitous Pohnpeians' rapid acquisition of some form of English:

In matters of any interest to them they readily acquire knowledge—as, for instance, the acquisition of the English language. Very many of them are quite familiar with that sailor's "lingo," which is almost the only one they have heard. Those . . . who have been to sea are among the very quickest of islanders in picking up facts and making themselves useful. They are usually favourites wherever they go abroad from their native island (Gulick 1862).

Hanlon (n.d.) notes that "to communicate with the ships, Pohnpeians acquired a pidgin trade language. Sailors stepping ashore on the island were often greeted with a 'Hello, Jack! Give us a chew of [tobacco]?'" He cites an interchange in which a Pohnpeian, "proceeding on to the ship, . . . climbed aboard and said to the captain in his best pidgin English: 'Look, Kepin, you see women? Stop at nan weleniahk' (the edge of the mangrove swamp)."

The women of Pohnpei and Kosrae would have been cultural and linguistic brokers as much as the Island men and the resident Europeans. After recounting how Island women and their male kin virtually lived aboard the whaling ships on the basis of liaisons with crew members, Hezel (1983: 141) goes on to describe a "young Kosraean woman who chatted with a crew member of the *Cavalier* about ice and snow and professed a desire to see America"—a wish "not unusual among the habituees of whaleships."

We learn more about the linguistic medium of these polyglot communities on shore and on shipboard if we turn to Kosrae, which was only slightly less overwhelmed by the whalers but after 1844 refused to accommodate deserters. Initially, Hezel (1983: 113) notes, "the growth of the white community—if the motley assortment of beachcombers could be called a community—was just as rapid on Kosrae as on Ponape; by 1835 . . . there were 'not less than thirty runaways on the island . . . and many of them convicts.'" But after several bloody ship attacks, an astute "King George" decided it was to his advantage to eliminate the foreigners as residents and accommodate them only as temporary business partners.* We learn from an 1843 newspaper article describing attacks on ships at Kosrae that "no white inhabitants were found upon the island, and what appears very remarkable, nearly every native could converse in good English" (Ward 1967: 559). An 1844 article about another ship attack notes that "the inhabitants of Strong's Island [Kosrae] speak English remarkably

*Europeans in the Pacific regularly promoted local chiefs into "kings," and often gave them European names when the local names were too difficult to render.

well. [The captain] states it as his opinion that, although there may be no Englishmen resident on the Island at present, there must have been at some previous time, as the natives are so well versed in the English language" (Ward 1967: 569, 572). Elsewhere, we learn more clearly what the nature of this "English" was:

Before the missionaries landed upon the island [in 1852], the natives had acquired a smattering of the English language. This was merely the result of their intercourse with foreigners, principally with seamen. They were able to employ intelligently a greater number of English words than those Hawaiians who have lived for years in foreign families in Honolulu. So great was their knowledge of English, that Mr. Snow endeavored for nearly four years after commencing his mission to preach in *broken* English, or Anglo-Kusaien. . . . But he finally abandoned the experiment, and fell back upon the vernacular of the natives. He found it to be exceedingly difficult to communicate religious truths in this mixture of Kusaien, English, Spanish, Hawaiian and other languages (Damon 1861: 50).

Hezel (1983: 117) notes, on the basis of his exhaustive search of documentary evidence, that "most of the population [of Kosrae] spoke a kind of pidgin that served adequately as a means of communicating with passing ships. Unlike Ponapeans, the Kosraeans had no need for whites to assist in their commercial dealings with foreign ships; the islanders themselves had always handled their own trade arrangements."

Unfortunately, few texts from Kosrae have turned up. One comes from "King George" himself, who after years of regular dealings with European ships' masters, and later Snow, very probably spoke something closer to English than the Anglo-Kosraean pidgin: "White man take plenty gal go aboard ship. In morning, kanaka go board ship; every kanaka: big island, small island, all go and kill every man board ship" (*The Friend*, November 1854, quoted in Hezel 1983: 114).

Gulick (1862: 241) gives another version of this text: "White man want to get gal go aboard ship. King no like. In night white man take plenty gal go board ship. White man kill some kanakas. Then kanakas take chests, small things ashore; then set fire to ship; burn sails, rigging, spars, casks, everything belonging to ship. Every white man was killed."

Two more useful texts come from Hiram Bingham (1866: 16, 35):

Plenty white man speak me, very good tap cocoanut tree, get toddy; me say, no; no good; plenty men get drunk on shore; too much row; me like all quiet; no tap cocoanut tree on Strong's Island.

. . .

Me think missionary stop board that ship. . . . Me want to go 'long pilot; look quick. Me no care nothing 'bout 'nother ship; tha's what for I want go; look plenty.

Some other fragmentary texts from the eastern Carolines come from a somewhat later period and will be examined shortly.

It would seem that observers found what was spoken on Kosrae to be "remarkably good English" partly on phonological grounds. Damon (1861: 51) goes on to write of his 1852 mission visit to Kosrae:

While at Strong's Island, we were surprised in mingling among the natives to find so many of them who were able to speak in the *jargon* which has been introduced. Their ability to pronounce some of the difficult sounds of the English language was very remarkable. . . . We found the Caroline Islanders much more readily acquiring a knowledge of the English language than the inhabitants of the Hawaiian Islands.

Pohnpei and Kosrae were by no means the only ports of call for the whaling and trading ships of the 1840s and 1850s. Mokil, ninety miles to the east of Pohnpei, was regarded as a more benign and peaceful place for Europeans to do business:

With men in trousers and women wearing cotton blouses and smoking clay pipes, the Mokilese, thought one observer [in 1852], offered an encouraging example of the benefits to be derived from the civilizing process. Captain Samuel James of the missionary packet *Morning Star* described the Mokilese as "an honest, industrious race for which much credit is due to the foreigners residing on the island for teaching them these qualifications" (Hanlon n.d.).

Similar early European populations, trade, and participation as crew members on whaling and trading vessels marked other parts of the central Pacific, including the Marshall Islands (where the Germans were to establish a strong presence and plantation centers) and Belau (Palau) to the west. For our purposes it is more important to shift our focus southward to the Gilberts, Rotuma, and Fiji.

For the Gilbert Islands, we have some evidence on similar processes under way in the same period. Thus MacDonald (1982: 20–21) notes:

Rather than making up their full complement from among the riff-raff of Sydney or Honolulu, some captains chose to recruit Pacific Islanders. Recruiting began in the Gilbert and Ellice Islands in the 1820s but it did not become common until the 1840s. Most recruits worked only for a season but there were a few who remained with their ships until they were discharged in Sydney, Honolulu or the ports of New England to await a working passage home. . . . Their observations and experience, shared with their fellow islanders, made them as important as agents of change as the Europeans who chose to settle in the islands. . . . While a few Europeans remained for several years, or even a lifetime, in the islands, most moved on within a year or two. There were frequent opportunities to sign on with passing ships. . . . Thus there was a constant turnover in the membership of [the] small European settlements, few of which ever had more than a dozen members at any given time. . . .

Generally their own preservation, and a perceived bond with their fellow Europeans on board ships made them honest middlemen and interpreters. However their presence in this role was seldom required because a number of Islanders, especially those who had worked on whalers themselves, were soon sufficiently proficient in English to conduct their own trade.

For Rotuma, we find similar evidence from the whaling and trading period:

Whalers found the luxuriant islands [an] excellent station for replenishing their stores, and it became a favorite stopping place. . . . Young men eagerly signed on board visiting ships as crew members, and sailed to the far corners of the globe. . . . A large number of deserters . . . found their way to Rotuma's hospitable shores. Several . . . took Rotuman wives and left a substantial progeny (Howard 1970: 15).

Alan Howard (personal communication, Sept. 18, 1986), who has assembled considerable historical documentation on Rotuma in the nineteenth century, notes that "there . . . were as many as 100 beachcombers on Rotuma in the early 1800s." Although little linguistic evidence of the early encounters has come to light, Jarman's 1833 visit to Rotuma shows that even at this early date Europeans and Rotumans managed linguistic encounters with reasonable success (Jarman 1838: 178, 181):*

As soon as we landed we were surrounded by little children, girls and boys, rivalling each other in pressing their little presents of young cocoanuts upon us. . . . The children would take our hands and beg for a small piece of tobacco, "fenam chaw tabac."

                                  . . .

After we had finished our repast [the Principal Chief, "Fang Menou"] invited us to return to his house so soon as we should feel again disposed to "ki ki"; "for" said he "plenty Rotumah man speak a you eat, for catch a tabac; that no Rotumah fashion."

For the puzzling "fenam," Howard (personal communication, Nov. 18, 1986) offers the suggestion that it "is actually *far nam*, which would translate in Rotuman as 'please give me a taste' or something like it; *fara* translates as 'to beg or request,' the root *nam* translates as 'to taste.'"†

---

*For this source, I am grateful to Fr. Francis Hezel.

†However, Rotuman students at the University of the South Pacific whom Epeli Hau'ofa queried on my behalf could suggest no such derivation, and the possibility remains open that this was a pidgin form of some sort—possibly even one ("find-um"?) with an early version of the transitive ending *-im*, used elsewhere by Europeans in "talking to natives," which came to play an important part in later Pacific pidgin.

Nor were the Polynesian islands cut off from the influence of the whalers and from a developing contact jargon. Polynesians continued to contribute to the multilingual "Kanaka" component of ships' crews, and their home islands were in continuous contact with visiting ships. We get a glimpse of such contacts, linguistic and social, in the account of Lamont, from about 1852. On Aitutake in the Cook Islands, Lamont (1867: 98) reports: "I was astonished here to find the natives all speaking more or less English. The island is becoming a great resort for whalers, as many as a hundred sail or more calling here annually." On Mangaia, Lamont encountered a young man named "Goliah" who told him: "Oh, by, by riko catch 'im putty 'im in calaboose" (p. 90). The significance of such an early occurrence, in the whaling period (about 1852), of these transitive suffixes and of the future-marking will emerge in the chapters to follow.

In the Marquesas in 1852, Lamont encountered a young woman who complained about the French presence there, telling him (1867: 25): "Eh, me see Nukaheva too mushy. . . . Eh, Nukaheva goody longa timey. By, by, Francy too much poo, poo [imitating action of firing a gun], Nukaheva no goody."

When Lamont set sail from California, his crew included two "Huahinean Kanakas," which apparently simply meant Polynesians. Another "Huahinean Kanaka" from Mangiki in the Cooks was signed aboard, then almost left behind. "Kanaka Bob" explained to Lamont why he had been put ashore (1867: 95–96): "Cap'n, speak me go shore. . . . Oh, me ship go Carifona [California], me likey go Carifona; ship he no go. . . . Oh! Cap'n speaky me he no likey more go Carifona, more good me go 'shore; 'spose me no go Carifona, me like go 'shore too quick." We will see at the end of Chapter 4 that some thirty years later, this early jargon English, somewhat elaborated through indirect contact with the pidgin of the Labor Trade, remained in use in parts of Polynesia.

We find no clear evidence in all these texts of nativization, in the sense of the children of alliances between island women and European men growing up on ships or around European shore colonies and acquiring a native command of the emerging and expanding linguistic medium being used between the islanders and Europeans. We may guess that such children acquired a native command of the languages of their island mothers; whether they acquired a fluent command of their fathers' language(s) is more doubtful, particularly since so many of the early alliances were seemingly transitory. I suspect that a substantial population of children growing up on and around the ships, and in shore trading bases and deserter communities, became natively fluent in the prevailing trade jargon (and perhaps in shipboard English as well). It seems doubtful that at this early stage, as minor actors on the social stage, they would have contributed much linguistically to a lingua franca still in its formative stages; but this remains an open question.

By 1850, Fiji was a center of Pacific trade and commerce, and the prevailing lingua franca was known and used by some Fijian cultural middlemen. John Jackson, in Fiji for several years in the mid-1840s, learned to speak Fijian fluently. His account of his adventures, published by Erskine (1853), describes a Fijian chief from Rewa (on Viti Levu) named Cakonauto, aged about twenty-eight, who was known to Europeans as "Mr. Phillips." He greeted Jackson "in English": "How do you do? Ah, you come see me; all white men see me; man belongen ebery place see me; me like um man belongen noder place" (Erskine 1853: 461). According to Jackson (ibid.), "Phillips . . . could talk almost fluently in Spanish, Tahitian, Tongan, and all the different dialects of Feejee."

Clark (1979: 31) goes to great lengths to explain away the occurrence in this text of the possessive "belong" and the transitive suffix *-um* as anachronistically early and not genuinely representative of the lingua franca of the time (he suggests they may be an import from Australia or elsewhere or "an extension" by a "linguistically gifted individual"). I believe that he is mistaken, and that we must take this as a crucial though fragmentary piece of evidence of the early appearance in Pacific pidgin of grammatical constructions that later become standard in all daughter dialects. I will argue that they also represent the first stages of an incorporation of Oceanic Austronesian grammar into this emerging pidgin. Indeed, Dana may have recorded the same transitive suffix from Hawaiians in San Diego in the previous decade, in "lock him up in chest." We have seen clear evidence of it from the Cook Islands in "catch 'im" and "putty 'im" in Lamont's text from the whaling period, less than a decade after Jackson recorded Cakonauto's speech.

Mühlhäusler, in a sketch of the history of English-based pidgin(s) in the Pacific (1985a: 38), comments that prior to 1860, "Islanders serving on board European vessels, and Europeans deserting to the islands and living among the natives are the exception rather than the rule." My reading of the evidence suggests that Mühlhäusler is wrong. The total population of Islanders serving on European vessels was quite substantial enough to constitute a potent force of linguistic (and cultural) innovation and transmission, particularly insofar as they communicated with one another as well as with Europeans, and insofar as their wanderings to distant places gave them a prestige and sophistication, and a role as linguistic and cultural brokers, far beyond their absolute numbers. The population of beachcombers, deserters, and shore-based traders was again not great in absolute terms, but by the mid-nineteenth century they too constituted a potent force toward cultural and linguistic brokerage and intermediation.

It is not a new insight that ships with mixed Island and European crews constituted a crucial setting for the early development of a Pacific lingua franca, or that sailors speaking a worldwide English-based (though far from uniform*) pidgin when they communicated with "natives" were important agents of linguistic diffusion and change. Reinecke, for instance, in his classic study of "marginal languages" (1937: 434), comments: "One of the most favorable situations for the formation of such dialects is found among merchant vessels which ply the seven seas—and indeed the seaman is a figure of the greatest importance in the creation of the more permanent makeshift tongues." More recently, J.-M. Charpentier (1979: 50–52) has written of the earliest phases of development of a Pacific trade jargon:

> Whaling, at first exclusively carried out by the British, began at the end of the eighteenth century. . . . The American whalers [then] became the most numerous and active. . . . They undoubtedly used a lingua franca to communicate with the indigenous inhabitants of the islands they visited, and above all with those who served as fellow crew members. . . .
> The whalers processed their catch at bases where they rendered the oil. This work required a considerable indigenous labor force. There are good reasons to believe that the lingua franca often known as "whaler's speech" was being used at these bases. . . .
> This contact medium must only have had a limited vocabulary needed for the limited and ephemeral contexts of interaction. . . .
> On the ships, men of every nationality were thrown together. . . . The lingua franca of these whalers, with its limited vocabulary focused on nautical matters, and cut off from prestigious linguistic models, constituted a jargon [*sabir*]. . . .
> [In the subsequent sandalwood period], in the shore bases where Europeans of diverse origin were thrown together with indigenous peoples of no less mixed origins, the only means of communication available was the jargon used by the whalers (my translation).

There are two points here that get rather tangled up in the literature. The first is that the European seamen themselves, who on English and American ships were predominantly English speakers, used distinctive (though far from uniform) dialects of working-class English in interacting with one another. The second is that they collectively carried with them a set of linguistic and cultural expectations and strategies for "talking to natives," which has a long and complex history (only partly explored and documented), and which represented a cumulative interlinking of the various lingua francas of the Atlantic, the Caribbean, the China coast, and perhaps the Indian Ocean. What Islanders, as fellow crew members or on shore, would have had as linguistic input comprised both the "na-

---

*On this point, see Mühlhäusler 1986: 97–99.

tive talk" produced by the sailors in dealing specifically with them and the distinctive nautical English the sailors spoke with one another.* More-over, one of the most important elements in this complex sociolinguistic situation was the need for Islanders who were speakers of diverse and mainly mutually unintelligible Oceanic languages to communicate *with one another*, in settings where their solidarity and their ability to commu-nicate other than through Europeans was probably crucial.

Mühlhäusler (1986: 39) comments that prior to 1860 there were "a number of unstable varieties of jargon English in various parts of the Pa-cific Ocean." But I see no strong evidence, linguistic or historical, sup-porting Mühlhäusler's contention that there were a multitude of different jargons. To be sure, speakers of different Pacific languages brought to an emerging lingua franca different phonological repertoires; and they prob-ably bent the constructions of a developing jargon/pidgin to their own grammatical patterns (see Chapter 13). And no doubt local media of inter-lingual communication incorporated indigenous lexical items and usages, whether Gilbertese, Tahitian, Hawaiian, Pohnpeian, or other. But it seems to me, given the sort of evidence for an early shipboard lingua franca I have sketched, that we misrepresent the map of the mid-nineteenth-century Pacific by, as it were, coloring in the widely scattered specks of land and leaving the ocean blank. The ocean, dotted with ships plying their trade and seeking their whales, provided a network of broad avenues connecting these scattered specks of land. We better capture the scenario by coloring in the ocean and leaving the specks of land as tiny dots on it. Islands that were hundreds of miles apart were not separate and un-connected settings for the development of distinct local trade jargons; and men from these islands were thrown together in settings far from their homes.

In taking this view of a Pacific-wide developing lingua franca, I agree with Robert Hall (1966: 10) when he writes:

In the South Sea islands to the north and north-east of Australia, English-speaking sailors, traders, whalers and recruiters of indentured labor . . . were pursuing their activities and teaching a pidginized English to the natives, from the New Hebri-des to the Carolines. This South Seas Pidgin came to be known as beach-la-mar.

We will see, however, that the processes of transmission and change en-tailed much more, on the Islanders' side, than just "being taught." This view of a Pacific-wide beach-la-mar is further expressed by Charpentier (1979: 53–54), who writes:

*And perhaps, in some cases, a register somewhere between the two, used by English-speaking seamen in dealing with crewmen who were speakers of, say, Portuguese, Spanish, or French, either in standard or creolized forms.

This jargon extended across virtually the whole of the south Pacific. . . . [quoting Hall]. The jargon was being employed from the New Hebrides to the Carolines. In New Caledonia and New Zealand, where many whalers sojourned, it was known as well, as it was in Polynesia. Thus the zone where this jargon was used incorporated the whole of the Pacific.

An early but relatively developed Pacific lingua franca was, I suggest, introduced from the central Pacific into southern Melanesia (the Loyalties, New Caledonia), where it underwent further expansion. This already quite grammatically developed pidgin provided a medium for the commencement of the Labor Trade in the 1860s, in which Loyalty Islanders, Rotumans, Gilbertese, Fijians, Pohnpeians, and other already fluent (and possibly in some cases native) speakers of pidgin acted as middlemen and brokers.

The quest for sandalwood led European ships—many of which had mixed-island crews from the central Pacific—into southern Melanesia. We need now to move our focus to the south and southwest.

CHAPTER 3

 The Sandalwood Period

THE EASTERN CAROLINES, the Marshalls, Rotuma, and the Gilberts, as well as Tahiti, the Marquesas, Hawaii, and other parts of Polynesia, were regular Pacific ports of call by the time sandalwood was found on Erromanga, in the southern New Hebrides, in 1825 (Shineberg 1967: 7). Indeed Peter Dillon, who first found the New Hebrides sandalwood, had done a lively trade in Fiji, where most of the sandalwood had been cut by 1816. We may surmise that both an early Pacific pidgin and Polynesian languages made their entry into the southern New Hebrides at this stage, since crews of the early ships had included (up to 1830) some 600 Polynesians and Rotumans (Shineberg 1967: 21), with whom the Europeans presumably used versions of the prevailing jargon. The Europeans presumably used it as well in their dealings with the fierce and politically fragmented Melanesian communities with whom they sought to establish peaceful trading relations (Shineberg 1967: 27).

The sandalwood trade did not begin in earnest in southern Melanesia until 1841. "It was then that the scramble for sandalwood commenced in earnest, and a veritable invasion of the islands by colonial vessels began. From that time, New Caledonia, the Loyalty Islands and the New Hebrides were constantly visited" (Shineberg 1967: 29).

Shineberg details the encounters between the indigenous peoples of the Ile des Pins,* with its Tongan-introduced dynasty, and the sandalwood traders, a trade that began in friendship (1841) and ended in bloody

*I use French spellings where islands and places bear French names (other than Nouvelle-Calédonie), but use phonetic renderings for the Melanesian names of islands in place of the orthographically clumsy and misleading French renderings (thus Lifu rather than Lifou, Uvea rather than Ouvéa).

attacks (1843). The accounts provide only limited information on the linguistic media of these encounters, and those that followed in the Loyalties. Polynesian languages provided one medium; some traders such as Cheyne acquired some knowledge of vernaculars; and the trade jargon by then acquiring the grammatical complexity and stability of a pidgin presumably was put to use by Europeans and picked up by islanders. In this process some further stabilization and elaboration of the jargon seems likely, at least within the limited zone of the Loyalties, Ile des Pins, New Caledonia, and southern New Hebrides. Shineberg (1967: 79, 84) notes:

> By the end of 1849 there was little of the New Caledonian coastline that had not been explored by the colonial sandalwood traders. From the middle of 1846 until the end of the decade Erromanga and the mainland of Caledonia divided the trade between them, with Efate and the Loyalties merely a secondary source of supply. All around the coast of the mainland the sandalwood or "beach la mar" English became the second language of the inhabitants and indeed remained so for many years.
>
>   . . .
>
> As the traders went from one island to its neighbour, they would try to take a man with them in the expectation—usually justified—that there would be someone at the new place who spoke the language of the old, or that the man himself had some smattering of the new. . . . As the regular boats were established and Melanesians took work on ship-board, "sandalwood English" . . . became the *lingua franca.*

The importance of ships as the primary context for the development and dissemination of this "sandalwood English" emerges in Erskine's important accounts of his experiences in southern Melanesia in 1850. Erskine (1853: 393) unsuccessfully sent someone to find "a native boy, now at the Ile des Pins, [who] had been on board the *Vanguard* at the time of the massacre [in 1847, near Noumea], and might serve as an interpreter, as he spoke English tolerably." Erskine describes the men of the Ile des Pins as "ready to embark in English vessels, where they . . . quickly acquire the language" (p. 400). The "chiefs" of these southern Melanesian islands dealt regularly with Europeans on their ships and often traveled with them. Erskine encountered the well-known chief "Basset" of Yengen, New Caledonia (near present Noumea): "Basset and his brother . . . had both visited Sydney and spoke a little English, the former sufficiently well to maintain a conversation tolerably well without the aid of an interpreter" (p. 354). He describes "the chief of another tribe," on Lifu in the Loyalties, named Sumako, who was "not . . . on friendly terms with the others, who assured us he was 'no good.'" Sumako, Erskine says, was "a sharp, intelligent fellow, but with rather a swaggering manner and an odious jabber of English slang words" (pp. 365–66).

In contrast with the sophisticates of the Loyalties, New Caledonia, and the Ile des Pins who had voyaged and dealt with Europeans,* Erskine in 1849 had been hard pressed to find interpreters and middlemen in the southern New Hebrides. He describes "the great want of an interpreter" on Aneityum (1853: 305), and on Tanna "our communication with the people was almost limited to signs on both sides" (p. 308). But where Erskine did manage to find interpreters on Tanna, all had acquired their Pidgin in shipboard contexts: "One or two men, who have made voyages in trading vessels, are said to speak English fluently, and during my last visit to Kaiassi many of the boys standing round jabbered a few words such as 'very good,' 'come along,' etc., etc., very distinctly" (p. 320).

In the mid-1870s Steel (1880: 184) encountered on Tanna a local man preaching Christianity, who had become Christian in Tonga and then had lived in Fiji.

We asked his history, and he told it to us in broken English. Fourteen years ago, when a young lad, a whaling vessel had called at Black Beach; he and some other boys had gone off to see her, and in her they were stolen from their homes. There [on the ship] he had lived for a year, and got plenty of work and very little food (as he expressed it, "Plenty work, plenty kicks, no plenty kyky").

The role of Loyalty Islanders in the spread and proliferation of a ship-based subculture, with an emerging English-based pidgin as its linguistic medium, seems to have been crucial, despite their relatively small numbers. Strikingly mobile, with a propensity to sail across the southwestern Pacific as crew members, the Loyalty Islanders became much more sophisticated in the ways of Europeans (and the English language) than their fiercely tribal contemporaries from New Caledonia and the southern New Hebrides. Howe (1977, 1978) gives us a good summary of these remarkable Loyalty Islanders, as sophisticated adventurers, inveterate travelers, and cultural middlemen:

Striking developments which began in the 1840s and continued into the twentieth century were the islanders' enthusiasm for travelling overseas [and] their eagerness and expertise in trading with Europeans. . . .
    The policy of recruiting Loyalty islanders to serve on English commercial ships was a long-standing one by the 1860s, for there were few English vessels working regularly in the south-west Pacific from the 1840s onwards without some Loyalty islanders on board. . . .
    Without doubt those Loyalty islanders who sailed about the Pacific would have formed a significant proportion of the [total Loyalty Islands] population of

*Including their own quota of deserters and beachcombers. Pisier (1975: 47) gives Cheyne's account of a young British deserter on Lifu, in the Loyalties, in 1842.

about 12,500 in the mid-1860s. . . . In 1857 the LMS missionaries reported: "Many of the young men . . . have been away in ships to California, Sydney, and other places," and the Marfits noted in 1861: "The passion for travel, to see other countries, to become like *whitemen*, to be admired, often takes possession of the young men; and many, leaving their islands, are happy to cross the seas." . . .

"The young men from the ships," said Jones [in 1888], "on board vessels going to Australia and the other parts of the world, pick up English, and they come back, and *almost all* have gone at one time or another" (Howe 1977: 85, 89–90, 91).

Scant wonder that by the time plantations were established in New Caledonia and subsequently in Fiji and Queensland, the sophisticated and adventuresome Loyalty Islanders wanted little part in the back-breaking toil of indentured labor in the fields: it was they who, as cultural brokers and sophisticated travelers of the southwestern Pacific and beyond, acted as middlemen in recruiting their Melanesian cousins from the New Hebrides and later the Solomons. Their role in the dissemination of a developing pidgin into the central and northern New Hebrides and Solomons must have been crucial. Whether they were important in the *creation* of the pidgin of the 1850s and 1860s or, as I suspect, inherited it relatively fully formed from Pacific islanders—Fijians, Rotumans, Polynesians—from further north and east, cannot be established with certainty from the meager documentary record.

The centrality and mobility of Loyalty (and especially Lifu) Islanders and the mixed-island nature of the ship and shore communities in the southwestern Pacific in the 1860s and beyond emerges if we glimpse some of the "South Sea Islanders" resident on Murray Island in the Torres Straits in 1885 (Queensland 1885):

Pidgeon Lifu: "Has been knocking about in Sidney, Port Denison, etc., for seventeen years."

Johnny Lifu: "Lived a good many years in various parts of Queensland and in Sydney; first came to the Straits in 1871."

Lewis Lifu: "Has lived six years in Brisbane and seven years in Murray Island."

Ben Moa: "From Tonga. . . . Had been a sailor and at one time had lived in Tasmania."

Joe Simeon: "A native of Rotumah; . . . has been to Sydney, New Guinea, and all over the South Seas for twenty years."

George Lackey: "Native of Rotumah, left his island twenty-two years ago; has been all over the south seas."

Bunny Fen: "Native of Rotumah; left eleven years ago; has been a sailor in South Seas and in Queensland ports."

William Bedley: "A native of Sandwich Islands; left eighteen years ago; was four years in an American whaler and fourteen years in Torres Straits."

We can usefully turn to the nature of the "sandalwood English" spoken on and around ships and along the coasts of southern Melanesia in the 1850s and early 1860s. A number of Europeans commented on the "good English" spoken in this zone. A close reading suggests that it was less a sophisticated use of English syntax that gained these southern Melanesians a reputation for speaking "good English" than their renderings of English phonology. It would seem that the ("aberrantly") complex phonologies of the Oceanic Austronesian languages of southern Melanesia allowed speakers of (at least some of) them to approximate English consonants more closely than other Pacific islanders did. Erskine (1853: 320, 360–61) observes that:

> The much greater harshness of the Tanese language enables them, I was told, to acquire the English pronounciation with greater facility than the Polynesian.
> . . .
> The capacity of the Tanese for the pronounciation of the English words . . . is not less conspicuous among the New Caledonians. . . . Words which a Polynesian could seldom hope to master were picked up with the greatest ease by any of the people.

Having shifted our focus to the southern islands of Melanesia, we need to remember that in the twenty years from the mid-1840s to the mid-1860s, the islands of the central Pacific that had been an earlier center for the development of pidgin remained part of the same dispersed speech community. The eastern Carolines, the Marshalls, the Gilberts, and Rotuma remained connected to the dispersed pidgin speech community into the 1880s, particularly through the many Islanders who served on crews, traveled or settled abroad, and eventually became a first generation of plantation laborers. Seemann, for instance, encountered a number of Rotumans in Fiji during his visit of 1860–61, and reported that "the Rotuma men can nearly all speak a little English" ([1862] 1973: 36). He writes of "the ruling chief [of Rotuma], a fine young fellow, having made a voyage to Sydney, where he was well received—even, if report be true, at Government House" (p. 35).

Archival evidence provides few solid examples of "sandalwood English," especially as used by Islanders themselves, in the 1850s and 1860s. We do have some texts from the central Pacific in this period, catalogued by Ross Clark (1979: 29–30):

> Oh, me live with one mission in Tonga; I learn English, I wash, my wife, he iron (Tongan in Fiji, 1851).

Very good; 'nother day's sun he come all right (Kosrae, 1860).

Me saba plenty (Kosrae, 1860).

Me too much sick (Gilberts, 1860).

You think carva [*kava*] been poison? (Gilberts, 1860).

Only he got using all the same pigeon (Kosrae, 1860).

He too much bad man (Kosrae, 1860).

Me think missionary stop board that ship (Kosrae, 1857).

Our textual evidence is slightly richer for southern Melanesia. Erskine (1853: 347) describes a chief of "Uea" (Uvea) in the Loyalties, who "spoke a little English," and had told Captain Oliver of HMS *Fly* in 1850:*

(1)   Great fool Uea man, steal little thing he no want, big ship come and kill him.

Clark (1979: 37) draws attention to another interesting set of texts from Lifu in the Loyalties, recorded by Nihill in 1850:

(2)   You see all Lifu man can't swim, by and bye me drowned.

(3)   Canoe too little, by and bye, broke—All man go away, canoe gone, very good me stop.

On Tanna, probably in 1859, McFarlane (1873: 106) recorded:

(4)   Suppose missionary stop here, by and by he speak, "Very good, all Tanna man make a work." You see that no good: Tanna man he no too much like work. By-and-by missionary speak, "No good woman make a work: Very good, all man he only get one woman." You see Tanna man no like that; he speak, "Very good plenty woman: very good woman make all work." Tanna man no save work.

From 1859, we have a fragmentary rendering of a sermon at Mare in the Loyalties by the missionary Paton, as recounted years later by his wife (Paton 1894: 6–7):

(5)   Jehovah very good. He love Black man all same White man. He send Son belonga him. He die for all man.

From a decade later she gives us fragmentary examples of the pidgin used by Melanesians at the inception of the Labor Trade:

*Henceforth, sentences exemplifying pidgin usages are numbered to permit convenient reference.

(6)   What for you make paper about man Aniwa? (p. 30).

(7)   That no gammon (p. 35).

(8)   What for you look me? (p. 35).

(9)   You plenty lie. You 'fraid me se-teal. Me no se-teal, me come wor-
        ship. What for you look me se-teal? (p. 39).

(10)   You plenty lie! You all same Tiapolo [Devil] (p. 39).

(11)   Misi make him bokis sing. Plenty man come hear you make him
        bokis sing (p. 77).

From an 1867 account from Tanna we have several sentences cited, although some sound suspiciously like those reported by McFarlane (Adams
1984: 173–74):

(12)   Suppose missionary come here, white man go away, where man
        Tanna get tobacco?

(13)   Suppose missionary come here, he want man Tanna put on clothes;
        no good man Tanna he wear clothes; very good white man he
        wear clothes, all the same as you. . . . Look at that man, he look
        well, he no want clothes.

(14)   Look here, Tanna man he lazy, he plenty lazy, he no like work, he
        like walk about. . . .

(15)   Suppose missionary come here, he say, very good man Tanna
        keep only one woman.

Many elements in these and the other sentences quoted for this period
probably represent misrepresentations by the English-speaking chroniclers, not only (predictably) of the phonology, but of constructions and
lexical items. This will prove a recurrent problem in interpreting the
grammar and lexicon represented in the early texts. Nonetheless, these
fragments give crucially important glimpses of a developing pidgin. Here
we have not only lexical items such as "gammon," "walkabout," "plenty,"
and "all same," but evidence of grammatical constructions that are pervasive in all modern dialects of Melanesian Pidgin, such as:

   1. Periphrastic causatives using *mek-em* to form Pidgin equivalents of
Oceanic causatives (a pattern that will turn out to be important in my
later argument).

   2. What seems to be verb serialization using the auxiliary *kam* ("come
worship"); constructions using *go* as an auxiliary may occur as early as the
1850s, in "Every kanaka, big island, small island, all go and kill every
man board ship" (Hezel 1983: 114).

   3. Use of a resumptive pronoun (*hi* or *i*) after noun subjects (the so-
called "predicate marker," which will be examined in later chapters).

4. The use of *bulong* for possessives.

5. The use of *baebae* preceding subject nouns and pronouns to indicate a future time-frame for the verb.

6. Embedded relative clauses, as early as 1850 (". . . steal little thing he no want").

7. Interrogatives derived from English "wh-" phrases, in "what for . . . ?"

I fail to see why we cannot call this lingua franca so widely spoken on ship and shore in the Pacific by 1860 a pidgin, rather than a "jargon" (Clark 1979); it is considerably more developed, by this early stage, than the "true pidgins" described by Bickerton (1981).

Indeed it is not implausible that incipient creolization was under way in this period, if we can define this in terms of children acquiring a pidgin as at least a coordinate first language. As Howe (1977: 88–89) notes, many whites sailing the New Caledonia coast and plying trade in the southwest Pacific had taken Mare and Lifu (Loyalty Islands) women as wives. This seems particularly to have been true of the masters of English vessels. Whereas "Captain Banner married a Lifu woman and sent their children to school in Sydney" (Howe 1977: 89), most presumably had children who grew up on shipboard. We can only guess at the socio-linguistics of such situations (the crews of such ships largely consisted of Loyalty Islanders, but a dozen languages are spoken in the Loyalties). It is far from improbable that an emerging pidgin, rather than Mare, Lifu, or Uvean dialects, or standard English, was the medium not only of ship-board work relations but of domestic life for parents and children, even though the children were native speakers of their mothers' languages. If so, the pidgin of the period would have been acquired by these children as fluent early-childhood learners. (Whether this constitutes "nativization" is irrelevant to my argument;* but the command such children acquire appears to be very different from the command acquired by adult learners in a context of plantation labor or its equivalent.) There is no linguistic evidence from this period to suggest grammatical elaboration and incip-ient creolization in this sense, beyond the kinds of constructions I have illustrated. But we would be unwise, I think, to assume that the prevail-ing lingua franca as used by adults was too impoverished to act as the primary medium of communication in miniature speech communities, learned with native fluency by young children participating in it. And we would be unwise, when our fragments of recorded speech come from Europeans with a highly imperfect command of the pidgin being spo-ken by Islanders themselves, to make assumptions about its grammatical

*I am grateful to Christine Jourdan for long and illuminating discussions on this issue.

impoverishment, considering that it already incorporated standardized grammatical markers and allowed constructions with embedded relative clauses.

A single early-Pidgin speech community, ship- and shore-based, solidly established within the zone of the Loyalties, Ile des Pins, New Caledonia coast, and southern New Hebrides islands of Erromanga, Tanna, and Aneityum, as well as in the central Pacific, provided, I suggest, a base for the further elaboration and stabilization of Pacific pidgin in the Labor Trade. By the end of the 1860s, with missionaries and traders established in the southern New Hebrides, more or less fluent command of the prevailing pidgin was increasingly widespread there, in contrast to the situation Erskine had encountered in the early 1850s. On Tanna in 1869, Palmer (1871: 46) encountered "Yaufangan, . . . the orator of the chief Yankarubbie [who] had picked up a little English in his contact with the traders." He describes how Nownun, nephew of "the principal chief of Port Resolution [Tanna] wanted me to catch [the perpetrator of an offense] and 'make him fast,' which, upon questioning him, I found meant hanging" (p. 50).

By this time, many of the Loyalty Islanders had gone well beyond this in their linguistic sophistication in interacting with English speakers. Palmer (1871: 117) writes of witnesses in an 1869 Select Committee hearing on the initial phase of the Labor Trade: "Lifou Dick, Bebbo, . . . and Kouma, three of the boat's crew, —and Fangai or Johnny Mare the cook; all these natives speaking English, and two of them men of considerable intelligence, being able to read and write." Of these, "Beppo had been in Queensland three years" (p. 216)—which takes us to the earliest phase of the Labor Trade.

CHAPTER 4

The Labor Trade

THE LINGUISTIC COMMUNITY that was established on and spread by the early trading ships was not confined to southern Melanesia. By the earliest phase of the Labor Trade, it had left scattered speakers of a developing pidgin in the southeastern Solomons, as attested by Brenchley's visit to Makira (San Cristobal) in 1865: "Having met two natives who spoke a little English, I immediately engaged them to serve me as guides. These men . . . are passionately fond of smoking" (Brenchley 1873: 265). Later "another native came also who spoke English" (p. 270); and "almost immediately on landing an elderly native, using coarse Hawaiian gibberish, no doubt derived from traders, made a proposal touching the other sex which I declined" (p. 272).

Even out-of-the-way specks of islands like Anuta, between the southeast Solomons and the Torres and Banks Islands, had by 1870 some experience in dealing with Europeans. There, Commander Markham encountered a young Polynesian who "had certainly been in communication with Englishmen, as he was able to say 'yes,' 'no,' 'good morning,' and 'no savez,' of which accomplishment he was not a little proud" (Markham 1873: 131).

By this time, the sophisticated islanders from the Loyalties, Fiji, the Gilberts, Rotuma, and other areas of the Pacific who served on ships' crews and acted as middlemen, recruiters, foremen, and traders were already fluent speakers of a developing Pacific pidgin. While it is true that the Labor Trade entailed the bringing together of speakers of a multitude of different—though as we will shortly see, grammatically similar—languages, it did not bring them together under conditions of radical sociolinguistic juxtaposition (such as Bickerton and his colleagues depict for

Hawaii), where they had in effect to invent a medium of communication from scratch. At each stage in the development of Pacific pidgin from the mid-1840s onward, fellow Pacific Islanders, fellow speakers of Oceanic Austronesian languages, who were already fluent speakers of a by-then-established and relatively expanded, stable pidgin played crucial roles as negotiators, recruiters, supervisors, foremen—and agents of language transmission.

Having examined the probable role of Loyalty Islanders and others from southern Melanesia, we need to remember that Islanders from the central Pacific continued to play crucial parts in the dissemination and development of Pacific pidgin. C. F. Wood interestingly describes the Island crew he acquired in 1872 (1875: 73) to replace "the four Rotumah boys that I had had with me":

I had now only two white men before the mast, and, I must confess, had about as nondescript and rascally-looking a crew as ever graced the deck of any pirate. To begin with, two natives of the Loyalty Islands. . . . Next to these [a] Solomon Islander [from Makira], anxious to go home. . . . Two natives of Rotumah, one from Rorotonga [Cook Islands], and three from Ellice's group [now Tuvalu]. . . . Later on I picked up two Spanish Malays, natives of the Philippines.

The Gilbertese, because in a crucial period they moved so widely as pioneer plantation laborers as well as crew members and intermediaries, deserve special mention. The first Island laborers recruited for Samoa, in the late 1860s, were Gilbertese; and they were joined, in the early 1870s, by a few Caroline Islanders (Moses 1973: 102). It seems likely that it was the pidgin of the central Pacific, already in use there by German traders as well as Islanders, that provided the initial linguistic medium of plantation communication in Samoa, later to change in parallel with the pidgin developing in Queensland.

As agents of linguistic diffusion, the Gilbertese may have played a role farther afield than Samoa. In the light of Goodman's challenge (1985) to Bickerton's claim that Hawaiian Creole emerged too late to have received any input from either Pacific pidgin or Atlantic creoles, and Goodman's suggestion that Hawaiian Creole may have taken shape in the 1870–80 period, it is worth noting that substantial numbers of Gilbertese were in Hawaii at just the right period to have had some impact (Hezel 1983; Bennett 1976). Hezel (1983: 239–40) notes that

by 1873, the worst of the blackbirding scourge in the Carolines and Marshalls [to Samoa and Fiji] was over. . . . Only in the Marshalls, where Jaluit was used as a depot for native laborers recruited in the Gilberts to work on the sugar plantations of Hawaii, did the labor trade continue to any appreciable extent. In the late 1870s, some Marshallese were shipped to Hawaii along with the Gilbertese who made up the vast majority of the recruits, but this practice had been discontinued in 1882 when it became apparent that Pacific islanders could not cope with the difficult work of harvesting sugar.

Recent research by Baker and Mühlhäusler on the role of Gilbertese in the dissemination of an early Pacific pidgin points to similar possibilities. In a forthcoming paper, Mühlhäusler (n.d.2) comments that

a significant number of Gilbertese, speaking a reasonably developed pidgin English by about 1840, were employed on trading and whaling vessels as well as on the plantations of Hawaii, Samoa, Queensland, and Réunion in the Indian Ocean. The Gilbertese may have acted as agents for the diffusion of certain lexical items and constructions.

This suggests the possibility that Gilbertese may have had some linguistic impact on the creole of Réunion in the Indian Ocean, the only place beyond the Pacific where the "predicate marker" (see Chapter 10) is clearly attested.

The dominant phase of the Labor Trade brought New Hebrideans and later Solomon Islanders to Queensland, Fiji, and New Caledonia. This represented a progressive harvesting of recruits to meet expanding demands for plantation labor that moved from the central Pacific southward and from the southern New Hebrides to the north and west into the central New Hebrides and northern New Hebrides, the Banks and Torres groups, and then into the southeastern and northern Solomons. The sweep from central Pacific to the south, then toward the north and west, was partly a concomitant of logistics and distance (in relation to Fiji, Samoa, and Queensland), and partly a supply-and-demand phenomenon. The latter factor operated in several ways. One was the depletion from death and disease of populations of young men in areas that had provided plantation workers for ten or fifteen years. A second was the increased sophistication of Islanders in these established sources of labor, which made young men reluctant to commit themselves to the physically difficult and dangerous regimen of plantation labor under conditions of long indenture. A third and related process was the saturation of areas such as Tanna, Erromanga, and Aneityum with the European goods—steel tools, guns, cloth—that had provided the lure for plantation labor. Finally, the sheer demand for labor required an expanding supply of recruits at a time when the old areas were providing fewer recruits and driving progressively harder bargains in a competitive market.

Missionary success in the southern New Hebrides and Loyalties was another factor, since the destructive consequences of the Labor Trade were the focus of a growing stream of moral criticism in the form of political propaganda (see Howe 1977 on the Loyalties and Adams 1984 on Tanna). A consequence of all these factors was that recruiters had to keep working their way into areas where less-sophisticated Islanders needed the trade goods for which recruiting was the only source, and where Christianity had not yet taken firm hold.

We find in the records of the early Labor Trade evidence of a small, scattered population, on the various islands, of men who by that time had acquired some sophistication in dealing with ships and some command (often minimal) of the shipboard pidgin. These men came to serve as local middlemen and brokers. Thus, when Capt. John Moresby visited the Banks Islands and New Hebrides in 1872 in command of HMS *Basilisk*, he encountered sophisticates who could assure him that labor recruiting was no longer a matter of kidnapping. On Santa Maria in the Banks, he

received a hearty welcome on landing from several hundreds of savages, who wore no clothes and were armed with deadly arrows. Amongst them we saw one who was the happy owner of a red shirt and a double-barrelled gun, and he spoke English well, and told us he had spent five years in Australia. We talked about kidnapping, and he observed, "All black men savy; no kidnapping now; if black man like to go he go, if he like to stop he stop" (Moresby 1876: 96).

In some areas the role of such sophisticates as opportunistic middlemen, who parlayed their capacity for intercultural communication into considerable local power, became virtually institutionalized. Local figures became well known to the recruiters and acted as their agents, negotiating for plantation recruits and extracting substantial rewards from the recruiters. The famous Kwaisulia and Foulanga ("Foulanger") of Malaita in the southeastern Solomons (Corris 1970, 1973) are type-figures in the literature.

These local sophisticates in turn became agents in the further spread of a developing pidgin. Some of them did not stay in the Islands, but moved on to serve on ships or plantations as recruiting middlemen or foremen. Siegel (1986: 64) cites 1869 testimony regarding the schooner *Daphne* in which "Charlie, 'a native of Amota Lava [Mota Lava in the Banks Islands] who speaks English' (and a well known recruiter in the labor trade), says: 'You no go long way; you stop Tanna, bye and bye you come back.'" By the mid-1870s, there were enough Queensland veterans in the central and northern New Hebrides that a knowledge of pidgin was no longer confined to a few opportunists.

The role of whites as pidgin speakers in this period merits preliminary comment at this stage. European recruiters acquired sufficient command of the prevailing form of pidgin that they were able themselves to communicate fairly successfully with Islanders who commanded "some English." But their records of their own pidgin utterances reveal that few of them spoke the pidgin of the day fully grammatically, however disdainful they may have been of the local savages. I will return in Chapter 7 to the respective roles of Islanders and Europeans in the formation of Pacific pidgin.

This process of brokerage in labor recruiting was one alternative for sophisticates with long experience to gain substantial rewards without the heavy costs of plantation labor. We have already noted the propensity of Loyalty Islanders to serve on crews of vessels working in and beyond the southwestern Pacific. Another alternative for those who had already worked as indentured laborers in Queensland, Fiji, or other areas was to stay on in these plantation areas, working as mobilizers, organizers, or supervisors of new indentured laborers, and commanding greater rewards and greater freedom than the latter (see Moore 1986 for Queensland). These "finish times," from the Loyalties, Tanna, Aneityum, and Erromanga and later, places like Ambae (Aoba) in the northern New Hebrides and Malaita in the southeastern Solomons, who had worked for a decade or longer in plantation areas, probably played an important part in the further development, elaboration, and stabilization of Pacific plantation pidgin even after the focus of recruiting had moved beyond their own islands. Many of them married in Queensland, Fiji, New Caledonia, or Samoa and remained there after the cessation of the Labor Trade at the beginning of the twentieth century. Their children probably grew up as native speakers of the prevailing pidgin. But I suspect that by the late 1880s, at least, pidgin was so fully developed that—as in modern Papua New Guinea (Mühlhäusler 1985b) and the Solomons (Jourdan 1985)— there was little room or need for children acquiring it natively to expand its syntactic possibilities.

Before looking at the textual evidence on the pidgin of the 1870s and 1880s, it will be useful to look at the sources of plantation labor during the Labor Trade. That will prove to be important when we consider the question of substrate linguistic models.

We have detailed information on the islands of origin of recruits for Queensland, compiled by Price and Baker (1976). A similar compilation for Samoa has been published by Moses (1973), although the breakdown of data is less specific in terms of language subgroups. Siegel (1986, 1987) reconstructs corresponding figures for Fiji. As far as I know, comparable data for New Caledonia are not available. Fiji was less important in terms of the emergence of an elaborated and stabilized Pacific plantation pidgin than Queensland, New Caledonia, and Samoa because, as Siegel (1986, 1987) has documented, a pidginized Fijian early emerged as the primary lingua franca of Fiji plantations (although Pacific pidgin continued to be

TABLE 4.1

Origins of Recruits to Queensland, by Five-Year Periods, 1863–1904

(Principal sources only)

| Period | Loyalties | New Hebrides | | | Southeastern Solomons |
		South	Central	North	
1863–1867	421	307	881	120	—
1868–1872	643	508	961	1,481	58
1873–1877	55	1,197	2,202	4,412	813
1878–1882	—	1,327	1,892	6,435	1,561
1883–1887	—	1,143	1,355	5,437	2,509
1888–1892	—	525	953	3,116	—
1893–1897	—	265	573	1,760	3,037
1898–1904	—	528	906	1,743	5,028

SOURCE: Price and Baker (1976), adjusted slightly for linguistic subgroupings.

the medium of recruiting in the islands, and a secondary medium of communication among island laborers).

Price and Baker's Queensland figures are here adjusted slightly (Table 4.1) so as to correspond with the linguistic subgroups that will be examined in Chapter 6. Price and Baker's data must be treated with caution on several grounds. First of all, as they acknowledge, their inferences in relation to the names of islands of origin require considerable guessing and extrapolation. Second, several authors have suggested that, especially for the early years of the Labor Trade, the figures (based as they are on officially recorded voyages and legal immigration) may be significantly lower than actual totals, partly because of the concerns of the French over incursions into "their" waters: "The first Queensland recruiting ships reached the Loyalty Islands in 1865 and until 1874 thirty-nine visits can be documented. The real number was undoubtedly greater because of the clandestine nature of recruiting necessary to escape hostile French attention" (Howe 1977: 90).

More important, the number *recruited* during particular time periods do not directly represent the numbers *present* in Queensland for these periods.* Even if laborers were only recruited for a single three-year term, the numbers would have to be substantially adjusted (so, for example, workers from the southeastern Solomons would not have actually begun to *outnumber* New Hebrideans in Queensland until about 1900). Given the fact that many workers had served two or three or more terms or were permanently established in Queensland, and the fact that these "finish times" tended to be in supervisory and leadership positions, the preponderant

---

*Christine Jourdan, personal communication.

importance of speakers of Central and Northern New Hebridean languages in Queensland is reinforced.*

Because the Labor Trade of the 1870s and 1880s to Queensland has been so extensively discussed with reference to the emergence of Melanesian Pidgin, I will cover this period in less detail. I will largely confine myself to looking at some aspects of the linguistic evidence from the Queensland period, seeking to establish that much of the grammatical complexity observed in Tok Pisin, Bislama, and Solomons Pidgin (the "elaboration" of Pidgin widely discussed in the literature) had taken place by the mid-1880s (much of it by the late 1870s, contra Mühlhäusler 1981).

A preliminary word about the evidence is needed. First of all, almost all observers have heavily anglicized their renderings of pidgin. Second, in their paraphrases of utterances by Islanders, often written long after the event but sometimes recorded in log books soon after their occurrence, Europeans undoubtedly further anglicized utterances in content and grammar. The trained eye can detect many apparent errors in recording due to code interference, selective perception, or faulty memory. However, to correct the primary texts—or even to transliterate them into their probable actual form—entails dangers as well. These are the only records we have of the period, and if we interpret them according to the pidgins known directly from the twentieth century, we might obliterate crucial evidence and impose our own interpretive biases. Hence, I have left the texts as they stand, but have noted in footnotes what I take to be probable errors of recording. Third, as I argue at some length in Chapter 7, the evidence indicates to me that it was Islanders, not Europeans, who by the onset of the Labor Trade were the fluent speakers of a developing pidgin; most Europeans spoke the pidgin badly. However, at least by the 1880s a bifurcation had begun in which a more anglicized register was being used by Islanders who had sustained contact with Europeans and modified pidgin in the direction of the superstrate language. We find this anglicized register in the textual record, as in the transcripts of the Queensland inquiries, identifiable by a different pronominal system and other features—sometimes interspersed with pidgin, or used by Islanders in quoting utterances by English speakers.

First, we can usefully borrow some of the pre-1878 passages dug out by Clark (1979: 39). I continue the numbering used in Chapter 3.

(16)   Captain, he buy him four boy belong a me (Nguna, New Hebrides, 1870).

(17)   Well, master, man Makura, he no want missionary (Makura, New Hebrides, 1872).

*I use capitals to refer to linguistic subgroups, which will be outlined in Chapter 6.

(18)   He say, canoe come, seven or eight men. Canoe break, men run
         away bush. He no kaikai him. He say, long time before he no
         kaikai man (Nguna, New Hebrides, 1876).

Evidence from a slightly later period, the first half of the 1880s, comes
from Rannie (1912):

(19)   We too close already; by and by when that fellow finish dance
         they fire up along you and me (Lihir Group, Bismarck Archi-
         pelago, 1844; p. 53).

(20)   What for Government Agent no let boat's crew help-'em boys
         when altogether want go Queensland? Suppose we been have 'em
         good fellow Government, we full up now (Lihir Group, 1884;
         p. 53).

(21)   All right, you give me ten stick tobacco and I give 'em you head
         belong my small fellow brother (Malekula, New Hebrides, 1884;
         p. 94).*

(22)   Paddy no good, he flash fellow, he savey too much lie (Simbo,
         Solomons, 1887; p. 292).

Wawn ([1893] 1973) also gives some useful examples, including renderings of his own conversations:

(23)   By-and bye, man-o'-war come; me speak cappen belong man-o'-
         war man Sandwich make big wind, big wind broke ship belonga
         me. . . . Yes, man Sandwich make him. All atime, big wind he
         come along here (Wawn, reporting his own utterance at Efate in
         1878; p. 144).

(24)   This fellow no all the same: he come along here. That fellow big
         wind, man Sandwich make him; he broke ship along island be-
         longa you. Me speak cappen belong man-o'-war, suppose you no
         look out (the local's quoted reply; he had "served a term in New
         Caledonia"; p. 144).

(25)   Very good you go look chief belonga me: he like spik you. . . .
         Chief he old man. No savey walk good (Efate, 1878; p. 143).

Giles ([1877] 1968) gives further useful texts, the first from an Ile des
Pins man who had lived in Queensland for three years:

(26)   Me bin work long-a Maryboro. Misse White my massa.† You
         savee Misse White, my word me plenty work long that fellow
         massa long-a-soogar. Misse White no good he plenty fight, too

---

*"My" here is highly suspect.
†Again, "my" is suspect, although the several occurrences of an English-derived possessive construction may indicate that it was an option introduced recurrently by superstrate speakers.

much kill 'em me, he bin give me small fellow boks, no good, me fine fellow man, very good you give me tambacco, me too much like-em-smoke (p. 37).

(27)   What name ship? Where he come? . . . You buy him yam? . . . You want to buy him boy, what name you give it belong a boy? Suppose you give me one fellow musket, me give you one fellow boy (Tanna, 1877; p. 40).

(28)   Me no care, me no belong this fellow place, man here no good— rogue. . . . What for you steal him man, you no been buy him that fellow? (ibid.).

(29)   You see Massa, you bin tell me altogether man fool put im red longa face. Me no fool, me put im blue (Emae, New Hebrides, 1878–79; p. 57).

From Queensland plantations in the late 1870s, we have various bits and pieces of evidence, among which these two brief texts are representative:

(30)   He plenty fight along'o boy. Master plenty whip him and fight him boy (Horrocks 1878).

(31)   Me sick me stop over there no more. Me stop no more there, me want to go along big fellow house;* too much sick there (*Mackay Mercury*, Sept. 1, 1877).

Coote (1882) gives a number of passages recorded in 1880:

(32)   Me speakee English, my name belong Black John, me been Porter Mackai, too muchee wark, my word, me no sleep all er time, plenty wark, big fellow wind he come, me plenty sick, me word, me no likee Porter Mackai, plenty sugar he stop, me carry him planty time, me get one feller bokus [box], one feller gun, plenty tambacca, me stop three feller year, my word to muchee work, me no sleep, me carry sugar, my word, me no likee him, no you give me tambacca, you come England? me savvy England, plenty far, good feller man he belong England, feller man belong Porter Mackai he no good (Torres Islands; p. 142).[†]

(33)   Here two man he stop. Here three feller man. Here woman stop (Torres Islands; p. 143).

(34)   No, he belong white man. . . . Oh, he belong oui-oui-man. . . . Oh, no; oui-oui-man no belong white man; oui-oui-man belong

*What is recorded as "want to go" is, judging by the distributional evidence, probably *wande go*, with *wande* used as a modal auxiliary. In the 1850s we have, from Kosrae, "White man want to get gal go aboard ship" (Gulick 1862: 241), which is the first apparent recorded instance of *wande* as an auxiliary.

[†]Coote says the "man was very communicative, and had a long sentence such as the following, which he repeated continually." "Feller man" is very probably an error (see Keesing n.d. 3). "My name" is suspect.

all same devil (the Loyalty Islander is responding to queries, in bad pidgin, by Coote himself; the question at issue is whether French are real "white men"; p. 194).

(35)   No, steamer he no come—steamer he stop on a stone—all man he go saltwater—plenty man he die—steamer he finish (New Caledonia; p. 197).

(36)   The Hailey, king belong Coolangbangara, big feller fighting man; me speak you; me kai kai ten one [11] feller man belong Esperanza; me take him altogether trade—musket, powder, tobacco, bead, plenty; me take everything; me make big fire, ship he finish. . . . White man allsame woman, he no savee fight, suppose woman plenty cross she* make plenty noise, suppose man-of-war he come fight me, he make plenty noise, but he all same woman— he no savee fight (Kolombangara, western Solomons; p. 206).

The recruiter Jock Cromar, whose recollections (published in 1935) turn out to be extremely accurate and must have been based on a detailed journal, gives several useful texts from his early visits to the New Hebrides and Solomons in 1882–86. In the context of his first trip to the New Hebrides in 1882, he comments (1935: 36) that in these islands "it was never necessary to carry interpreters, for so many men had been to Queensland that *beche-de-mer* English, the pidgin of the Pacific, was already the *lingua franca* of these islands." Cromar gives us texts, probably from 1884 (although the exact date is uncertain), that not only are interesting linguistically but prefigure my documentation in the next chapter of how German recruiting for Samoa spanned the same islands (and presumably used the same linguistic medium) as recruiting for Queensland, well into the 1880s:

(37)   Me fellow keep him. By and by me fellow buy'em gun along man-we-we [i.e., Frenchman: "man oui oui"] and German man (pp. 117–18).

(38)   Me savvy. You all right. You new-chum along Maratta. You buy-em boy along shoota (musket)? . . . [Cromar replies in the negative.] Me think you can't catch-em boy. S'pose German man and man-we-we pay-em shoota, him catch-em altogether boy. Man Maratt like'm shoota too much. You can't catch-em boy along tabac (Malaita, 1884 or 1885; pp. 138–39).

Elsewhere, Cromar provides various local commentaries on sexual relations between Europeans and indigenous women:

*The "she" is highly suspect here, although probably some of the reported occurrences are genuine, and reflect the divergence of registers on which I have already commented: that is, accommodation by Islanders to the usages or expectations of English speakers.

(39)   S'pose you try for take'm mary, man Maratt must kill you (Ma-
        laita, 1884 or 1885; p. 137).

(40)   You no like'm me? . . . Me like'm white man. You come (Malo,
        New Hebrides, ca. 1885; pp. 180–81).

Florence Young (1926), writing of Queensland plantations in the late
1880s, gives a number of texts, of which two can be taken as illustrative:

(41)   He no like-'im school, because he no savee. By-and-by he like-'im
        plenty, he come all the time (Bundaberg, 1886; p. 46).

(42)   Me no want-'im school. Suppose me come along school, by-and-
        by me no savee fight. Me go home along Island, man he kill-'im
        me. Along Island altogether man he row, row, row all the time.
        Man he go sleep along bed, he hold-'im spear, bow and arrow,
        gun along hand. Suppose he go got-'im gun, some-fellow man he
        come, he kill him quick (Bundaberg, 1886; p. 47).

Kay Saunders (1979) has unearthed several pidgin texts from Queensland dealing with employer-servant relations, of which one fragment,
from 1884, can be taken as representative:

(43)   Mi see him overseer that time he been hit him Cao first time. He
        been kick him long boot. Overseer say "What name you? No
        work quick." When he kick him, Cao, mi say, "What for you hit
        him?" Cao no savey talk. New chum. . . . He then hit me first
        time long face two fellow time (1884; p. 170).

Finally, we have bodies of testimony from the various commissions of
inquiry set up in the 1880s to investigate alleged abuses of the Labor Trade, of which two passages quoted by Wawn ([1893] 1973) are
illustrative:

(44)   Cappen, you been take me along three year. Me, sandfly, both
        speak, three year. By-and-by, boy belong island he speak: "What
        for you speak three *year*? Very good, you speak three *moon*. Sup-
        pose you no speak three moon, altogether boy, he stop Queens-
        land three year. No good." Me think all the boy want to kill me;
        then me, sandfly, go back and speak we come along three moon
        (Milne Bay, New Guinea, 1885; p. 373).

(45)   He belong Buri-Burrigan; he know he come alonga Ceara; he
        come three years, work alonga sugar cane. . . . When he go
        alonga sugar cane in* Queensland, he too much work; no like
        him; suppose he work strong fellow, white fellow he no hit him;
        suppose he lazy, he hit him a little fellow. Sun, he come up, he go
        work; sun, he go down, he go sleep, no get him plenty ki-ki;

*"Long" is much more likely to have been the preposition here.

plenty boy die; he think he die, too, wants to go alonga home
(ca. 1884; p. 349).

Before summarizing the grammatical patterns attested in the pidgin of
the Labor Trade, it is worth pausing to examine some fragments of contemporaneous pidgin from the central Pacific and Polynesia. These texts
show both continuities with the developing pidgin of the Labor Trade
zone and discontinuities, as from the early 1870s onward the incorporation of these areas into the Pacific pidgin speech network progressively
attenuated.

We can begin with the Gilberts, for which we have an account from
MacCallum (1934), who visited the Gilberts with Robert Louis Stevenson in 1889. He gives several fragments of the speech of Gilbertese, both
of "kings" who were in regular contact with Europeans and spoke in a
relatively anglicized register and of others who spoke something closer to
standard shipboard pidgin. MacCallum reports "King" Tubureimoa of
Makin as saying: "Me, I got power, . . . Tembinoka, I think I like fight
him" (p. 252). This gives an interesting early glimpse of a "me, I" sequence, a phenomenon that will be of interest in Chapter 10; and it
shows an apparent instance of the pervasive incorporation of the transitive suffix, in what appears to be *faet-im*—a pattern that will be of interest in Chapter 8.

Tembinoka was the elderly ruler of Apemama, another island in the
Gilberts, who had long had close relations with Europeans. MacCallum
(1934) records:

> When he had distinguished visitors, he used to don the most gorgeous outfits
> his savage heart could conceive; often a red or green short jacket of silk plush
> over his singlet, while his fat legs were covered with a pair of cotton pants, or just
> a native ridi, as his fancy chose. At one time on the occasion of Stevenson's
> farewell, he appeared dressed in the coat of a navy captain. . . .
>
> His ideal of kingly power of majesty was "Victoreea," as he called England's
> queen. Sitting in his house one night he told me "Me got plenty powa, just like
> Victoreea." . . . The king spoke English, but a variety entirely his own. It was
> quite different from the Beche-de-Mer of the wild islands, or the pidgin English
> spoken by the Asiatic Polynesians (pp. 262–63).
>
>   . . .
>
> Right then and there I [MacCallum, as ship's cook] was taken to Tembinoka's
> heart. He told the captain, "I likum mobetta, my cook no savee how, bimby cook
> he come my outchhe, get good boone (wife)." . . . The king's answer was "I
> likum, how much?" . . . Captains . . . who . . . were no longer welcome in Apa-
> mama were catalogued as "Cheat too much mo plenty" (pp. 268, 277, 278).

Although Tembinoka's speech may have been unique, we have other attestations of his use of the transitive suffix, as in the slightly earlier (1887) fragment from Moss (1889: 132): "Think me better shoot him."

We get a fragment of speech from the ordinary Gilbertese "natives" later in MacCallum's account: "Him fella along hole flenny sick, catchem die." The "him fella" may be incorrectly reported, or may represent a sporadic extrapolation from the demonstratives "dis-fella" and "dat-fella" for which there is good early textual evidence (see Keesing n.d. 3). Otherwise, it sounds much like the common pidgin coin of the Pacific realm, with "along" (*long*) as locative and "catch-em" with transitive suffix.

For the shipboard English of the period, we get a tiny sample from an Islander named Tatoma, a member of the crew of the *Equator*, who is reported (MacCallum 1934: 250) as saying "That Murray, he make difference." The resumptive pronoun here is further evidence of its increasingly pervasive use: a phenomenon that will concern us in later chapters.

Nor had pidgin disappeared in Rotuma. Sir John Thurston's correspondence chronicled a Rotuman chief named Riamkau, who had served in 1861–62 on the crew of the *James*. In 1873, Riamkau wrote to Thurston attesting that the latter had not killed a Rotuman: "No mister Thurston, me know Mr Thurston he very good man" (Scarr 1973: 19–20). A somewhat later text comes from a Rotuman named Albert, whose pidgin probably is relatively anglicized as well as recorded though the filter of an English-speaking chronicler, H. H. Romilly. In 1880, Romilly (1893: 101) recorded a letter dictated by Albert:

> Me all same brother you. The time Mr. Romily stop Rotumah me look out all same you when he stop England. Me wish me savey you, but think be no good. Suppose ship go you write me. Suppose Mr. Romilly go you sorry me. Send letter. This my letter you. Time Mr. Gordon stop Rotumah good too much. Mr. Romilly all same. Mr. Romilly same my boy, you same my brother. Suppose you wish something Rotumah you write your brother. Me make him. . . .
>
> Me savey you got three son, two daughters. Me got three son, three daughter. My fam brother your fam, all same you brother me.

Elsewhere Romilly records Albert as saying: "Suppose man do good, give plenty copra mission, he go heaven too quick. Suppose do bad, Devil catch him, take him Helly" (p. 109).

From a slightly later period, we get fragments of pidgin from Polynesia. In Manihiki in the Cooks in 1887, Moss (1889: 109) recorded a young man pointing to the "king," called Apollo by Europeans, and saying: "That fellow king."* He called to the "king": "Aporo, Aporo, this man he want see you."

---

*On verbless equational sentences in Melanesian Pidgin and Oceanic languages, see Chapter 10.

We can now turn back to the pidgin of the Labor Trade zone, as represented in the texts we have examined. Most of the essential syntactic and semantic/lexical patterns of Melanesian Pidgin are represented in the texts from the 1870s and 1880s (and the earlier texts we have seen), despite the thick filter of European preconceptions and misconceptions. It is worth pausing to summarize some of these linguistic patterns.

   1. In terms of global syntax, a preferred SVO order of constituents.
   2. Relatively complex syntactic potentialities. By 1850 (sentence 1) relative clauses could be embedded; by 1878, a direct object could be topicalized by fronting (sentence 24)—as will be seen, a characteristic Oceanic Austronesian pattern. In sentence 24, the fronted direct object seems to be used to embed a relative clause ("That fellow big wind Man Sandwich make him he broke ship").
   3. A standardization of grammatical devices for linking clauses, such as *sapos* to introduce a conditional clause (a construction and form represented in all dialects of Melanesian Pidgin and recorded in Pacific jargon as early as 1835). The form *wen* is used here (sentence 20) to introduce an embedded temporal clause, where contemporary dialects characteristically use *taem*.
   4. A standardization of modals within verb phrases, notably *save* and its negation *nosave* (sentences 4, 25, 43) or *kaen* (sentence 38) 'be unable to,' and *wande* plus infinitive 'want to' (sentences 17, 20, 27, 44, 45), and *trae fo* plus infinitive (sentence 39)—patterns manifest in all dialects of Melanesian Pidgin.
   5. A standardization of tense/aspect-marking, with *bin* (past or nonpresent marker manifest in Tok Pisin and Bislama) and *bambae* (future, irrealis, or nonaccomplished mode marker manifest in Tok Pisin, Solomons Pidgin, and Bislama). *Bambae* canonically preceded a subject pronoun, but it could either precede or follow a noun subject (the former the canonical pattern in Bislama, the latter the canonical pattern in Solomons Pidgin; see Keesing 1986, and Chapter 11). The regularity of *bambae* as a future/irrealism marker closely linked to the subject pronoun in these texts of the 1870s and 1880s suggests that during the Labor Trade it was becoming grammaticalized and was not merely a "temporal adverb" (although the English superstrate model dictated its usual clause-initial position; cf. Sankoff and Laberge 1973).
   6. The standardized use of a transitive suffix *-em* or *-im*, with and without a following noun object. This usage is represented in all dialects of Melanesian Pidgin.
   7. At least a partial standardization of a pronominal paradigm incorporating *mi, iu, hem/i, iumi, mifela*, perhaps *iufela*, and *olgeta* (or *ol*), forms represented in all dialects of Melanesian Pidgin. Use of short pro-

nouns derived from English subject pronouns "I," "we," and "they" (*ae, wi, de*) is a recurrent theme through the long history of Melanesian Pidgin (see Chapter 10) and is represented here in several sentences (e.g., 19, 20, 21). No doubt such usages did occur, but they must be treated with caution, given that Europeans who spoke pidgin imperfectly were our scribes; all these sentences came from Rannie (1912). I examine the development of the Pacific pidgin pronominal system in detail in Chapters 9 and 10, and in Chapter 12 examine the pronominal pattern of Solomons Pidgin.

    8. Use of the grammatical element -*fela* in a set of quite regular syntactic slots:

        a. As a determiner quantifying nouns (sentences 27, 32, 33, 42, 43).

        b. As a suffix to attributive adjectives modifying nouns (sentences 20, 21, 26, 31, 32).

        c. As a suffix to attributives used as stative verbs (sentence 22).

        d. As a demonstrative determiner, preceding nouns (sentences 26, 28).

        e. As a demonstrative pronoun (sentences 19, 24).

        f. As a suffix to nonsingular pronouns (sentence 37, etc.).

        g. In adverbial constructions, apparently as a second, stative verb in compound constructions (sentence 45).

I discuss this highly regularized pattern in Keesing n.d. 3, showing that Mühlhäusler's claim that "fella" remained grammatically unstable through the nineteenth century is incorrect (see Chapter 8).

    9. The use of *bulong* plus noun or pronoun in possessive constructions (first attested in 1844 and represented in sentences 5, 16, 21, 24, 25, and 44).

    10. The use of the third-person plural ("they") pronoun as plural marker for nouns designating humans, manifest either as *olgeta* (sentences 29, 38, 42, and 44) or *ol* (sentences 2, 3, 4, and 44). This pattern, whose congruence with patterns in substrate languages I will discuss in Chapter 8, was manifest by the beginning of the 1850s; it is represented in all dialects of Melanesian Pidgin, often with both forms in use, even by the same speaker (as in sentence 44). Particularly interesting, in view of Mühlhäusler's reconstructed scenario for the relatively late and separate development of *ol* or *olgeta* as a plural marker with nonhuman nouns (1981; 1986: 182–83), is the occurrence of *olgeta* as plural marker for a nonhuman noun ("trade," referring to trade goods) in sentence 36, recorded in the Solomons in 1880. The same pattern turns up in the 1890s in texts from the New Hebrides.

    11. Periphrastic causatives with *mek-em*, used as early as 1869 (cf.

Mühlhäusler 1980: 38–42). I will discuss the implications of this in Chapter 8.

12. The standardization of clause-initial interrogatives derived from English "wh-" phrases, such as *wanem* (sentences 27, 43) and *watfo* (sentences 6, 8, 20, 28). The labels and/or semantics of these interrogatives have shifted somewhat in the course of a century, but their syntactic slot and functions remain the same.

13. The regularized use of the so-called "predicate marker" *i* after noun subjects, in maintaining reference across clauses and in embedding relative clauses. In Chapter 10, I will suggest an alternative analysis of the "predicate marker."

14. The regularization of *long* as an all-purpose locative particle, manifest in all dialects of Melanesian Pidgin.

15. The use of "say" (*se*) as a complementizer (sentence 18), with quoted utterances, prior to 1880 (cf. Mühlhäusler's discussion, 1986: 188–89, of the development of *se* as complementizer in Tok Pisin, as if it were a separate development).

16. The adoption (from English) of an array of forms, many with distinctive Melanesian semantic shadings, pervasively in use in dialects of Melanesian Pidgin, among them *olsem*, *nomoa*, *stap*, *kas-em* ('to reach [a place]'), *gat-em* ('to have, possess'), *fastaem*, and *wokabaot*.

By the first half of the 1880s, and in many cases well before 1880, the essential patterns of Melanesian Pidgin—syntactic, semantic, and lexical—were thus well established. The anomalous degree of standardization and expansion characteristic of this pidgin is a development not of the twentieth century, but of the nineteenth, a development the most striking features of which were established more than a hundred years ago. Whereas some authors have placed these developments spatially in New Guinea and the adjacent islands, the brief historical sketch I have given makes clear that we must look farther to the east and north in space, as well as further back in time. We are still left to ponder why the patterns I have summarized are found in all dialects of modern Melanesian Pidgin, including Tok Pisin.

CHAPTER 5

The Tok Pisin Lineage

MÜHLHÄUSLER'S HYPOTHESIS regarding the separate origins of New Guinea Pidgin (Tok Pisin) has been advanced in a series of provocative papers (Mühlhäusler 1976, 1978a, 1985a; Mosel and Mühlhäusler 1982). He argues that by 1870 a form of English-based pidgin had become established on the German plantations in Samoa. While the initial form of this pidgin may have had some connection to the pidgin used in the earliest phases of the Labor Trade to Queensland (a point on which he is never very specific), he views "Samoan Plantation Pidgin" as having had a substantially separate linguistic history from 1870 onward. It was this Samoan Plantation Pidgin that was introduced into the plantations of German New Guinea, initially in the Bismarck Archipelago; and that there developed, with some influence from the Melanesian languages of the Bismarcks, into Tok Pisin. (Mühlhäusler has also documented the existence of a Queensland-based dialect of pidgin in Papua, which eventually disappeared; see 1978b.) Mühlhäusler acknowledges that the hypothesis of a substantially separate origin for the New Guinea Pidgin lineage was initially articulated by Richard Salisbury, in a brief 1967 article.

Mühlhäusler's hypothesis has received remarkably little critical scrutiny, either from historians or from pidgin specialists. However, Clark (1979: 39–40) gives an assessment with which I am in general agreement. It is worth quoting at some length:

If we consider Melanesian pidgin to have developed and spread, like South Seas Jargon, within a dispersed network of communities at least partly seaborne, then the New Hebrides and Solomon Islands were connected to this network more or less continuously throughout the period 1865–1900. The connection of New Guinea with this network, on the other hand, was limited and brief. In

1878, . . . the first Melanesians (83 New Hebrideans) arrived on the German plantations of Samoa. The first labourers from New Britain and New Ireland came the following year, but for the next few years the New Hebrideans and Solomon Islanders were numerically dominant. . . . Many of the New Hebrideans and Solomon Islanders had probably learned the evolving Melanesian pidgin, either during previous service in Queensland, through contact with ships in their home islands, or en route. Not only were they a solid majority of the labour force in Samoa; their pidgin, through 15 years of development in Queensland, was probably a superior linguistic instrument to whatever form of South Seas Jargon the Gilbertese and New Guineans may have known. It was thus natural that the southern Melanesians would dominate linguistically, and their pidgin be adopted by the New Guineans.

After 1882 the situation changed rapidly. The numbers of New Guineans recruited to Samoa increased rapidly, and from 1885 on there appears to have been no further recruitment from southern Melanesia. New Guinea's connection with the Melanesian pidgin network thus lasted no more than seven years.

I will suggest that the close connections both between the southern recruiting grounds and Samoa and between Queensland and the Bismarcks lasted almost to the end of the 1880s. But more important, many of the crucial grammatical expansions and stabilizations of Melanesian Pidgin had taken place by 1885.

The most glaring problem with Mühlhäusler's argument for the essentially separate development of the Tok Pisin lineage is that virtually all the syntactic patterns of Tok Pisin, including many for which Mühlhäusler himself has proposed specific developmental hypotheses (e.g., periphrastic causatives, use of third-person pronoun as plural marker), are found as well in the Bislama of Vanuatu and in Solomons Pidgin. I have noted some aspects of this problem in Chapter 4 and will return to it in some detail in Chapter 8.

Here Mühlhäusler is caught in a cleft stick he has fashioned himself. If the Tok Pisin lineage and the Queensland Pidgin–derived lineage had in fact been separated, then there are two possible explanations for the scores of complex syntactic patterns they share: (1) they derive from an ancestral dialect spoken prior to 1880 (or perhaps from the common superstrate language, i.e., English); or (2) they have evolved separately and in parallel in the two separate sets of pidgins. The first possibility seems to be ruled out by Mühlhäusler's own argument (1980: 38) that the simplicity of Pidgin grammar prior to 1880 precluded the development of such grammatical patterns as periphrastic causatives. If so, these patterns would have to have evolved separately, but in exactly the same ways, in the two pidgin lineages. These syntactic parallels go far beyond the fairly abstract patterns claimed by Bickerton (1981, 1984) to be common to "true creoles," which he attributes to innate linguistic faculties: they would, I think, represent the most massive manifestations of parallel grammatical development in the history of our species.

I will show that there is a much simpler set of explanations:

First, that the pidgin initially introduced into Samoan plantations was the same dialect being used by Islanders on ships' crews throughout the central and southwest Pacific—the dialect that was the initial medium of communication to take root in Queensland. That is, in the early 1860s there was a single dialect of Pacific pidgin, largely shipboard-based, which provided the linguistic input into plantations in Queensland, Samoa, New Caledonia, Fiji, the Marshalls, and other areas. I have shown that this shipboard-based dialect already incorporated many of the grammatical patterns later recorded in Samoa and Queensland. Gilbertese were among its speakers, but so, too, were Caroline Islanders, Rotumans, Polynesians, Fijians, Loyalty Islanders, and others.

Second, that until the end of the 1880s, the plantation speech community of Samoa was continuously connected to the plantation speech community of Queensland. Most of the connections were indirect, representing the speech patterns of the Islanders who served as boats' crews and recruiters on the water pathways connecting the plantations. These patterns of speech spread through the common recruiting grounds in the New Hebrides and Solomons, the sources of labor for both plantation communities. It seems likely that there was also a considerable movement of multiple-term laborers between the two areas: the very experience that made Islanders fluent in pidgin led them to be sought after as foremen, cooks, and other more-than-menial employees and gave them considerable bargaining power over their movement between as well as within the separate plantation communities. Linguistic developments, including grammatical elaboration and standardization, spread through this entire system of interconnected plantation speech communities, even though each area developed special local lexical innovations (from, e.g., Samoan, French, and Aboriginal languages).

Third, that until the end of the 1880s, there was close and sustained linguistic contact between Queensland plantations and many parts of the Bismarck Archipelago, so that the dialect of pidgin used in Queensland was already established there when German plantations in New Guinea expanded. That is, when the pidgin of Samoa reached New Guinea, it was essentially the same as the pidgin already spoken in some areas that had long been in contact with the Queensland recruiters and plantations, and earlier traders. It was after the closure of this border, at the end of the 1880s, that Tok Pisin underwent drastic relexification—a relexification that entailed replacement of many English forms with forms from indigenous Bismarcks languages, creating the illusion that this was the most genuinely "Melanesian" form of Melanesian Pidgin and that the other dialects represented anglicized attenuations of an original pattern.

Mühlhäusler's articulation (1985a) of his hypothesis of a separate lineage for Tok Pisin deriving from Samoa does not completely rule out contacts between Samoa and the Bismarcks on the one hand and between Samoa and Queensland and its recruiting grounds on the other. But it depicts these contacts as indirect and relatively unimportant: "Salisbury's arguments seem to be conclusive enough to exclude the possibility of strong *direct* influence of Queensland Plantation Pidgin on Tok Pisin. However, . . . such influence could have been exercised by a number of less direct routes."

Mühlhäusler sets out a diagram showing "direct influence" between Queensland and New Hebrides and Solomons, no link between Samoa and Queensland, and a "direct influence" between both New Hebrides and Solomons and Samoa. He goes on to explain that "this model suggests that the relationship between the main plantation areas was indirect, i.e., via shared recruiting areas. It further suggests that Tok Pisin is much less directly related to Queensland Plantation Pidgin than are Solomons Pidgin, New Hebridean Bichelamar and Papuan Pidgin English" (Mühlhäusler 1985a: 43–44).

Having argued for the development of a Samoan Plantation Pidgin separate from (and deserving a different label as a language from) Queensland Plantation Pidgin, Mühlhäusler goes on (p. 44) to depict Tok Pisin as having a specific year of "birth"—1884.

The year 1884 marks an important event in the history of Tok Pisin; one could almost call it the year of its birth. In 1884 the German Reich, in order to protect German trading interests in the area, formally annexed the Bismarck Archipelago, part of the Solomon Islands, and the north-eastern part of the New Guinea mainland. The most immediate result of the declaration of a protectorate over German New Guinea was that the labour trade between this area and most plantation areas in the Pacific was brought to an abrupt halt.

The Pacific Islanders who by the 1870s were occupying the key positions in the Labor Trade and the organization of plantation labor, as recruiters, boats' crews, interpreters, and middlemen were, we may guess, the central agents of language transmission. As crucial (and well-rewarded) interpreters and brokers in securing future laborers, and in their positions of responsibility as second-, third-, and subsequent-term workers supervising the labor of new recruits on plantations, those sophisticates moved widely through the entire dispersed plantation speech community. They must have played a key part not only in providing the linguistic input for recruits to the various plantation areas—since it was mainly they, not Europeans, who dealt routinely with the "new chums" on the ships and on arrival at the plantations; they must also have been agents in the transmission of pidgin to boys and young men who aspired to become recruits when they reached maturity. Wawn ([1893] 1973: 41) noted in 1879 in the New Hebrides that "children pick up South Sea English very quickly; and I have known boys who came on board my vessel converse fluently, having acquired the language from returned labourers and by visiting trading and labour vessels."

We have already glimpsed evidence that by the time the Labor Trade commenced there was a substantial population of Islanders already much too sophisticated (and sought after and well rewarded for their skills as linguistic and cultural brokers and middlemen) to be interested in menial and poorly paid manual work in the hot sun. Hence we cannot assume that because the first wave of plantation workers, whether in Samoa or New Caledonia or Queensland, were from a particular area, the pidgin they brought with them was a local dialect spoken in the islands from which they came. Probably the dominant linguistic models came not from those who went to do the plantation work, but from those sophisticated Islanders who recruited them and organized their work.

With a common Pacific pidgin apparently being used on the ships, and being diffused into the various recruiting grounds and plantations, our most important questions must concern not direct connections between the plantations—Queensland, Samoa, New Caledonia—which were divided by political barriers and rivalries; but rather indirect connections through the ships and common recruiting grounds.

The clearest evidence that the Samoan plantations constituted part of a single speech community (or system of interconnected subcommunities) in which local variants of a common dialect of pidgin prevailed, at least through the 1880s, comes from documents of the Labor Trade showing German recruiting in the New Hebrides and southeastern Solomons.

The Government Recruiting Agent Rannie, recounting his experiences in the Labor Trade in the 1880s, comments (1912: 123–24): "I have often heard the account of how the one-eyed master of a Queensland Labour vessel and the one-legged master of a Samoan Labour vessel filled up their ships with recruits from Tanna. . . . Before sundown both ships had their full complement of recruits, the one for Queensland and the other for Samoa."

Wawn, recruiting in the New Hebrides and Solomons, found himself both in competition with and mistaken for German recruiters seeking workers for German plantations. At Pentecost in the northern New

Hebrides in 1879, Wawn ([1893] 1973: 190) encountered "another schooner, . . . the *Mary Anderson*, [of] Captain Schultze. . . . This proved to be a British vessel, commanded by a master of German nationality. He held a recruiting license from the British Consul in Samoa, and carried no recruiting agent. He was recruiting labourers for German employers in the Samoa islands." He notes also that "the French schooner *Aoba* . . . was in company with us, recruiting labourers for Noumea" (p. 191).

This recruiting continued well into the 1880s. The figures compiled by Moses (1973) show a total of 985 New Hebrideans and 425 Solomon Islanders (in comparison with 612 Gilbertese) recruited to Samoa in the period 1878–82. In the subsequent years, 216 New Hebrideans and 193 Solomon Islanders were recruited, although the balance had begun to shift toward the German-controlled Bismarcks (from which 261 recruits had come in the same period).

In 1880, Wawn's green-hulled ship was mistaken for a German recruiting vessel in southern, central, and northern New Hebrides. In Tanna, "the steam and the vessel's green paint combined caused them to set her down as a Samoan. . . . The cruise of the Samoan was . . . recent. . . . . . . Further north, the natives frequently refused to believe that we were recruiting for Queensland, expressing their belief that, if they were engaged by us, they would be taken to Samoa" (p. 197). At Port Stanley (Malekula), Wawn was greeted with "You go away! You no belong Brisbane. You no good! Me savez you!" (p. 199). And farther northwest, in the Banks Islands: "At last, one morning, when it was almost calm, I steamed round to the west end of Motalava, one of the Banks Is. . . . When they could make out the green-painted hull, they concluded she was from Samoa, and were excited accordingly" (p. 199). Finally, at Espiritu Santo, Wawn repainted the *Jabberwock*: "After that she was no more mistaken for a Samoan" (p. 201).

The politics of boat painting became quite intricate. In 1884 a regulation was passed requiring British vessels to be painted a dull red with black band: "Subsequently, French and German ships cruising in the New Hebrides and the Solomon Islands also took to carrying red-painted boats, with which they could pass themselves off as coming from Queensland" (Wawn [1893] 1973: 332).

This continuity between Samoa and the areas of the New Hebrides and southeastern Solomons that were the primary recruiting grounds for Queensland and Fiji continued at least until 1890. Thus Wawn ([1893] 1973: 358) notes that "the German vessel *Maria*, recruiting in 1890 for Samoan planters, at Port Adam, Maramasiki I., engaged 72 boys, giving a snider and ammunition for each: the *Ubea* (German) took forty boys from Tiarro Bay, Guadalcanal I., the same year." In 1890, in the New Hebrides, Wawn noted that "beside the *Dart* and the *Touganini*, I spoke [sic] or sighted some half-dozen other vessels, British and French, and one German schooner recruiting in the group" (p. 427).

Are we to imagine that crews of the Samoan-based recruiting ships that were so anxious to pass as Queensland recruiters were using a "Samoan Plantation Pidgin" distinct from the pidgin of the New Hebrides and of Queensland? Or that when they arrived in Samoa, recruits—and foremen, and recruiters, and plantation managers—had to learn a new dialect? I see no evidence, linguistic or historical, for separating Samoan pidgin of the latter 1880s from the pidgin spoken elsewhere in the southwestern Pacific.

Indeed, German recruiting of Solomon Islanders for Samoa—and not merely from Bougainville and Buka, within the German orbit of political influence, but from the old Queensland and Fiji recruiting grounds—continued into the twentieth century. I have noted (Keesing 1978: 69, citing the research of S. G. Firth, and O'Connor 1968) how a substantial number of indentured laborers recruited in 1907 from the southeastern Solomons (mainly Malaita) were in Samoa in 1913–14, were stranded there by World War I, and were finally repatriated in 1920–21. At what period, then, was Samoa separated from the rest of the southwestern Pacific plantation speech community, including Queensland?

Scant wonder, then, that the dialect of pidgin Mühlhäusler characterizes as Samoan Plantation Pidgin was essentially identical (judging by the limited linguistic evidence available) to the pidgin being spoken in Queensland in, say, 1890. No doubt there were Samoan-derived lexical items, just as there was a French lexical component to the pidgin spoken in New Caledonia. These special local lexicons were quickly learned by Islanders who commanded the general syntactic and lexical repertoire of the pidgin prevailing through the entire region. Given what happened in Fiji (Siegel 1987), we might have expected a simplified, pidginized Samoan to have emerged. But the sociolinguistic situation in Samoa seems to have fostered the use of Pidgin English, with an eventual acquisition of Samoan, initially as a second language and eventually as a first language, as recruits who stayed on were absorbed into the Samoan speech community.

Governor Solf's 1895 diary, translated by Mühlhäusler (1978a: 72), gives:

Whatfore you no speak me: calabos belong raty [rat trap], suppose you speak me all the same me savee.

Master, him fellow white man he no savee speak English, suppose me speak along you, you savee me no speak lies.

Solf himself was in no doubt that this was the same pidgin being used elsewhere in the southwestern Pacific (and, we may surmise, on the German plantations in the Marshalls):

Thus, in what way do the workers from such different places and islands communicate, when thrown together in Samoa? They use that Volapuk of the South Seas, which has become international among whites and coloureds: Pidgeon English. . . . It is incredible how quickly all blacks learn this lingua franca and how extremely clever they are at paraphrasing concepts for which they have no word. . . . In this intelligent way the blacks can communicate over the whole South Seas, both among themselves and with the whites (Mühlhäusler 1978a: 72).

Mühlhäusler's claim that Samoan Plantation Pidgin was transmitted into the Bismarcks as the Germans established an internal plantation system in New Guinea must also be tempered by the evidence of communication between the Bismarcks and German northern Solomons and Queensland, at least until 1887. If, as I surmise, Samoan Plantation Pidgin was essentially the same dialect as the pidgin of the Queensland/ Fiji/New Caledonia Labor Trade, then such communication is neither surprising nor linguistically significant. The point is to establish a common linguistic community in the plantation areas until about 1890, after which the Tok Pisin lineage had a largely separate history. Well before that stage, by the first half of the 1880s, the pidgin broadly common to all the plantation communities of the southwestern and central Pacific (though only of secondary importance in Fiji) was expanded and stabilized to a striking degree, incorporating the syntactic patterns (including the pronominal system, causative pattern, embedding of relative clauses, and grammaticalized future- and past-tense marking) common to all daughter dialects.

Hernsheim, who was the German Consul in the Marshalls when he provided information on pidgin to Schuchardt in 1883, had encountered the common Queensland-Samoa dialect in several parts of the Pacific, and had no doubt that it represented a single dialect—or that it had taken hold in the Bismarcks from a Queensland as well as Samoan source. Schuchardt ([1883] 1980: 17–18) wrote:

The German Consul in Jaluit [in the Marshalls], confirms that it [Pidgin English] is spread over the whole of Western Oceania, including Queensland. . . . In New Britain, . . . upon his arrival seven years ago [1876], no native had been able to understand a European language, [but] nowadays nearly everybody, above all the children, speak this variety of English, some of them with great fluency. He had even heard natives frequently talking among themselves in this language when they spoke about whites or things having to do with whites.

Rannie (1912: 41–50) writes of his trips as recruiting agent to Buka and the islands off the New Ireland coast (Tabar Group, Tanga Group, Lihir Group) in the 1880s. There, in 1884, he encountered young men who knew "English" from working in Samoa:

We secured the services of an islander here [Buka] as an interpreter. He was the only one able to speak any English. . . . He had worked for Mrs. Farrell in Samoa. . . . Three [on Nissan] had a smattering of English, having formerly worked in Samoa. . . . At Caen Island [Tanga] an interpreter . . . told us that a few islanders wanted to go to Queensland; that he had been to Queensland. . . . He also said that a great many women wished to go to Queensland, as their men had gone in former vessels. . . . Ambulull, . . . the Chief of Sawmill and the most influential chief in the Caen group, . . . had heard so much about Queensland, and so many of his men had gone there, that he had quite made up his mind to emigrate to Queensland also.

Ambulull accompanied Rannie's vessel to the "Gerrit Denny Group" (the Lihirs), where he induced nine men to sign up for Queensland (p. 55). Rannie notes that "there were not many natives from New Ireland in Queensland altogether. All recruiting stopped immediately after Germany annexed the islands" (p. 262). But he tells of the repatriation of a Queensland recruit in Nolam in the Lihirs, and his wife. This man "had been married to a woman who was a native of Noosa, a village in the Stuffen Straits, which separate New Ireland from New Hanover. The marriage took place at Cairns, Queensland" (p. 271).

That the pidgin learned in Queensland and Fiji by plantation workers from the Bismarcks did not simply vanish when the Germans sealed the frontier is attested by Cayley-Webster's observations (1898: 289–90) on "the island of Kung" (New Hanover, off New Ireland) in 1897:

I was astonished at so many of the natives speaking pidgin English, and on making inquiries found that years ago a great number of them had worked on the plantations of Fiji and Queensland before Germany took possession of these islands. . . . They could not have worked for Englishmen since 1884, when Great Britain ceased to protect the archipelago, and yet they have retained their knowledge of the language, and in some instances spoke it most fluently.

In the same year, in the "St. Charles Hardy Islands" east of New Ireland, Cayley-Webster (1898: 333–34) noted that "gathering as many natives as possible together I interrogated them, finding that pidgin English was not unknown to several."

In 1887, Wawn repatriated workers from Queensland to their homes in the Bismarcks. "Besides visiting the British Solomons, we had seen the greater part of the German possessions in the Solomons group and the Bismarck Archipelago. . . . The contingent here objected to being divided, as they were all from the islands adjacent to New Ireland, or New Britain" ([1893] 1973: 308). Wawn discounts "a letter from Hernsheim in the Queensland papers, in which he complained that Queensland labour vessels had been supplying the New Britain natives with firearms in his neighbourhood. . . . It is well known Snider rifles—which may be counted by the thousand—now in the hands of natives of the Solomon Islands, . . . have been sold to the natives by German traders" (p. 289).

Wawn here is being a blatant propagandist for Queensland-based recruiting ships; but his evidence regarding the presence of Queensland recruiters in the Bismarcks and German recruiters in the southeastern Solomons—both using the prevailing plantation pidgin in use throughout the southwestern and central Pacific as linguistic medium—can be taken at face value. In 1891, when the Queensland Labor Trade had been temporarily halted, he asked rhetorically: "Since the trade has been stopped, will the islanders remain at home? No! Samoa and its German plantations, New Caledonia and its French ones, continue to employ them and reap the benefits of their labour" (p. 439).

Because Queensland Pidgin was already spoken in a substantial zone in the Bismarcks, including so many of the smaller islands (which then provided linguistic sophisticates the Germans could call on as their plantations expanded), it is no wonder that the texts from these islands in the 1890s reflect a pidgin substantially the same as that spoken in Queensland, the Solomons, and the New Hebrides in the same period. Thus, for example, we have a short text from Cayley-Webster (1898: 273), who recounts how an Islander from Outuan, in the St. George group between New Britain and New Ireland, described a dangerous fish: "That fellar he savey too much, he ki-ki along o' me plenty, me die finish."

In 1890 Fritz Rose, the German Imperial Commissioner, underlined the contempt Islanders felt for the punitive actions carried out by warships by quoting a New Irelander—in a pidgin that could perfectly well have been recorded in Queensland or its recruiting grounds in the same period: "What name you speak belong man-war? Man-war he all same one bloody fool, he no save kill'em kanaka. He make fire house, never mind. He no save go bush. Kanaka he no 'fraid belong man-war. Man-war he come, kanaka he go bush alright" (Hempenstall 1978: 171).

But by the 1890s, the German firms in the Bismarcks were seeking their own pool of plantation labor over which they could exercise direct and repressive political control. The plantation pidgin that had entered the Bismarcks and northern Solomons from both Samoa and Queensland was to undergo mainly separate, and very different, developments in German New Guinea, subject to the superstrate influence of German and the substrate influences of the Oceanic Austronesian languages of the Bismarcks and the New Guinea coast, and of Papuan languages.

I have noted in passing the ironic situation the relexification of Tok Pisin from the end of the nineteenth century onward has created. The Pacific pidgin spoken, with minor dialectal variants, across the whole range of connected plantation communities in the 1880s was lexically derived almost entirely from English and nautical pidgin. Yet the relexified, Tolai-ized, historically aberrant New Guinea offshoot of this lineage has been taken—and partly by virtue of its Melanesian-derived lexical forms, which are replacements for the original English ones—as the genuine and canonical dialect. The pidgin dialects of Vanuatu and the Solomon Islands that (in their "bush" variants) preserve the common ancestral pattern so much more directly have been interpreted as aberrant, and in effect debased by anglicization.

CHAPTER 6

Oceanic Austronesian Languages

WE ARE NOW in a position, having roughly located the emergence of a Pacific pidgin in time and space, to ask what substrate languages might have shaped the structure of an emerging pidgin.

The focus on Tok Pisin as the canonical dialect of Melanesian Pidgin has drawn attention, when considering possible substrate models or motivation for Pidgin syntactic patterns, to the extremely diverse linguistic environment of New Guinea and the immediately adjacent islands. Even if we direct our attention further back in time and farther into the central Pacific, we might be led by the vast scale of the Pacific and the diversity of its islands and cultures to assume a corresponding separation and diversity of indigenous languages. Thus, as I noted in Chapter 1, Goodman (1985: 119) correctly refers to the antecedent of Tok Pisin as "an earlier Pacific-wide nautical pidgin"; but he incorrectly infers that this early lingua franca emerged "in a very heterogeneous linguistic milieu both genetically and typologically."

In this chapter I shall show that the substrate languages that could have provided models for an emerging Pacific pidgin at successive stages in the nineteenth century, while spoken over a vast area, are far from "heterogeneous," genetically or typologically. Rather, they all fall into the Oceanic subgroup of Austronesian; and most of them apparently fall into a single putative subgroup of Oceanic, provisionally identified as "Eastern Oceanic."

In Chapter 8, I will argue that the "major [syntactic] choices" (Bickerton 1984) that characterized Proto-Oceanic, and that are most clearly preserved in languages of the putative Eastern Oceanic subgroup, are embodied to a striking degree as "major choices" underlying the structure of

Melanesian Pidgin. To do so requires that, in addition to sketching the connections between Oceanic Austronesian languages, I briefly describe the syntactic patterns in these languages on which my subsequent analysis will focus.

For convenience in explicating the grammatical structures of Oceanic languages—what they have in common and how they differ—I will refer to reconstructions of Proto-Oceanic (and Proto-Eastern Oceanic) grammar, and to hypotheses about the processes of grammatical development in Oceanic. But an argument for substrate influence on a developing pidgin cannot of course appeal to ancient languages, actual or hypothetical. It was languages spoken by Pacific Islanders in the nineteenth century, not their ancient antecedents, that could have helped to shape a developing Pacific pidgin.

The linguistic resources Pacific Islanders brought to their encounters with Europeans and with one another were natural languages, genetically related but individually diverse. None of these speakers of Oceanic languages had any more access to hypothetical ancient languages than contemporary speakers of the Indo-European languages have to Proto-Indo-European or Proto-Anglo-Frisian; hence these hypothetical languages cannot directly serve any legitimate theoretical purposes of linguistic or sociolinguistic argument regarding Pacific pidgin.

However, a linguist who attempts to reconstruct the grammar of an inferred ancestral language by comparing the grammars of daughter languages is engaged in an exercise that can be illuminating for quite different purposes. Such a reconstruction points toward patterns that may be shared, at least at an abstract level of underlying structure, by daughter languages; and/or to patterns that may be represented in some putative subgroups and lost in others. It may point toward patterns that are preserved directly in some putative subgroups and radically transformed in others. And purely for purposes of exposition, reconstructions may be useful in characterizing structural similarities and differences among daughter languages. The important point here is that for the quite different purposes of the analyst seeking possible sources of substrate models, it is not the inferred linguistic history that matters (and often that is the most problematic part of the historical linguist's argument), but the structural comparison of what is common to, or different among, genetically related languages, on which reconstructions have been based. The reconstructed proto-languages, in lieu of pages of comparative data, sometimes provide convenient expository pegs on which to hang an argument that has nothing to do with ancient linguistic history.

In the pages to follow, using data from a wide range of real languages, I attempt to show that there is a set of syntactic patterns, particularly in the structure of verb phrases, that at an abstract level are common to a large number of Oceanic languages spread across a vast expanse of water. I fur-ther attempt to show that in much of this area, what is shared comprises a very substantial system of morphological units (transitive suffixes, subject-referencing pronouns, clitic object-referencing pronouns) that are clearly recognizable, both to speakers of these languages and to linguists, as cog-nate. In other regions, the same pattern occurs at an abstract level, but the elements that mark this pattern characteristically are condensed or radically modified (e.g., by cliticization). At times it will be a useful economy of exposition to describe these patterns in terms of the com-parativists' subgroupings and reconstructions, hence to cite reconstructed pronominal paradigms or transitive suffixes. But our interests do not lie in or depend on the inferences about history the comparativist draws from the exercise that yielded the reconstructions.

Otto Dempwolff's hypothesis that the Austronesian languages of the Pacific islands would prove to compose a single subgroup of Austronesian (in contrast to the Western Austronesian languages) has been strongly supported by recent work. A number of phonological and morphological innovations have now been shown to mark all the Austronesian lan-guages spoken east of longitude 136 degrees East as belonging to a single subgroup: what Dempwolff called "Melanesian," and contemporary Aus-tronesianists class as "Oceanic."

Proto-Oceanic (POC) appears to have been spoken at least as early as 2000 B.C., probably in western Melanesia. Following its breakup, as Aus-tronesian speakers moved through the Melanesian islands and eventually out into the central Pacific and up into the northern Pacific, a series of geographically based subgroups began to diversify. Subgrouping of the Oceanic languages is still highly provisional, and is complicated by a number of difficulties:

1. Very few of the Oceanic languages of Melanesia, the area of great-est diversity, have been adequately described, lexically or grammatically.

2. Some processes characteristic of Oceanic-speaking communities impede conventional methods of subgrouping and reconstruction. These include highly complex processes of chaining at the level of language as well as of dialect, pervasive borrowings between neighboring languages, and word tabooing (Keesing and Fifi'i 1969; Simons 1982).

3. Some Oceanic languages are highly conservative of POC features, lexically, phonologically, and grammatically, whereas other daughter lan-guages have been characterized by extreme degrees of lexical replace-ment, phonological change, and grammatical innovation and diversifica-

tion.* Subgrouping is impeded on the one hand by bewildering diversity, rendering cognates few and difficult to recognize, and on the other by the preservation of POC features in the more conservative languages, features that could be mistakenly taken as the bases for narrower subgroupings. These languages, Grace (1976: 108) suggests, "have conserved an atypically large percentage of the original vocabulary and structure [of POC]. They might represent not a linguistic subgroup at all but just the set of the most conservative languages within Oceanic."

A relatively cautious subgrouping advanced by Grace (1955 and subsequent revisions) is given in Figure 1. In 1972 Andrew Pawley advanced a hypothesis, already prefigured in Grace's subgrouping, that the languages of the northern and central New Hebrides, Fiji, Rotuma, Polynesia, and the southeastern Solomons form a single subgroup, which he labeled "Eastern Oceanic" (EO). Pawley subsequently decided that there was insufficient evidence for including the Southeast Solomonic languages in this subgroup (Pawley 1977a). He proposed that the remaining subgroup be relabeled "Remote Oceanic," and hypothesized that the Nuclear Micronesian languages would fall into the subgroup, although the evidence for their inclusion was still inconclusive.

The picture outlined by Grace and Pawley has been clarified by subsequent research. First, Malcolm Ross's research (1986) on the Oceanic languages of the northern Solomons, western Solomons, Bismarcks, and New Guinea coast points to emerging subgroups that tie together a number of Grace's separate subgroups (see Fig. 2). Second, the linguistic picture of southern Melanesia is being clarified and simplified. Some evidence points to the New Caledonia and Loyalties languages falling into a single subgroup. Further, there are now some grounds for connecting the diverse and less conservative languages of the southern New Hebrides with the languages of the northern and central New Hebrides (as Grace had originally suggested). Rather than falling within Remote Oceanic, these southern New Hebridean languages seem more likely to fall within a higher-order subgroup including Southeast Solomonic and some Solomons outlier languages (Lynch and Tryon 1985).

Third, although the position of Nuclear Micronesian languages is still not clear, their subgrouping with the EO languages has been reinforced by subsequent work.

The position of Southeast Solomonic remains unresolved. However,

---

*In some areas the influence of Papuan languages has been a major factor (see Lynch 1982). However, there also seem to have been processes (discussed by Grace 1981 and Pawley 1981) promoting rapid linguistic change and exaggerating diversity in some areas, and inducing conservatism of POC features in others.

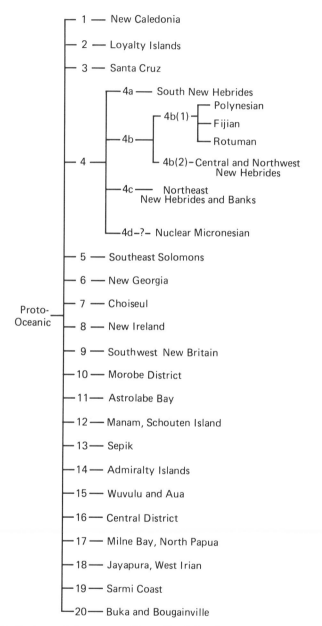

Fig. 1: A Preliminary Subgrouping (Partial) of the Oceanic Languages (Grace 1955)

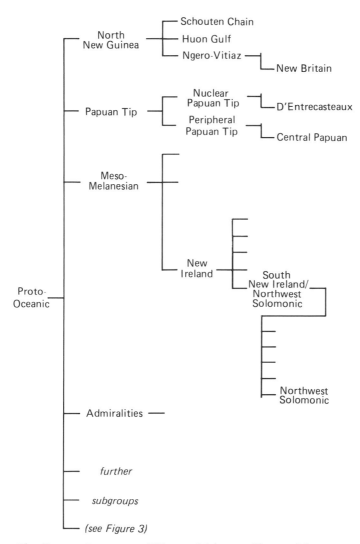

Fig. 2: The Oceanic Languages of Western Melanesia (Ross 1986)

the striking conservatism of the Southeast Solomonic languages and their
EO cast lexically, phonologically, and grammatically has led several specialists to proceed on the expectation that Southeast Solomonic languages would turn out to fall into a subgroup roughly equivalent to
Pawley's original EO, but including Nuclear Micronesian languages. This
is an expectation I share with Geraghty (1983), Blust (1984), and

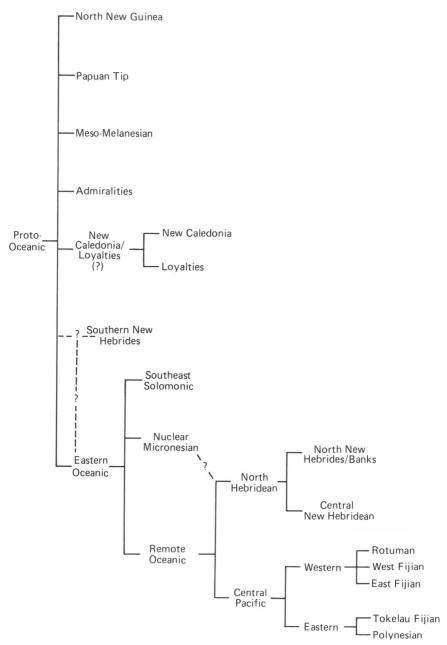

Fig. 3: Oceanic Subgrouping: A Tentative Synthesis (Keesing, Modified from Pawley 1981)

others.* A plausible subgrouping (modified from Pawley 1981) is given in Figure 3.

For our purposes, what matters is that there is a vast zone—extending from the central and eastern Carolines all the way across Polynesia to Easter Island and Hawaii, and down the central Pacific through Fiji into all or most of the New Hebrides, through the Banks and Torres Islands, and through the southeastern Solomons—within which relatively closely related Oceanic Austronesian languages are spoken. In most of this zone, the languages are strikingly similar in a number of grammatical, lexical, and phonological respects. Although neither precise subgrouping hypotheses nor inferences about proto-languages and their grammars are, strictly speaking, necessary for my arguments about possible substrate models, we may presume (as comparative linguists and prehistorians have) that such distributions are the result of substantial periods of shared history, despite the wide dispersion of these languages in space.

It is particularly significant that the languages spoken in the eastern Carolines, Rotuma, Fiji, and the Gilberts—which I have suggested were central in the first stage in the emergence of a distinctive Pacific pidgin—strikingly preserve most of the syntactic patterns reconstructed for POC and PEO. So, too, do the languages of the central and northern New Hebrides, whose speakers provided the bulk of plantation laborers through the critical phases of the Labor Trade; and so do the languages of the southeastern Solomons, which became the principal source of plantation workers in the 1890s.

We have seen that in the sandalwood period (late 1840s to mid-1860s), the southern islands of Melanesia, and especially the Loyalties, were a regional focus for the spread of pidgin (although I have suggested that speakers from these islands may have contributed little to its *linguistic* development). In these islands, too, and in New Caledonia, Oceanic Austronesian languages were spoken. In these languages, as will be seen, most of the "core" POC syntactic pattern is preserved, though often in modified, condensed, or frozen forms.

We can now turn to a first look at the grammars of Oceanic Austronesian languages. I will focus on what I take to be the core syntactic structures of Oceanic languages—structures that, I will argue, closely parallel those of the Pacific pidgin. These core structures represent a system of marking subject-object relations through the use of pronouns incorpo-

---

*Blust (1984) has proposed a close link between the Southeast Solomonic languages of Malaita and the Nuclear Micronesian languages. But the apparent innovations they share seem likely to turn out to represent retentions of a common EO or even OC pattern.

rated, as agreement markers, within verb phrases. One pronominal element within the verb phrase, marked for person and number, references the subject (agent, actor, or experiencer) of the verb. This pronominal element precedes the verb, separated from it by aspect markers or other verbal particles. This pronominal element either references an explicit noun subject by reiteration or maintains subject reference anaphorically or indexically in discourse.

A second pronominal element, in transitive sentences, is suffixed to a transitive verb (which is itself usually marked as such with a transitive suffix). This pronominal element references the direct object, which in turn may be specified or implicit in a context of discourse. Since neither subject noun phrase (NP) nor object NP needs to be specified (referenced as both are by agreement-marking pronouns within the verb phrase), the core of a (verbal) Oceanic sentence is a VP, with its obligatory pronominal constituents. The subject and object NPs are "optional adjuncts" (Wolff 1980). This Oceanic pattern in which pronouns within the VP reference subject and object prevails all the way from center to south in the island Pacific—from Kosrae to the Loyalties.

The slot where a subject NP fits may, in Oceanic languages, precede or follow the VP (most languages have an unmarked preferred order). A pronoun rather than a noun may fit into this subject-NP slot; and when it does, we have two pronouns referencing the subject (as in French *moi je*). In the Oceanic languages, as in French, the two pronouns are distinguished by case marking. The obligatory pronoun, in the Oceanic pattern, occurs in the VP and (among other things) marks the base that follows as a verb; the optional and semantically redundant one fits in the subject-NP slot (whether that precedes or follows the VP). Grammarians of Oceanic are far from agreed on how the two sets of pronouns are best analyzed, or labeled. I shall follow a relatively neutral path, since the resolution of these questions is not essential to my argument. I refer to the obligatory pronominal element in the VP, referencing a noun or pronoun subject, as a *subject-referencing pronoun* (SRP); and I refer to the optional pronoun that fits into the subject-NP slot (and serves to emphasize, topicalize, or reiterate the pronominal reference) as a *focal pronoun* (FP).

Characteristically, the singular forms in the two sets are phonologically distinct; nonsingular forms of FPs and SRPs tend to be similar, with the SRPs often a shortened version or phonological variant of the FPs. These two sets of "subject" pronouns (and two other sets of "object" pronouns) have been reconstructed for PEO by Pawley (1972). He points out that the singular FPs resemble object pronouns in their phonological shape; the singular SRPs resemble the pronominal clitics used as possessives and

TABLE 6.1

Proto-Eastern Oceanic Subject Pronouns

Number and person	Pronoun	
	Focal (FP)	Subject-Referencing (SRP)
Singular		
1	i-nau	ku
2	i-koe	ko, o
3	inia, ia	na
Dual		
1 inclusive	kitadua[a]	tadua
1 exclusive	kamidua	(ka)midua
2	kamudua	mudu
3	(k)idadua	dadua
Trial		
1 inclusive	(ki)tatolu[b]	tatolu
1 exclusive	kamitolu	mitolu
2	kamutolu	mutolu
3	(k)idatolu	datolu
Plural		
1 inclusive	kita	ta
1 exclusive	kami	kami
2	kam(i)u	m(i)u
3	(k)ida	da

SOURCE: Pawley (1972:37).
[a] dua 'two.'
[b] tolu 'three.'

suffixed to prepositions. The paradigm of FPs and SRPs reconstructed by Pawley (1972: 37) for PEO, in slightly simplified form, is set out in Table 6.1.

This system, and the two sets of "object" pronouns also reconstructed for PEO, are preserved among most subgroups of daughter languages. Thus, for Nuclear Micronesian, Sheldon Harrison (1978: 1080) notes that "the grammars of most Melanesian languages recognise four pronominal subsystems, paralleling those reconstructed (Pawley 1972) for earlier periods in the development of Oceanic: possessive suffixes, subject markers [SRPs], object markers, and absolute pronouns [FPs]." However, as will be seen in data from New Hebridean languages, there has been a drift in some languages toward a loss of the semantic information encoded in the SRPs, so they have lost some or all of the marking for person and number. This development will prove important to our understanding of the Melanesian Pidgin pronominal system.

Before looking at the pattern of marking agent-object relations through transitive suffixes and object pronouns, it is worth briefly examining further the structure of the VP in Oceanic languages.

In the characteristic Oceanic pattern, the obligatory subject-pronominal constituent of the VP (the SRP) is preceded and followed by verbal particles marking mode, mood, tense, and aspect. These often are free particles, but they may be marked on the SRP with bound particles. (See Pawley 1972, 1973, and 1977b for some suggestions about structures of the VP, and about the forms of and slots for these particles, in POC and PEO.)

In Oceanic languages, modals marking negativity, possibility, or impossibility characteristically appear as particles separating the SRP from the verb that follows. Thus, for example, in Pohnpeian:

i   sohte   pahn   mwadongo
SRP(I) NEG   ASP(unreal)   play
I won't play.

Marking of tense and aspect is not extensively developed in Oceanic languages. Frequently a distinction is drawn between an (unmarked) accomplished mode and a nonaccomplished (or sometimes irrealis) mode that is used to characterize probable future events or hypothetical events. A common pattern (attributed by Pawley 1972 to PEO) is for the nonaccomplished or irrealis mode to be marked on the SRP with a bound suffix. The verb slot following the SRP is commonly followed by various postverbal particles marking aspect, mode, or directionality.

Before we turn to verbs in Oceanic languages, it is worth briefly noting a pattern that will be of some interest in our analysis of the development of Pacific pidgin: the existence, in some Oceanic languages, of sentences with nonverbal predicates. In some Oceanic languages, equational sentences ("X is a chief") are nonverbal and consist simply of two NPs without a connecting copula. In some Oceanic languages, sentences with locative (or other prepositional) predicates ("X is on the beach" or "X is with his sister") contain no verb but consist simply of a subject NP and a prepositional phrase. Whether either pattern is attributable to POC or PEO is unimportant for our purposes (the lack of good grammatical descriptions precludes our assessing how widespread these patterns actually are). But it is important to look at some examples, not simply in relation to Pacific pidgin, but to clarify what the SRPs are, and what they do syntactically. An SRP is an element of the VP, and (among other things) it marks the base that follows as a verb. If an equational or prepositional sentence has no verb phrase, and no verb, it cannot utilize an SRP to mark the subject. How, then, does one say "He is a chief" or "She is on the beach"? In languages using these patterns, we find that nonverbal sentences with pronominal subjects use the FP, not the SRP, in the subject NP slot. Some examples will be useful.

In Pohnpeian (Rehg 1981: 158–59):

kowe   ohl   loalekeng
FP(you)   man   intelligent
You are an intelligent man.

Here, the corresponding SRP in Pohnpeian would be *ke*. Note that in Pohnpeian, and in most other Oceanic languages, some attributive adjectival forms (such as *loalekeng* '[be] intelligent') can be used both as stative verbs and directly as preposed or postposed modifiers of nouns.

In Kwaio (Malaita, southeastern Solomons):

ngai   wane   naa   ba'e
FP(he)   man   of   shrine
He is a priest.

and

'aga'a   i   asi
FP(they2)   LOC   sea
The two of them are at the coast.

In these last two sentences, without VPs, the FP rather than the corresponding SRP is used.

At this point, we can usefully turn to verbs in Oceanic languages. We can begin with the contrast between active and stative verbs. Pawley (1973: 112), in his reconstruction of POC grammar, hypothesized that "POC verbs are either stative or active. . . . Active verbs divide into optional transitives, obligatory transitives, and obligatory intransitives. This classification is based on privileges of occurrence in sentence structures, chiefly with respect to case-marking."

In this Oceanic pattern, a stative sentence consists minimally of a stative VP. This VP includes an SRP referencing the experiencer of the state and a stative verb; an NP slot denoting the experiencer may be filled, but no further NP "denoting actor or goal" can be added (Pawley 1973: 113).

What is significant, in regard to questions of Melanesian Pidgin to be examined in Chapter 8, is that "adjectival" meanings are typically expressed in Oceanic languages with verbal predicates, that is, with stative verbs preceded by pronouns referencing the experiencer of the state. Thus, in Kwaio:

gala   ba'ita   no'o
SRP(they2) be big   PRF
The two of them are grown now.

Or, with the subject NP slot filled:

fou   lo'oo   e   gelo
stone DEM   SRP(it)   be heavy
This stone is heavy.

As noted, it is common in Oceanic languages for a subclass of attributive stative verbs to be used as well to modify a noun directly, either preposed or postposed to it. In Kwaio *wane ba'ita* is 'big man' but **fou gelo* could not be used for "heavy stone."

We can now turn to active verbs. First, it is worth noting that there may be two active verbs in sequence, not one. With the emergence of finer-grained descriptions of Oceanic languages, we have more and more evidence of the pervasiveness of serial- and other compound-verbal constructions in these languages. Among the (putatively) EO languages of Melanesia, for example, Crowley (1986) and Keesing (1985) give extended discussions of serial (and other compound) verbs in Paamese (Central New Hebridean) and Kwaio (Southeast Solomonic).* We shall see that there are apparent echoes of these serial-verb constructions in Melanesian Pidgin.

Active verbs, in Pawley's (1973) comparative schema, are those that can be accomplished by NPs "denoting actor or goal." In the typical pattern of Oceanic languages that Pawley has attributed to POC, some verb roots are always used intransitively and some are always used transitively; but the largest class comprises verbs that can be used either intransitively or transitively. Their use as transitive verbs is marked by a transitive suffix (or by affixation of a clitic object-referencing pronoun directly to the verb root).

In this pattern, the VP itself is syntactically and semantically complete.† The subject reference is marked by the SRP; the object reference (in a transitive sentence) is marked by a pronominal clitic suffixed to the verb root or to a transitive suffix; or, as will be seen, it may in some languages be zero-marked morphologically as an implied "it." The VP is essentially complete by itself. Either the subject-NP slot or the object-NP slot, or both, may be filled; but both may be empty. Kwaio will serve to illustrate.

---

*I have suggested, in analyzing Kwaio, that what have been treated as adverbs in some Melanesian languages may represent a pattern where stative verbs are used as the second elements in compound-verb constructions.

†As long as pronominal reference is contextually clear.

ku   aga-si-a   naaboni
SRP(I)   look-TRS-it   yesterday
I saw it yesterday.

ma'a   a-gu   ka   aga-si-a   naaboni
father   POSS-me   SRP(he)   look-TRS-it   yesterday
My father saw it yesterday.

ka   aga-si-a   boo   naaboni
SRP(he)   look-TRS-it   pig   yesterday
He saw a pig yesterday.

ngaia   ka   aga-si-a   boo   naaboni
FP(him)   SRP(he)   look-TRS-it   pig   yesterday
He saw a pig yesterday.

Here we see how a subject-NP slot may be empty (the first and third sentences), with the subject referenced by the agreement-marking SRP; or may be filled with a noun (the second sentence) or an FP (the fourth sentence). We further see, with transitive verbs, how the clitic object pronoun attached to the transitive suffix may be followed by a direct-object NP (the third and fourth sentences) or may reference an implicit object (the first two sentences). In Kwaio, when the direct object is human (or higher-animate), a pronominal clitic marked for person and number is used to reference the direct object:

ngaia   ka   aga-si-'adauru
FP(him)   SRP(he)   look-TRS-us(incl)
He saw us.

These examples serve effectively to introduce the nature of transitive suffixes and object-marking pronouns in Oceanic languages, which are important for an understanding of Melanesian Pidgin syntax.

Two transitive suffixes are pervasively represented in Oceanic languages. One is the form that appears in the Kwaio examples. In POC, it is reconstructed as $*-i$;* this transitive suffix seems to have marked the semantic role of the following NP as patient, or less often, as goal or stimulus.

A relatively small class of transitive verbs in POC seems to have been marked as such not with the transitive suffix $*-i$, but by direct suffixation

---

*Most EO languages have lost the final consonants of disyllabic bases, so that consonant/vowel combinations of the form CVCVC are represented as CVCV. In these languages, the transitive suffix is characteristically manifest as -Ci (with the consonant possibly reflecting or replacing the dropped consonant of the base; these languages often manifest several allomorphs of -Ci).

of the clitic object-referencing pronoun to the verb stem. In some daughter languages (e.g., Kwaio), this pattern has become more generalized.

The syntactic functions of the second transitive suffix, reconstructed as *-aki(ni)*, are less clear. Pawley (1973; Pawley and Reid 1979) suggests that in POC this form of the transitive suffix, which he calls "remote," marked several other semantic roles of the following NP, such as concomitant, cause, instrument, or beneficiary. However, this interpretation of *-aki(ni)* has been questioned by Harrison (1982), who suggests an alternative origin of this suffix from a POC verb. We need not, in any case, be concerned with questions of linguistic history per se: it is the manifestations of these patterns in daughter languages, especially EO languages, that concerns us. The second transitive suffix is of interest in relation to Pacific pidgin, but only in a negative way: in showing how, even where substrate influence seems to have been at work, distinctions pervasive in substrate languages may be neutralized in the development of a pidgin as simplified lingua franca.

One specific use of transitive suffixes in Oceanic languages bears brief mention at this time; we will return to it as providing a clue about the development of Melanesian Pidgin syntax. So-called "prepositional verbs" (discussed by Pawley 1973: 142) are disyllabic bases that "connect a verb with its grammatical object" as prepositions, but follow the morphological pattern of transitive verbs (including transitive suffixes and/or clitic object pronouns). Examples are Kwaio

fe'e-ni-a	'with'
fono-si-a	'against'
fa'a-si-a	'away from'
suri-a	'along, about'
'ani-a	'with (instrumental)'

This pattern is a striking feature of Oceanic grammar, one that probably evolved from serial-verb constructions.*

A closer look at the clitic "object-referencing pronouns" will be useful at this stage. Pawley (1973) attributes to POC a pattern in which clitic pronouns attached to the verb-plus-transitive suffix referenced a following object NP, specified or implied. Because the transitive suffix itself implied an "it" object, and the clitic "it" implied transitivity, use of *both* the transitive suffix and the "it" form of the clitic object pronoun entailed some redundancy. Characteristically, daughter languages have dropped one or the other, either relying on the object-referencing pronoun to mark tran-

---

*This development may well antedate the separation of Oceanic, since similar patterns turn up in some Western Austronesian languages.

sitivity (as Kwaio does, with a very large class of verbs) or using the transitive suffix with zero-marking to indicate an implied "it": "Most daughter
languages [of POC] have opted for the less redundant transitive suffix
only, or objective suffix only" (Lynch 1985: 251). Where reference is to
"me," "us," "you," or "them," this is indicated with the appropriate object pronoun following the transitive suffix.*

What matters for us is that in Oceanic languages the transitive suffix
can be thought of as embodying a third-person "it" reference. In many of
these languages, this "it" is marked with what seems to be a monosyllabic
pronominal element. In many others, it is zero-marked but implied by the
transitive suffix itself, in the absence of a following pronoun marked for
person or number; we will see that the Melanesian Pidgin transitive suffix
operates in exactly this way.

We are now in a position to approach the complex question of the preferred order of constituents in Oceanic languages, a question of some importance in considering the issue of substrate models for Pacific pidgin.
Once more Pawley (1973: 117 and passim), as pioneer, has given the
"standard" interpretation, which he and others have then refined or
challenged:

> In most Oceanic languages examined, the preferred word order is subject + verb
> + direct object (SVO). Notable exceptions are the Fijian languages, the non-
> outlier Polynesian languages, Roviana, and most of the New Guinea Oceanic
> languages. Since Oceanic languages which prefer SVO are much more wide-
> spread in terms of regions and subgroups than the exceptions, it is probable that
> SVO was the preferred order in POC. This conclusion is consistent with the pref-
> erence for SVO order in certain Eastern Indonesian languages which may be the
> closest relatives of Oceanic.

An original verb-initial order has been suggested for Proto-Austronesian (in contrast to Proto-Oceanic) by Pawley and Reid (1980), Wolff
(1980), and others. There are some reasons to surmise (as Simons 1980
and Wolff 1980 do) that the verb-initial pattern was the original one in
POC, as well. However, Pawley and Reid (1980) may well be correct in
maintaining Pawley's original (1973) interpretation, and reconstructing
SVO as the unmarked order of constituents for POC. For our purposes,
the historical sequence is irrelevant. But given our concern with the linguistic resources Pacific Islanders brought to their nineteenth-century encounter with nautical pidgin and with English, it is important to note
that even in the Oceanic languages with preferred verb-initial ordering of

---

*Once more, Harrison (1978) has challenged prevailing wisdom, suggesting that what
Pawley had reconstructed as an "it" clitic pronoun in POC was in fact part of the transitive
suffix, which was dropped when the following object-pronoun slot was filled.

constituents, the minimal sentence consists of a verb phrase, and that in these languages the order of constituents *within* the VP is subject-initial. That is, as Pawley (1973: 117) points out, "the SVO order is still obligatory for pronominal subjects [SRPs] and objects [the clitic pronouns]."

Fijian will serve to illustrate (Schütz 1981: 197–98):

au   sā   lako
SRP(I)   ASP   go
I go.

o   sā   lako
SRP(you) ASP   go
You go.

era   qito   na   gone
SRP(they) play   ART   child
The children are playing.

The last sentence illustrates how the SRPs, as obligatory constituents of VPs, carry a heavier functional load in VP-initial languages than in SVO languages. That is, in Fijian or the VP-initial Polynesian languages, the sentence begins with a subject pronoun (although in some of these languages a third-person singular pronoun is zero-marked but implied by an aspect marker). As the third sentence illustrates, the SRP at the beginning of the VP may contain essential semantic information not embodied in the following optional subject NP.

In Fijian, as in many of the Oceanic languages with a preferred VP-initial syntax, the subject NP can be fronted. In the Fijian case there has been some debate whether, given the constructional options, the VP-initial one can be taken as representing the dominant or underlying structural pattern. This issue need not concern us.

In those languages that have SVO order as the unmarked form, the pronominal referencing of the subject within the VP is seemingly more redundant than in the VP-initial languages. If the initial subject-NP slot in a sentence is filled, either with a noun or with a pronoun, the following SRP is semantically redundant. Not surprisingly, in many of these languages there is a tendency in discourse for a speaker to have the option of not using an SRP following a subject NP, especially one with a noun as head. SRPs serve to maintain reference to this noun subject across subsequent clauses or sentences. Thus in To'aba'ita (Southeast Solomonic), Lichtenberk (1984: 13) notes: "A verb may appear without a subject marker [SRP] if the referent of the subject is recoverable from the context, either linguistic or extralinguistic." In some Nuclear Micronesian languages, the SRP is (obligatorily) used when the subject-NP slot is empty, and obligatorily omitted when it is filled. Thus, in Pohnpeian (Rehg 1978: 255):

Subject pronouns may . . . occur in a verb phrase . . . only when the subject noun phrase of the sentence is not present. . . .
Soulik peren.
'Soulik is happy.' . . .
e peren.
'He is happy.'

In neighboring languages, however, what has been reconstructed as the original pattern is preserved. Thus in Woleaian and Marshallese the corresponding sentences are (Rehg 1978: 256):

Soulik   ye   ker
Soulik   SRP(he)   be happy
Soulik is happy.

Soulik   e   monono
Soulik   SRP(he)   be happy
Soulik is happy.

The optional or obligatory pattern (in SVO languages) of dropping the SRP in a clause where the subject NP is specified is not surprising, if we view the SRP in functional-grammatical terms as a device for maintaining pronominal reference across clauses.

Such a functional-grammatical perspective leads to further insights. Particularly in languages in which an SVO order is standardized, it would not be surprising to find another development: the progressive loss of the semantic information encoded in SRPs. That is, once reference has been established with a subject NP, it is possible (until reference is changed) to reiterate it anaphorically in subsequent clauses with a pronominal element less-than-fully marked for person and number. When reference is switched, or an embedded clause creates ambiguity, an FP or noun can be used to establish the new reference and/or to reiterate the old one.

It should not surprise us, then, that in some Oceanic languages (and here, it is EO languages that are of particular interest to us) SRPs are less fully marked semantically for person and number than in the paradigms reconstructed for POC or PEO. Because this phenomenon, and the maintenance of reference anaphorically in discourse, will be important in the analysis of Melanesian Pidgin, it is worth examining the subject-pronominal paradigms of some EO languages—first, languages in which the full semantic information marked on FPs is marked on corresponding SRPs, and then at languages where the SRPs are progressively less com-

TABLE 6.2

The Subject Pronouns of Kwaio (Southeast Solomonic)

Number and person	FP	SRP
Singular		
1	(i)nau	ku
2	(i)'oo	ko
3	ngai(a)	ka, e
Dual		
1 inclusive	('i)da'a	golo
1 exclusive	('e)me'e	mele
2	('o)mo'o	molo
3	('i)ga'a	gala
Paucal[a]		
1 inclusive	('i)dauru	goru
1 exclusive	('e)meeru	meru
2	('o)mooru	moru
3	('i)gauru	garu
Plural		
1 inclusive	gia	ki
1 exclusive	('i)mani	mi
2	('a)miu	mu
3	gila	(gi)la

[a]Morphologically trial pronouns that have lost the semantic sense of "three" and imply limited number beyond two, or simply plurality.

pletely marked for person and number than the corresponding FPs. We can first look at Kwaio (Table 6.2), a Southeast Solomonic language that preserves completely the hypothesized OC/EO pattern with a full semantic marking of SRPs; and then at New Hebridean languages that preserve it in attentuating degrees.

In a series of Central and Northern New Hebridean languages, we can see a progressive simplification of the PEO subject pronouns, and particularly of the encoding of semantic information in SRPs. In some of these languages, SRPs are marked for aspect and so there are two or more sets; the forms given are the unmarked sets. In Nguna (Table 6.3), the inferred EO system is clearly preserved, although the trial pronominal series has disappeared. Although the marking of the distinction between dual and plural number on FPs is apparently optional, only the second-person singular and plural SRPs have lost their distinctive contrast.

Tangoan (Table 6.3), a Northern New Hebridean language spoken on a small island off Espiritu Santo, has preserved the full EO pattern for FPs and has preserved marking for person in the SRPs; but only a distinction between singular and nonsingular forms is expressed in the SRPs. Put an-

TABLE 6.3

The Subject Pronouns of Nguna and Tangoan

Number and person	Nguna		Tangoan	
	FP	SRP	FP	SRP
Singular				
1	kinau	a	enau	na
2	nigo	ku	egko	ko
3	nae	e	enia	mo
Dual				
1 inclusive	nigida(-rua)	toro	enRarua	Ra
1 exclusive	kinami(-rua)	aro	kaMamrua	kaMa
2	nimu(-rua)	koro	kiMimrua	ka
3	nara(-rua)	ero	enrarua	la
Trial				
1 inclusive			enRatolu	Ra
1 exclusive			kaMamtolu	kaMa
2			kaMimtolu	ka
3			enratolu	la
Plural				
1 inclusive	nigida	tu	enRa	Ra
1 exclusive	kinami	au	kaMam	kaMa
2	nimu	ku	kaMim	ka
3	nara	eu	en(i)ra	la

SOURCES: *Nguna*, Ray (1926: 206, 215); *Tangoan*, Camden (1979).

other way, the dual/trial versus plural distinction is marked on FPs, not on SRPs.

A further apparent loss of semantic information in the SRPs emerges if we look at the Northern New Hebridean language Maewo (Table 6.4). Here we find striking confirmation that the functional-grammatical perspective taken toward the SRPs is appropriate. In Maewo, we find two sets of SRPs. One, labeled A in the table, is minimally marked for either person or number; it is used in "a simple indicative sentence" or an initial clause (Codrington 1885). SRPs in this set may have aspect markers affixed, but they remain only minimally (and ambiguously) marked for person and number. Presumably, they are used when the reference is clear from a preceding NP. SRPs in the second set, labeled B, which partially preserve the semantic marking for person and number, are used for subsequent clauses conjoined to an initial clause that contains an SRP from set A.

An even more striking example of the attenuation of the anaphoric-referencing function of the SRP, in Northern New Hebridean languages, comes from Mota (Table 6.4), in the Banks Islands. Here the PEO

TABLE 6.4

The Subject Pronouns of Maewo and Mota

Number and person	Maewo FP	Maewo SRP A	Maewo SRP B	Mota FP	Mota Predicate marker
Singular					
1	(i)nau	i	ne	(i)nau	i
2	(i)niko	u	go	(ini)ko	i
3	ia, ni	i	ti	(i)neia	i
Dual					
1 inclusive				(i)narua	i
1 exclusive				(i)karua	i
2				(i)kamurua	i
3				(i)rarua	i, we
Trial					
1 inclusive				(i)natol	i
1 exclusive				(i)katol	i
2				(i)kamtol	i
3				(i)ratol	i
Plural					
1 inclusive	(i)gida	i	te	(i)nina	i
1 exclusive	kami	u	ge	(i)kamam	i
2	(i)kamu	i	ge	(i)kamiu	i
3	ira	i	ge	(i)(ne)iru	i

SOURCE: Codrington (1885).

subject-referencing pronoun set has essentially lost all its marking. The invariant form *i* serves simply to reiterate a previously established subject reference, and (presumably) to mark the base that follows as a verb.*

    Whether the original development of SRPs as agreement markers was a concomitant of a VP-initial syntactic pattern is for our purposes irrelevant. What is important is that in the zone I have suggested was crucial in the several successive stages of the development of Pacific pidgin, including eastern Micronesia, the New Hebrides, and the southeastern Solomons, an unmarked SVO ordering is standard in the great preponderance of languages. Fijian, most Polynesian languages (derived from the Fiji cluster), and a few southern Melanesian languages have VP-initial syntax. This must, however, be qualified in two respects.

    First, as we have seen, in the Oceanic pattern the VP begins with a subject pronoun (the SRP), even where the subject NP optionally follows the VP. This produces a surface convergence with an SVO pattern, a point that will be important in interpreting the development of pidgin in

*It is thus not surprising that Anglican missionary linguists working in the shadow of Codrington, and using Mota as a grammatical standard for other Melanesian languages, were slow to appreciate that SRPs were in fact pronouns.

the Pacific. Second, in most of these languages where subject (and object) NPs normally follow the VP, a subject NP can optionally be foregrounded by fronting to sentence- or clause-initial position. In standard Fijian, for instance, although "they play the child(ren)" is the unmarked word order, "the child(ren) they play" is grammatical, serving to emphasize the reference to the children.

We can usefully illustrate patterns of global syntax and the use of SRPs by looking at three southern Melanesian languages, all of which have quite radically changed the inferred POC pattern in some respects (notably, a phonological condensation of particles into affixes), while preserving its essential relationships and syntactic markings, and most features of its ordering. The examples illustrate clearly how SRPs, even in bound form, maintain reference anaphorically, and how they are functionally related to subject NPs (whether these precede or follow the VP).

We may take as examples Iai, one of the Loyalty Island languages (spoken on Uvea), and Sie, spoken on Erromanga in southern Vanuatu, as manifesting a pattern of pronominal subject marking basically common to all of these languages. In Iai (Tryon 1968: 62–63; I have dropped some of the diacritics not essential to the data and modified the orthography):

> When the subject is a common noun, it must always be accompanied by a tense-marking pronoun [i.e., an SRP marked for tense]:

than   a   aNO   ke   walung
chief   he(PST)   make   a   noise
The chief made a noise.

This clause would be nonsensical if the pronoun were omitted. Thus a kind of double subject is required where the doer of the action is a common noun, but only a single subject [i.e., the SRP] is found if the doer of the action is pronominal, e.g.:

a   aNO   ke   walung
He   made   a   noise.

In Iai, as in a considerable number of these southern Melanesian languages, the global order of constituents is different in intransitive and transitive sentences. In intransitive constructions (Tryon 1968: 62):

> (a) With pronominal subjects, the subject always precedes the predicate, e.g.:

oigeme   long
I   listen

> (b) With common-noun subjects, the obligatory pronominal tense marker [the SRP] occurs before the predicate, while the common noun itself follows the predicate, . . . e.g.:

ame   tEnge   than
he(PRES)   cry   chief
The chief cries.

Even with plural common-noun subjects, the pronominal time marker [the SRP] remains in the singular, e.g.:

ame   laba   eang   lakuk
he(PRES)   stay   here   my-children
My children stay here.

With transitive constructions (Tryon 1968: 63):

(a) With pronominal subjects, the subject always precedes the predicate, e.g.:

oigeme   ham   tusi
I   give   the book.

(b) With common-noun subjects, the common noun and the pronominal time marker both normally precede the predicate, . . . the common noun preceding the pronoun which agrees with it for number, e.g.:

than   a   aNO   ke   walung
chief   he   make   a   noise
The chief made a noise.

je   than   Orine   aNO   ke   walung
the   chiefs   they(PRES)   make   a   noise
The chiefs make a noise.

In Sie, spoken on Erromanga in the southern New Hebrides (Lynch and Capell 1983: 57–58):

The basic intransitive clause has the structure Subject + Verb. Where the subject is a pronoun, or a noun phrase which has appeared in an earlier part of the discourse, it may be omitted, since the person and number of the subject are marked by prefixes to the verb [i.e., cliticized forms of the Oceanic SRPs]. Indeed, in this context, a subject is normally present only when the speaker wishes to place strong emphasis on it. . . .

Narai   y-agan
Narai   he:TNS-angry
Narai was angry.

etm-en   yi-velam
father-his   he:TNS-come
His father came.

yogo-tu-ampe
I:TNS-NEG/IRR-go
I won't go.

The basic transitive clause has the structure Subject + Verb + Object. . . . When the subject is a pronoun or [has] been mentioned, it may be deleted, and usually is. Similarly, when the object is a pronoun, it appears as a suffix to the verb and not as a free noun phrase; and when the object is a noun phrase which has already been mentioned, it may be omitted, though the transitive suffix remains. . . .

```
etm-en      yi-tai         lou
father-his  he:TNS-make    canoe
His father made a canoe.
```

```
g-ogh-or
he:TNS-see-them
He saw them.
```

The SVO pattern prevails in some other New Hebridean languages, such as that spoken in southwestern Tanna (Lynch 1982). In other New Hebridean languages, such as Anejom, spoken on Aneityum (Lynch 1982), the verb-initial pattern is manifest. But once again a pronominal clitic marked for tense and mood is obligatorily situated in the VP, referencing an implicit or explicit noun subject. Thus in Anejom (Lynch 1982: 132):

```
et       man   cin   wamatec     a     kikad
he:TNS   ASP   eat   sweet pot.   SM    pig
The pig ate the sweet potatoes.
```

In the SVO languages characteristic of Nuclear Micronesia, the central and northern New Hebrides, and southeastern Solomons, the unmarked preferred order of constituents places a subject NP (if explicit) first, the VP (containing an SRP) second, a direct-object NP third, and any peripheral arguments of the predicate (prepositional phrases), or temporal phrases, in sentence-final position. Any of the arguments of the predicate, or temporal phrases, can be moved into sentence- (or clause-) initial position through left dislocation, hence foregrounded or topicalized. Thus in Kwaio,

```
(nau)    ku       aga-si-a      boo a-mu       naaboni
FP(me)   SRP(I)   look-TRS-it   pig POSS-you   yesterday
I saw your pig yesterday.
```

can have topical emphasis shifted by fronting:

```
boo a-mu       ku       aga-si-a      naaboni
pig POSS-you   SRP(I)   look-TRS-it   yesterday
About your pig, I saw it yesterday.
```

Or:

naaboni	ku	aga-si-a	boo a-mu
yesterday	SRP(I)	look-TRS-it	pig POSS-you

Yesterday (but not today) I saw your pig.

The fronting of object NPs and the referencing through SRPs allows the embedding of relative clauses without relative markers:

boo a-mu	ku	aga-si-a	naaboni	ka	'akwa
pig POSS-you	SRP(I)	look-TRS-it	yesterday	SRP(it)	ran away

Your pig I saw yesterday ran away.

The complex person- and number-markings on pronouns allow a subtle system of pronominal reference that is more than a simple agreement-marking for (explicit or implicit) subject and object NPs. Consider the following constructions in Kwaio, equivalents of which have been reconstructed for Eastern Oceanic (Pawley 1972):

la	Tome	ma	la	Diki	ta-meru	age-a	gani
ART	Tom	CON	ART	Dick	FUT-SRP(we3E)	do-it	tomorrow

Tom and Dick and I will do it tomorrow.

Here the SRP is the first-person exclusive trial form, indicating that the agent is not merely Tom and Dick, but includes Harry, the speaker. Compare

la	Tome	ma	la	Diki	ta-gala	age-a	gani
ART	Tom	CON	ART	Dick	FUT-SRP(they2)	do-it	tomorrow

Tom and Dick will do it tomorrow.

In the first sentence, the SRP within the VP does not simply copy person and number of the surface NP, as in the second, but marks the underlying subject as Tom, Dick, and the speaker. In discourse, once Tom and Dick have been identified, reference can be maintained with the VP alone:

ta-meru	age-a	gani
FUT-SRP(we3E)	do-it	tomorrow

We'll do it tomorrow.

The same subtleties of pronominal reference can occur with the clitic object pronouns:

ta-la	aga-si-'ameru	la	Tome	ma	la	Diki	a-i
FUT-SRP(they)	see-TRS-us(E)	ART	Tom	CON	ART	Dick	there

They'll see Tom, Dick, and me there.

In Oceanic languages, the FPs characteristically can incorporate noun subjects semantically. Again, a Kwaio example will be instructive:

'e-meeru	la	Tome	ma	la	Diki . . .
FP(we3E)	ART	Tom	CON	ART	Dick . . .

We, Tom, Dick and I . . .

(In Kwaio as in most EO languages using morphologically trial as well as plural pronouns, the "we three" forms do not have a strict reference to three, but are used for a small, limited number, and may simply indicate plurality; Pawley and Geraghty call these morphologically trial pronouns "paucal.")

At this stage, some of the questions I will address in the chapters to follow regarding the structures of Melanesian Pidgin in historical context can be introduced by examining how older speakers of Solomons Pidgin (who learned it on plantations) would render the sentences illustrated for Kwaio. (It was in pondering parallels such as these that I began the exploration that led to this book.)

First, consider the topicalization of direct object NPs and temporals, comparing Kwaio

ku	aga-si-a	boo	a-mu	naaboni
SRP(I)	look-TRS-it	pig	POSS-you	yesterday

I saw your pig yesterday.

with Solomons Pidgin

mi	luk-im	pikipiki	bulong	iu	astade
I	look-TRS	pig	POSS	you	yesterday

I saw your pig yesterday.

The morpheme-by-morpheme correspondence needs no comment at this stage. Compare the constructions when the direct object is topicalized, and the subject pronoun/SRP serves to embed a relative clause (for the moment, I avoid giving grammatical labels to the Solomons Pidgin pronouns; see Chapters 9, 10, and 12). Kwaio:

boo a-mu	ku	aga-si-a	naaboni	ka	'akwa
pig POSS-you	SRP(I)	look-TRS-it	yesterday	SRP(it)	run away

Your pig I saw yesterday ran away.

Solomons Pidgin:

pikipiki	bulong	iu	mi	luk-im	astade	i	ranawe
pig	POSS	you	I	look-TRS	yesterday	it	run away

Your pig I saw yesterday ran away.

Again, the morpheme-by-morpheme correspondence needs no comment at this stage.

Solomons Pidgin uses pronouns in exactly the same way as Southeast Solomonic (and other EO) languages to reference implicit subject NPs. Thus

la	Tome	ma	la	Diki	ta-meru		age-a	gani
ART	Tom	CON	ART	Dick	FUT-SRP(we3E)		do-it	tomorrow

Tom and Dick and I will do it tomorrow.

would be rendered, in the pidgin of older Solomon Islanders,

Tome	and	Diki	bae	mifala	du-im	tumora
Tom	and	Dick	FUT	we(E)	do-TRS	tomorrow

Tom and Dick and I will do it tomorrow.

As in EO languages, in Solomons Pidgin the equivalent of an FP may be used in surface constructions to, in effect, incorporate nouns: "mifala Tome ana Diki," 'Tom, Dick, and I,' exactly corresponding to Kwaio *'e-meeru la Tome ma-la Diki*.

Essentially the same constructions as these Solomons Pidgin equivalents of the Kwaio occur in Tok Pisin and Bislama (just as constructions equivalent to the Kwaio ones I have illustrated occur in the other EO languages of the central and southwestern Pacific). How could such a situation have come about? How is it that speakers of Southeast Solomonic languages such as Kwaio—or of New Hebridean languages such as Tangoan (Camden 1979)—use a pidgin that is seemingly calqued so directly onto their native languages, often on a morpheme-by-morpheme basis? Are they, in so doing, producing pidgin so idiosyncratic that speakers from the next island find it opaque? Not at all. In so doing, they produce common coin of the polyglot plantation community, essentially fully acceptable and intelligible to one another. Indeed, old men from Tangoa or southeastern Malekula in the New Hebrides, and old men from the Malaita mountains, who learned their pidgin in the 1920s or 1930s, would still be able to communicate comfortably with one another in what was then still virtually a common pidgin. It was this paradox and puzzle that led me to this book.

We now have some of the means, historical and linguistic, to solve the puzzle, at least in a partial and preliminary way. We need now to turn to some questions of theory, before returning to the data.

CHAPTER 7

Substrate, Superstrate, and Universals

IN THIS CHAPTER, I shall examine the processes that contributed to the emergence, by the late 1880s, of a remarkably stabilized and expanded pidgin in the Pacific, with particular attention to the roles of substrate and superstrate languages, and universal grammatical relations and faculties, in this development. With this theoretical background, we will then be in a position to examine in some detail the grammatical structures of Melanesian Pidgin.

It is useful at the outset to contrast the Pacific situation with that of Chinook Jargon. Silverstein (1972: 378) notes that Chinook Jargon was the medium of interlingual communication among "unrelated Indo-European, Athapaskan, Salishan, Penutian and Wakashan-speaking peoples of the Pacific Northwest." He contrasts the syntax of Chinook, a major source of the lexical and grammatical material of the Jargon, with that of English. The underlying syntax of Chinook, with its ergative structure and highly complex cross-referencing system of pronouns marked on verbs and nouns, contrasts strikingly with that of English. Examining the surface syntactic patterns of Chinook Jargon, Silverstein concludes that in one sense Jargon has no grammar—or at least no coherent single syntactic system. Rather, surface strings that constitute acceptable and intelligible coin within this polyglot speech community can be produced by participants using markedly different grammatical models. Speakers of different and genetically unrelated languages produce and interpret sentences with reference to the grammatical resources and patterns of their native languages—in the process, stripping off much of their surface marking and syntactic richness. The constructions produced through these multiple grammars represent a process of "interlingual convergence." Silverstein (1972: 605) shows how mutually intelligible and acceptable constructions may be produced using quite different grammars.

> What is comparable to grammatically acceptable Chinook is almost grammatically acceptable English. . . . We can produce sentences whose surface forms from both points of view have [a greater than expectable degree of] one-to-one, unit-by-unit interlingual identifiability. It would be possible, then, . . . to produce intelligible interlingual sentences without complete concession by speakers using one system to those using the other.

This mutual acceptability and intelligibility is not achieved merely through simplification or peeling down through layers of transformational derivation toward underlying universals. Rather, for the speakers of different languages in this speech community, particular surface constructions in Jargon require quite different analytical operations at different derivational depth: "Rapprochement can be achieved to different degrees at different stages of derivations—not always pointing to identical deep structures—and by employing different optional styles of speech from among those in a native speaker's large repertoire" (Silverstein 1972: 603).

In such a speech community a jargon for interlingual communication must remain quite simple, neither extensively elaborated nor standardized; and its participants may use a range of sharply contrasting grammars to produce acceptable common coin. Silverstein (1972: 619–20) argues that the process of convergence not only limits the derivational depth of syntactic constructions but pushes them in the direction of implicational universals based on hierarchies of markedness of the sort set out by Greenberg:

> The functioning of universal marked/unmarked categories should be useful in explaining why they are represented in characteristic distributions in Jargon sentences. . . . We should . . . expect that the unmarked categories will have a high representation in Jargon. . . .
>
> [Moreover] what is fundamental to communicative situations, and hence expressed for language by nonimplicational universals, should be reflected in the very grossly communicative situation typical of Chinook Jargon, and hence in the Jargon surface structures which result from the convergence of types. If each speaker retains in his grammar for Jargon sentence production essentially these more basic and expectable features of his primary language, then of course we expect the surface forms to merge as a result of universal tendencies.

Today Silverstein would doubtless use a rather different framework for syntactic analysis, but the conclusions to which he points still seem compelling. I will argue that the same processes have contributed to the development of Pacific pidgin—and that in many respects we would err if we sought to identify either English, the main superstrate language, or the

Oceanic substrate languages as the source of particular syntactic patterns, or to describe the Pacific pidgin speech community at different time periods as "a language community with an essentially shared grammatical system" (Silverstein 1972: 623). It is fundamental to my analysis that Oceanic speakers and English speakers were analyzing and producing mutually acceptable sentences using different grammars.

Yet I have sought to show that in some respects the situation in the Pacific was very different from the one where Chinook Jargon developed. Rather than belonging to four genetically unrelated language families, as in the Pacific Northwest, the indigenous languages of the central and southwestern Pacific were all genetically related. The languages whose speakers seem to have been predominant in the sequential stages of Pacific pidgin development were members of a single putative subgroup of Oceanic, characterized by a striking retention of a common grammatical structure.

Moreover, this common Oceanic grammatical structure produces surface strings that in many ways parallel those of English, in ways that I will illustrate in some detail in the next chapter. Furthermore, in some striking ways the structures of Oceanic languages parallel those of Atlantic (and Indian Ocean) creoles, which through the medium of a nautical pidgin would seem to have provided much of the linguistic input to Islander-European interaction in the early decades. The grammatical pushing, bending, simplifying, and rearranging necessary for English and Oceanic Austronesian speakers to meet in the middle was thus much less extreme than that required of Chinook speakers and English speakers (and presumably speakers of many other languages within the Pacific Northwest speech community unrelated to either).

Much of the accommodation, I shall suggest, was of speakers of (particularly Eastern) Oceanic languages *to one another*, rather than to English speakers. This entailed no possibility of "complete concession"; and in many respects, it required no simplification down to universal, unmarked patterns. The challenge, to the extent that it involved interlingual communication *among* (Eastern) Oceanic speakers, was partly to simplify down to common denominators deriving from a common ancestral language. While the retention of basic patterns within a language family is obviously related to implicational universals and functional constraints, the "few major choices" (Bickerton 1984: 184) embodied in the ancestral language are likely to shape daughter languages in ways distinctive of that language family.

But what of superstrate influence? One of the thrusts in recent writings on pidgins and creoles has come from theorists of language acquisition such as John Schumann and Roger Anderson. A number of scholars in this emerging tradition have viewed the formation of pidgin languages as in some fairly direct way relatable to a putative pidginization stage in the acquisition of a second language by adult learners, with English (or some other superstrate language) as the "target language" in situations of interlingual contact. As Anderson (1983a: 19) notes, in some cases "hardly any of the incipient pidgin speakers (those creating the pidgin language) have direct access to native speaker input. The major part of their input must be second language output of other pidgin speakers like themselves."

If an individual language learner only has access to the speech output of non-native speakers of the language he is acquiring, the structure he infers from their speech will be [far] removed from the original native source. Pidgin and creole speakers usually find themselves in this situation. Because the pidgin or creole language arises from the need for a common means of intergroup communication, it is in fact the speech of his fellow nonnative speakers in this intergroup linguistic system more than the speech of the few native speakers (if indeed there are any) that he must understand. Thus the usual input that a learner in an incipient pidgin or creole community receives and processes is nonnative input (Anderson 1983: 15).

But native speakers of *what*? This literature often implies (though, as above, does not say explicitly) that in such situations (at least with pidginization) the "native speakers" who ought to have been there but often were not, were speakers of English, or French, or Portuguese—and that the European "target language" was acquired in an imperfect, pidginized form because of a restricted input. Is this what was happening in the Pacific in the 1850s? the 1860s? the 1880s?

I have avoided giving labels such as "Jargon English," "Sandalwood English," and "Beach-la-Mar" to the interlingual medium in the Pacific at various historical stages. Such labeling gives a spuriously discontinuous developmental picture, and implies that we know more than we do about the linguistic character of the codes in use at various stages.* But in terms of the processes involved in the development of this interlingual medium, several stages have to be roughly distinguished, during which different processes seem to have predominated.

Before about 1850, I think, English was in a quite direct sense the target language, to which Islanders approximated in ways constrained by their limited access to native speakers' input, the particular nature of the input they did receive (with a heavy content of nautical pidgin/"foreigner talk"), and the social/political contexts of its use. In this period (and to

---

*And also that we have clear linguistic criteria for distinguishing jargons, pidgins, and creoles; on the absence of such clear criteria, see Collins 1980 and Mühlhäusler n.d.2.

much lesser and decreasing extent in the subsequent two decades), the linguistic and sociolinguistic processes envisioned by the theorists of second-language acquisition were operating fairly directly.

The Islanders from places such as Kosrae, Pohnpei, Rotuma, the Gilberts, Fiji, Tonga, the Marquesas, Hawaii, and Tahiti were dealing—on ship and shore—with English speakers in situations the latter largely controlled and dominated. When Islanders were incorporated into ships' crews, or hung around the trading and whaling ships and the shore bases, they acquired a partial command of English that depended on the input available to them (on which more shortly) and particularly on the extent and duration of their direct interaction with English speakers. No doubt a substantial number of the Islanders who hung around the ships and shore bases as young children acquired a native or near-native command of shipboard English; adults acquired an imperfect command, phonologically and grammatically, of the medium in which English speakers were communicating to them.

Was this medium English? The English to which (most) Islanders were exposed in this period seems to have been "foreigner talk" modified radically not only in its simplification, but in its incorporation of many elements from a nautical pidgin embodying conventions used by English speakers for "talking to natives." This repertoire, the exact history of which is a matter of much controversy, included elements such as *save* and *pikanini* (ultimately of Mediterranean/Iberian/Romance origin), elements derived from Atlantic pidgins/creoles, elements such as *-um* as a verb ending that are probably of American frontier origin, and a number of elements with a seeming origin in China-coast pidgin (see Clark 1977, 1979, for a useful summary of the evidence on these elements). The last influence is hardly surprising, given that the sandalwood and trepang obtained by trade in the Pacific was being transported directly to the China coast. (No doubt a good many Pacific Islanders, as crew members, had direct contact with this China-coast pidgin.) It is hardly surprising that the medium of interlingual communication evolving in the period up to 1850 was a jargon quite different from standard (shipboard) English.

We have no direct evidence that in this period some Islanders acquired a fluent (and in some cases native?) command of the English (as opposed to nautical pidgin) then used on the ships of the nineteenth century *as well as* a command of the developing jargonized form of the period, with its "native-talk" elements such as "savvy," "fella," and "um." But I believe that this is very likely for at least a small number of Islanders who, as youngsters, hung around ships and their crews and trading or beachcombing colonies. We may guess that such was the case of the son of "King George" of Kosrae, who as a boy amazed visitors with his ability to recite the names of all the American Presidents and the accomplishments of each. I believe that this point, inferential as it must remain, is important: for it would have represented the beginning of a bifurcation between two codes of interlingual communication used by Pacific Islanders—(standard) English and a developing pidgin. I will suggest that in subsequent decades, substantial numbers of Islanders (e.g., the many who spent long periods in Sydney or Brisbane, and those who worked closely on a sustained basis with missionaries) acquired in varying degrees a command of standard English and at the same time had a fluent command *of a pidgin that was very different from standard English,* which they used with fellow Islanders. I believe that the literature is marred by a failure to distinguish between the two quite different target languages coexisting in the Pacific, and by the erroneous assumption that throughout the nineteenth century, speakers of pidgin were *trying to learn English* but were limited in their access to it. I will suggest that at least from the 1860s on, the fluent speakers of Pacific pidgin whose speech served as the target language (both for Islanders and for English speakers) were Pacific Islanders.

The evidence on the sandalwood period in southern Melanesia summarized in Chapter 3, although far too incomplete to permit confident sociolinguistic and linguistic inferences, strongly suggests to me that a significant number of Islanders from the central Pacific and southern Melanesia were by the 1860s fluent speakers of a pidgin acquired in childhood (probably in a good many cases natively, in addition to an Oceanic mother tongue). This process was to go on: recall Hernsheim's comment that by 1880, in New Britain, "nowadays nearly everybody, above all the children, speak this variety of English, some of them with great fluency," and Wawn's comment that in the New Hebrides in 1879, "children pick up South Sea English very quickly; and I have known boys who came on board my vessel converse fluently."

My guess is that a generation of Pacific Islanders from the Gilberts, Rotuma, Fiji, the Loyalties, and Polynesia born in the 1850s and early 1860s was crucial in the expansion and stabilization of a Pacific pidgin. This pidgin became rich enough lexically and syntactically to serve as a primary language of daily communication in the "communities," mainly shipboard settings, where it was used, in what may have been a phase of at least incipient and partial nativization (if we choose to mean by this the acquisition of a language by young children with native fluency, although it may be the primary language of none of them). In the subsequent twenty years, as they became young adults, these Islanders born in the 1850s and 1860s who had learned the prevailing pidgin with childhood fluency moved widely through the Pacific and beyond. We find their mark on the developing pidgin linguistically and sociolinguistically.

It is this generation of fluent pidgin speakers, I have suggested, that spread the lingua franca into the recruiting areas when the Labor Trade began. Recall the mixed population of Islanders from Lifu, Rotuma, Tonga, and Hawaii on Murray Island in the 1880s, products of this generation, who had spent years away from home on ships and in port. Fluent pidgin speakers of this generation seem to have brought the lingua franca into Samoa and Queensland; they may have brought it into the cane fields of Hawaii as well. They played a critical role as intermediaries in the development of plantations and the expansion of the Labor Trade, as middlemen and cultural and linguistic brokers. It is they who were speaking the "target language" both fellow Islanders and Europeans were trying, with more or less success, to emulate.

English speakers were providing a target language for them, too—but a different language. Recall from the 1869 Select Committee hearings "Lifou Dick, Bebbo, . . . and Kouma, . . . and Fangai or Johnny Mare the cook: all these natives speaking English, and two of them . . . able to read and write." Recall the Lifu and other Loyalty Islanders, and the Rotumans, who had lived in Sydney, Brisbane, or San Francisco. Like contemporary speakers of Caribbean English, these speakers were probably acquiring a repertoire for communicating, more or less fluently and grammatically, with English speakers, in addition to their fluent command of a lingua franca they used with one another. Islanders who were more sophisticated in terms of their experience in speech communities where standard English was the common linguistic coin had one register for interacting in that world and another for interacting in the social world of fellow Islanders (in which native English speakers were marginal participants). I believe this bifurcation can be traced through the late nineteenth century. We find some direct evidence for it in the court interpreters of 1885 and elsewhere in the documentary materials of the Labor Trade. My own texts from elderly Solomons Pidgin speakers reveal striking contrasts in register, often from the same speaker, when talking about or quoting Europeans with whom the speaker had sustained contacts through mission or police work.

We should not be misled here by the fact that the Islanders themselves, and the Europeans, considered both registers to be forms of "English," one with higher status and one with lower status; the same has been true in the Caribbean. For well over a century in the Pacific, Islanders have regarded the prevailing pidgin as English (for most, the only version of it to which they had access); and Europeans have regarded it as a bastardized form of English. Neither "side" in this sustained linguistic encounter has realized that the lingua franca was grammatically a language quite distinct from English (and as I will show, Oceanic in many respects). Moreover, the ideological portrayal of the lingua franca, sub-scribed to (it seems) by both Islanders and whites, has been that whites were its creators and "proper" speakers. A lexicon that in the nineteenth century came almost entirely from English and nautical pidgin, and the surface syntactic parallels between Pacific pidgin and English, both lent themselves to such a portrayal. But there can be, and in this case has been, a wide gulf between an ideology framed in circumstances of colonial domination and capitalist exploitation, and sociocultural and socio-linguistic realities.

In much of contemporary Melanesia, speakers of Melanesian Pidgin dialects continue to subscribe to this ideology, in which Pidgin is a bas-tardized and low-status form of English that should be transformed into "proper" English (although there is now a countervailing nationalist rhetoric in Papua New Guinea and Vanuatu promoting the legitimacy of pidgin dialects). While such an ideology is fully intelligible in a historical context of colonial domination, there is no reason why linguists floating second-language-acquisition theory into the Pacific should subscribe to or perpetuate it. By the 1870s, at least, Islanders were not struggling ineptly to learn English, thwarted by their limited input from native speakers and their disadvantages as adult second-language learners. *They* were the flu-ent speakers of a language they had (I shall show) largely created, which Europeans learned incompletely and spoke badly, thanks to massive code interference and *their* disadvantages as adult second-language learners.

If the scenario I have suggested is roughly accurate, then two processes were under way that demand further explication. One is the process of co-creation by Oceanic Austronesian speakers of a grammatical system that, as I shall illustrate in the next chapter, incorporates in a simplified way the core grammatical system more or less common to their native (mainly Eastern) Oceanic languages; in this process, English speakers were politi-cally dominant but sociolinguistically secondary participants. In the next chapter, I explore the interplay between substrate models and universal lin-guistic faculties and patterns. The second process parallels that sketched by Silverstein for Chinook Jargon with which the chapter began: a process whereby mutually acceptable and intelligible surface strings were pro-duced and interpreted by Oceanic and English speakers using different grammars.

It seems to me absolutely fundamental that the ability of Oceanic speakers to create a pidgin grammatical system incorporating the "core" structures of Oceanic Austronesian grammar (in some cases, at a rela-tively abstract level) is not only compatible with developing theories of universal grammar; it urgently demands recourse to them, as I shall seek to show in the next chapter.* The Islanders themselves spoke diverse and mutually unintelligible languages, and the excavation of "major syntactic choices" and unmarked constructions would have entailed the elimination of surface marking and language-specific patterns. Hence, the process of language creation in the Pacific would have required the participants to rely heavily on universal linguistic faculties for simplifying and mutually accommodating through minimally marked constructions, and excavating deep syntactic and logical relationships (though not necessarily universal ones) underlying surface diversity.

In the historical circumstances I have sketched, the development of an expanded Pacific pidgin not only demanded a stripping off of much of the surface marking of individual languages to "find" or "create" abstract, simpler, minimally marked structures underlying them; it further required that the elements so "identified" be lexified from an alien source, and that the constructions so created be acceptable and intelligible to the superstrate speakers who ultimately were politically dominant, and whose ships and plantations constituted the settings for pidgin and its raison d'être.

The pathways for the creation and elaboration of pidgin grammar depended on the fit (or lack of it) between the lexifying superstrate language and substrate languages, on the availability of unbound forms (see Goodman 1985), and on universal relations of markedness of the sort discussed by Silverstein (1972) and faculties of simplification of the sort discussed by Kay and Sankoff (1974). In establishing a general theoretical position and developing heuristic hypotheses for interpreting particular grammatical constructions, we should seek to find what Mühlhäusler (1986: 132–33) describes as

conspiracies . . . between the different forces, . . . (1) superstratum and universal tendencies; (2) substratum and universal tendencies; (3) substratum and superstratum; (4) all three factors. Such combinations can occur at all levels of grammar. [In preference to any single-causal explanation, one should seek out] the much more likely explanation of a conspiracy between universal processes, simplified input and substratum factors. Where these factors coincide, the cognitive cost for those in the business of developing a pidgin or creole is least, and it is for this reason that pidginists and creolists should be on a constant look-out for such developmental conspiracies and the linguistic syncretisms resulting from them.

The capitalist and paranoiac metaphors may not in the end be essential to theoretical progress, but the search for such confluences constitutes, as Goodman and Mühlhäusler both emphasize, the needed reorientation for a field long polarized by the advocacy of supposedly mutually exclusive or

*See Mufwene 1986.

contradictory modes of analysis and explanation (see also Mufwene 1986).

It is worth posing a speculative linguistic and sociolinguistic question at this stage. What would have happened had substantial populations of speakers of mutually unintelligible Eastern Oceanic languages found themselves in circumstances requiring them to work and live together where they were not under the political, economic, and technological domination of a minority speaking a genetically unrelated language? What would have happened if there had been no linguistic superstrate? Perhaps some single Oceanic language would have emerged as the major lexifying source language, on the basis of demographic or political domination. But we may surmise that nonnative speakers would have learned and used that dominant language not in its standard form but in a pidginized form that neutralized many surface features and dug back toward underlying syntactic patterns that had three convergent properties: (1) being broadly common to the languages spoken by significant numbers of participants; (2) being unmarked (e.g., expressing generalized inalienable possession as opposed to alienable and semialienable possession); and (3) being in other respects relatively simplified, with limited surface marking and relatively shallow derivations, so as to be easy to learn and easy to communicate with despite an imperfect command.

We might further guess that such an emerging lingua franca would be relatively limited and simple lexically, relying on a core of common nouns and verbs that could be used, with qualifiers and circumlocution and contextual cues, to reduce ambiguity and generate new labels situationally.

However, it would be likely to differ from pidgin languages arising among speakers of languages not closely related genetically, in (1) incorporating specific syntactic patterns that are not part of a universal (unmarked) syntax (and hence might be reached by a radical simplification), but rather are broadly common to the particular language family or subgroup (see Mufwene 1986: 145); (2) stabilizing more quickly than would occur where speakers brought to the pidgin radically diverse native grammars, as in the cases discussed by Bickerton (1981, 1984) for Hawaii and Silverstein (1972) for Chinook Jargon; and (3) elaborating more quickly, in terms of the complex syntactic constructions made possible by specific grammatical devices common to the contributing substrate languages.

In the case of EO languages, we might guess that the pidgin language created through such a hypothetical historical scenario would have certain features, common to these languages, of a sort we would not otherwise find in a pidgin. These might include (1) a transitive suffix to mark agent-object relations; (2) a set of short subject pronouns used within VPs to reiterate an explicit subject NP and reference a subject indexically or anaphorically in subsequent clauses; (3) the use of these pronouns to embed relative clauses, allowing an early syntactic elaboration not found in Bickerton's "true" pidgins growing out of radical interlingual contact; and (4) representation, in these pronouns, of semantic distinctions (inclusive vs. exclusive, dual and trial vs. plural) that are drawn in the contributing languages but are so marked (in terms of universal hierarchies of markedness) that they could not be incorporated in a "true" pidgin (see Mufwene 1986: 141–44).

It is further possible that in pidgin developing among speakers of closely related languages, in the absence of a "superstrate" language, that we would find even more specific syntactic or morphological patterns widely distributed within these languages; thus in the Oceanic case, we might find a causative prefix converting stative and intransitive verbs into causative transitive verbs.

I shall show in the next chapter that all of these patterns (with the partial exception of the causative prefix, as will be seen) are found in all Melanesian Pidgin dialects, and must have been incorporated in the pidgin of a century ago. Some of them—the transitive suffixes, the embedded relative clauses—have been specifically noted by Bickerton (1984: 187) as distinguishing Melanesian Pidgin from "true pidgins," and also from the creoles that he presumes have developed from them through nativization.

In fact, from Siegel's analysis of Pidgin Fijian we have direct evidence of a scenario not so different from the imaginary one I have sketched. Although the plantation pidgin of the Labor Trade got an early foothold in Fiji, for various reasons it was replaced as the lingua franca of the plantations by a pidginized form of Fijian (see Siegel 1986, 1987). Recall that Fijian is an Eastern Oceanic language, so that speakers of New Hebridean and Southeast Solomonic languages found themselves surrounded by fellow EO speakers. The Fijians, numerically preponderant, physically intimidating, politically more tightly and hierarchically organized, in their own communities led by elders and warriors, had a dominance that went beyond being on their home turf, in contrast with the young men from scattered islands. Many of the Fijians were by then Christianized and sophisticated in dealing with Europeans. Moreover, many Europeans were themselves trying to learn Fijian so as to teach, preach, and rule through it. Little wonder that Fijian emerged as the main language of plantation work in Fiji.

But as Siegel (1987) brilliantly shows, this Fijian was a kind of EO Pidgin Fijian, stripped of many of its surface features, marked distinctions, and distinctive constructions (in contrast to other EO languages spoken by the New Hebrideans and Solomon Islanders), and rendered syntactically and lexically simple for the adult second-language learner. It comes as no surprise to find, in Siegel's analysis, many kinds of "sim-plification" in Pidgin Fijian that parallel those of Pidgin English in the southwest Pacific.

Pacific Pidgin English was, of course, not created solely by Pacific Islanders: the massive adoption of the lexicon from English, the absence of constructions we might have expected from a (solely) Oceanic lingua franca, and the presence of constructions lexified from English that follow an English, not Oceanic, syntactic pattern (e.g., "by and by" as a clause-initial time marker) attest clearly enough to that. But I will show in the following chapters that Pacific Islanders have left an unmistakable lin-guistic impress, both global and specific, on this language of domination, collective survival, and collective work.

The creation of Pacific pidgin was a dialectic of co-creation to which speakers of English and Oceanic languages contributed in different and complementary ways, commensurate with the radical contrast in their sociolinguistic and political-economic position. The Islanders were domi-nated and exploited by invaders with a superior technology, who could demand subservience and punish resistance. At first, and long before the Labor Trade, the odd Pacific Islander on a crew of a whaling or trading ship was forced to learn and use as best he could the prevailing seamen's English and whatever simplified "foreigner talk" was used with him. But increasingly, Islanders of mixed origin had predominated, and apparently they largely controlled and defined the nature of "shipboard culture" de-spite formal command structures. Later, the very circumstances of the ex-ploitation and inhumanity of the Labor Trade—the life-devouring plan-tation capitalism, with its imperatives to find ever-expanding sources of cheap labor, and the European racism, entailing the marginalization of Islanders and their relegation to semihuman status—created conditions in which Islanders became isolated from their European "masters" and in-teracted in most cases more with fellow Islanders than English speakers.

The evidence from the nineteenth and early twentieth centuries sug-gests that English speakers who learned and used Pacific pidgin seldom approached the fluency, grammatical repertoire, or phonological patterns of those Islanders who were its fluent speakers. The way Europeans who had spoken the language for years in a wide range of communicative situa-tions recorded it suggests that they were massively subject to code inter-ference from English, both phonologically and grammatically: using "al-together" instead of *olgeta*, "by-and-by" instead of *babae*,* and "what name" instead of *wanem*. They were using the wrong pronouns (usually

---

*The phonological shape of this form in Melanesian Pidgin varies considerably; I use *babae* or *bambae* according to context in the chapters that follow.

getting the exclusive/inclusive distinction wrong), were using "-em" where it did not belong and omitting it where it was required, and were using "fella" indiscriminately or as a noun rather than as a grammatical particle. That is one reason why the textual records from Europeans are so difficult to interpret. We will see in the next two chapters that we learn more about the way Islanders fluent in pidgin actually spoke from the few observers who were not English speakers—notably Pionnier (1913), a French-speaking missionary in the New Hebrides through the 1890s— than from the English-speaking chroniclers of the period. Pionnier's native French often provided clumsy means to represent the sounds he heard ("pastaïme," "bambaïlle," "olguita," "ouanème," "no ouanedème"); but unlike English speakers, he at least tried to represent the sounds he heard, not the English forms from which they were ultimately derived.

That can usefully bring us back to the question, raised by Silverstein (1972) with regard to Chinook Jargon, of whether English speakers and Oceanic speakers were producing and interpreting mutually intelligible surface strings using different grammars. I have no doubt that they were.

Expressions such as Pionnier's "pastaïme" and "ouanème" were undoubtedly analyzed by English speakers as "first time" and "what name." Consider the analysis of Pionnier's "solouara i go daoune" ('the tide is going out'). Judging by old "bush" Solomons speakers, the probable analysis by the New Hebrideans was

solowara	i	godaon
sea	SRP(it)	descend

where for English speakers it would have been "salt water he go down."

In the Melanesian analysis, the sentence consists of three morphemes; in the English analysis, of five. In the Melanesian analysis, the pronoun is in the verb phrase and is the obligatory subject constituent of the sentence. In the English analysis, it redundantly echoes the subject noun phrase and carries no syntactic load; for English speakers, these redundant resumptive pronouns would have been a stylistic oddity used by and with the "natives."

To take another small example, *ating*, derived from English "I think," occurs in Tok Pisin, Bislama, and Solomons Pidgin, with the same meanings of 'maybe.' In the 1880s, Pacific Islanders must have been treating *ating* as a single morpheme.* At the same time, Europeans must have been analyzing constructions with *ating* as containing an "I think" clause

---

*It would strain our credibility to infer that Islanders had originally analyzed the form as "I think" and that the three dialects underwent parallel reanalyses, particularly since the "I" pronoun had such a sporadic occurrence in nineteenth-century pidgin (Chapters 9 and 10).

that, for the Islanders, did not exist. The two parallel analyses continue into modern times.

In my view, the processes described by Silverstein (1972) for Chinook Jargon, whereby similar and mutually intelligible surface strings were produced by speakers of European and indigenous languages using different grammatical analyses, must have been going on in the Pacific. It is not that English and Oceanic speakers were using the grammar of their native languages to produce and understand pidgin. Rather, their respective grammars of pidgin were achieved by modifying, simplifying, and extrapolating from the grammars of languages spoken natively, drawing upon the repertoires of alternative constructional possibilities in these languages. I will show in the next chapter that the contrasts in surface strings and underlying grammatical relations between Oceanic languages and English seem much less drastic than those dividing Chinook and English. The bending, twisting, and extrapolation required to meet in the middle would have been correspondingly less extreme. I will show that in many syntactic respects, as with the global SVO pattern, we need not choose English or Oceanic languages as the source model for Pacific pidgin; and little bending was required on either "side." This did not mean that the sentences had to be simple.

It will usefully both illustrate this point and lead to the data of the next chapter if we consider some examples from Pionnier's texts from Malekula (New Hebrides) in the 1890s, with complex embeddings of clauses—embeddings that exactly follow an Oceanic pattern, but are quite transparent to English speakers (though they probably would seldom themselves have produced such sentences in pidgin). Here the numbered block is the sentence recorded by Pionnier (1913); beneath is my analysis of it—which the reader is asked to accept on faith in advance of the analysis of the next two chapters:

1. You fraïlle naou ol tigne i no goud you mèkèm bifore
   (kiaman, sitil, kil), ol tigne i no goud (p. 198).

iu	frae	nao	ol	ting	i	nogud	iu	mek-em	bifo
you	reject	now	PLU	thing	it	be bad	you	do-TRS	before

You reject all the bad things you did before,

(kiaman,	sitil,	kil),	ol	ting	i	nogud.
lie	steal	kill	PLU	thing	it	be bad.

lying, stealing, killing, all the things that are bad.

2. Blad ia i goud, i ouach ol tigne
   man i mèkèm no goud.

blad	ia	i	goud	i	wash	ol	ting
blood	DEM	it	be good	it	wash	PLU	thing

This blood is good, it cleanses the sins

man　i　mek-em　nogud
man　he　do-TRS　be bad
of men.

3. Big fala Masta i stap onetap, i mèkèm ol tigne,
i louk ol tigne, i peïme bèle long man i mèkèm goud,
long plèce i very goud onetap;
i kapsaïll bèle bilong man i mo mèkèm goud long plèce,
i no goud, long faïa, ol taïme, no finish (p. 197).

big-fala　masta　i　stap　antap,　i　mek-em　ol　ting
big-ADJ　master　he　stay　above　he　do-TRS　PLU　thing
The great master up above, who made all things,

i　luk　ol　ting,　i　pei-em　bel　long　man　i
he　look　PLU　thing　he　reward-TRS　soul　POSS　man　he
who sees everything, rewards the souls of men who

mek-em　gud　long　ples　i　verigud　antap
do-TRS　good　LOC　place　it　be good　above
do good in heaven above;

i　kapsae　bel　bilong　man　i　no　mek-em　gud　long　ples
he　dump　soul　POSS　man　he　NEG　do-TRS　good　LOC　place
he throws the souls of sinners in a place

i　nogud,　long　faia,　oltaem,　no　finis
it　be bad　LOC　fire　continuously　NEG　end
which is bad, with eternal fire, forever.

The last sentence, in particular, requires some of its embedded clauses to express meanings that in a natural language would be conveyed lexically. However, the syntactic pattern is perfectly Oceanic, and sentences equally complex and identical in their embedding patterns are common in Southeast Solomonic languages (and, as we will see, in bush dialects of Solomons Pidgin). Yet the syntax, using what I will argue in Chapter 10 are SRPs to embed relative clauses, is quite transparent to English speakers despite the lack of relativizers marked as such. The possibilities of "interlingual convergence" were conveniently at hand when Europeans penetrated the Pacific, and linguistically at least, "complete concession" was not an issue (at least until the modern era of mass education in English and French).

These circumstances—both the essentially similar grammatical structures of substrate languages and the surface parallels with English—created the possibility of a scenario of linguistic development very different from the ones characterized by Bickerton (1981, 1984) and by Givón (1984: 290–91), who believes:

Pidgins have only a *minimal syntax*, with virtually no complex/embedded constructions or morphology. . . . The Pidgin . . . is a rather *restricted* communicative code, in terms of expressive power, topics of discussion, speed of communication and independence of immediate context. The parent generation thus displays imperfect learning of a second language. Given both the variability and limited expressive range of the parents' Pidgin, the children never try to acquire it. Rather, they extract the only reasonably stable feature from the Pidgin—the lexicon, and then go on to *invent the Creole grammar* from scratch.

Bickerton knows that what happened in the Pacific was quite different—though in the light of what has been written by such scholars as Mühlhäusler and Sankoff about the elaboration of Tok Pisin in the twentieth century, he might be surprised at the complexity of the sentences given by Pionnier.* Bickerton's original guess, discussed in Chapter 2, that Pacific pidgin underwent a period of nativization in the mid-nineteenth century, and that the Labor Trade entailed its repidginization, may well be correct. However, like Bickerton vintage 1986, I doubt that the number of native speakers during the sandalwood and Labor Trade periods was great enough, or their political position strong enough, to make a strong impact on the language. Whether or not substantial numbers of Pacific Islanders were native speakers of pidgin in the 1860s, 1870s, and 1880s, Islanders who had grown up on and around ships and shore bases were certainly its most fluent speakers in terms of "expressive power, topics of discussion, speed of communication and independence of immediate context." Theirs was the "target language" of which English speakers (and plantation recruits) were imperfect adult learners.

*He assures me (personal communication, July 1986) that he is not.

CHAPTER 8

 Structures and Sources of Pidgin Syntax

AS BICKERTON (1981, 1984) notes, one of the problems inherent in most past claims that substrate models have had a strong formative influence on particular pidgins or creoles is the ad hoc and unsystematic character of the arguments advanced. Whereas languages form systems whose "major choices" syntactically have entailments manifest throughout the grammar, "substratophiles" have tended to pull out individual features or patterns and find analogues of them in substrate languages. Another frequent difficulty in claims of substrate influence has been a failure to fix clearly a time-frame and a set of substrate languages in which the hypothesized sociolinguistic processes could plausibly have taken place.

The two most serious attempts to assess the nature and degree of substrate influence on Melanesian Pidgin, Camden's (1979) comparison of Bislama and Tangoan and Mosel's (1980) comparison of Tok Pisin and Kuanua (Tolai), have been quite systematic and have looked across a wide range of syntactic, morphological, and semantic evidence. Although these studies have given substance to the distinctiveness of Melanesian Pidgin, in terms of the possible importance of substrate influence, they also, I think, have had a curious reverse effect. There is a disquieting impression that one can take any language from the southwestern Pacific and use it to show substrate influence on Pidgin (an impression strengthened by other less global and systematic comparisons of substrate languages and Melanesian Pidgin dialects, such as those advanced by Walsh [1978] and Charpentier [1979]). How can substrate models have come from so many languages in so many places? A comparison between Kuanua and Tok Pisin is partly immune to such criticisms, since the indigenous languages of the Blanche Bay area, including Kuanua, clearly had a substantial impact (at least lexically) on Tok Pisin. But Kuanua can hardly be a source of syntactic patterns found in the pidgin dialects of Vanuatu and Solomon Islands (and in some cases, Torres Strait Creole) as well as Tok Pisin.

In short, the game played by substratophiles has been a game with no rules; and that is one basis for Bickerton's objections. Substratophilia has been a weak position, in terms of linguistic theory as well as in terms of history: it seeks to explain the general in terms of the particular, to explicate wholes in terms of token parts. At the outset, we must define some of the rules of argument.

I have sought to provide a framework in time and space within which plausible sociolinguistic processes of substrate influence, in "conspiracy" with superstrate influences and universal constraints and faculties, could have operated; and I have looked at the languages spoken in the zone from which we would expect substrate models, if any, to have come, showing the relative homogeneity of superstrate languages, very different from the situation with Chinook Jargon. In doing so, I have provided a plausible explanation of why it is possible to take any Oceanic language of the southwestern Pacific and, in comparing it with a dialect of Melanesian Pidgin, make a case for substrate influence.

I will suggest that there is a temporal stratigraphy of substrate influences in Pacific pidgins—for this is a process that has continued through the entire period through which pidgin dialects have been learned by adults in multilingual settings. The patterns established early in Pacific pidgin, and represented in all modern dialects of Melanesian Pidgin, reflect structures broadly common to Oceanic languages. These structures tend to be preserved most strikingly in languages of the putative Eastern Oceanic subgroup from the central and southwestern Pacific. If so, then we will find some form of these patterns in any Oceanic language we choose for comparison with a Melanesian Pidgin dialect; and the more conservative our target Oceanic language is of these ancient patterns, the more of these correspondences we will find.

If we narrow our focus to a particular subgroup of Oceanic languages, among which pidgin has undergone a period of separate development, we could anticipate finding in this dialect of pidgin the impress of patterns specific to this subgroup. In Chapters 11–13, I will show striking evidence for such substrate models in Solomons Pidgin, models represented in Southeast Solomonic languages. (We might also expect to find the impress of syntactic patterns from particular sets of Papuan languages in regional variants of Tok Pisin.)

This begins to introduce some rules for seeking substrate models. Kuanua, for example, is a plausible source of models for constructions in Tok Pisin not found in Bislama and Solomons Pidgin; but contra Mühlhäusler, who sees Kuanua (Tolai) as Tok Pisin's "principal substratum language," it is not a likely source of models for constructions common to all the dialects of Melanesian Pidgin, either historically (since its influence would mainly have been post-1885) or linguistically (since this subgroup of Oceanic languages does not clearly manifest many of the Oceanic patterns represented in languages to the east and north, patterns whose impress on all dialects of Melanesian Pidgin I will illustrate here and in the chapters that follow).

In establishing ground rules for argument, another problem has to be squarely faced at the outset. In some respects, the global syntax of Oceanic Austronesian languages quite closely parallels the global syntax of English. This is one reason why linguists who are not Oceanic specialists, looking from the outside, assume an English superstrate source for Melanesian Pidgin grammar (and nowadays may invoke fashionable explanations about second-language learning). It is also one reason why English speakers in the Pacific could for more than a century speak pidgin imagining that it was a simplified form of English (modified in the direction of "Kanaka talk"), while Pacific Islanders could speak it following the grammatical pathways of their native languages. That is, the parallels between substrate and superstrate languages have themselves been a powerful mechanism in generating the syntactic patterns of an emerging Pacific pidgin, and in many respects make it unnecessary for us to opt for one source or another of a particular constructional pattern. The convergences between English surface syntax and Oceanic surface syntax create the conditions for "developmental conspiracies" (Mühlhäusler 1986) and the sharing of linguistic coin by both "sides" in a sustained interlingual encounter.

An example will serve to illustrate this process. Melanesian Pidgin dialects create conditional sentences with *sapos* 'if,' followed by the conditional clause: thus, *sapos iumi go long taon maet iumi lukim*, 'If we go to town, we might see him' (Solomons Pidgin). This clearly parallels English conditional constructions, with "suppose" substituted for "if" (presumably on the basis of the expectations about talking to "natives" that European seafarers brought to the Pacific, drawing on other pidgins and creoles of the northern hemisphere). Oceanic languages characteristically form conditional sentences in exactly the same way. In Nuclear Micronesian languages, we find *ma* or some similar form in sentence-initial position:

Pohnpeian:

ma   e   peien   kondo
if   srp(he)   mod(happen-to)   come
If he happens to come . . .

Mokilese:

ma sud lakapw kisai joah jeila loakjid
If it rains tomorrow, we won't go fishing.

In Southeast Solomonic, we find forms like Kwaio (Malaita) *lauta*

lauta   e   nigi   gani
if   srp(he) arrive   tomorrow
If he arrives tomorrow . . .

and Lau (Malaita) *leaso*:

leaso   gomolu   dao   kou
if   srp(youPLU) arrive   DEI
If you arrive . . .

In the Loyalties, we find forms like Nengone *nei* (Tryon 1967):

nei ey ma co kaka ibetu
If we eat immediately . . .

We could go through a similar exercise for initial modals where Melanesian Pidgin dialects use *maet* 'maybe'* (and English uses "maybe"), and Oceanic languages use forms like Pohnpeian *mwein*:

mwein   ohlo   aluhla   Kolonia
maybe   man   walk   Kolonia
Maybe the man walked to Kolonia.

These patterns are not, of course, confined to English and Oceanic Austronesian. Their "naturalness" has led to the incorporation of similar patterns in a wide array of the languages of the world. "Suppose" is an old form in nautical pidgin, and is represented in "suppose one got money," recorded from Hawaiians in San Diego in 1835 (Dana 1840: 24). The point is that for such patterns we do not want to argue narrowly for either a superstrate derivation from English or nautical pidgin or a substrate derivation, but for convergence of speakers of both sets of languages on a path that is a "natural" unmarked pattern. But we also need to exercise caution in inferring (as seems sometimes to have been the case) that such patterns

---

*Or, less commonly, *ating*, a form initially adopted from English "I think" but used as a monomorphemic modal 'if' in all three major Melanesian Pidgin dialects.

in Melanesian Pidgin are directly derived from English, without examining the Oceanic side of the coin.

While such parallels between Oceanic syntax and English syntax are historically important in the formation of Pacific pidgin, some of the patterns that superficially appear to follow English constructions reveal on closer analysis their fundamentally Oceanic derivation.

There are even more-striking parallels between the structure of Oceanic languages (especially the conservative EO languages) and structures common in many Atlantic (and Indian Ocean) creoles. A case in point is the syntactic position of "adjectives." Bickerton (1981: 68–69) notes:

In a number of creoles the adjective has been analyzed as forming a subclass of stative verbs. . . . Originally, all writers on Indian Ocean creoles . . . treated verbs and adjectives as distinct classes and posited an underlying copula before predicate adjectives, which was subsequently deleted. However, in an insightful article, Corne (1981) renounces his former analysis and sets up a class of "verbals" which would contain predicate adjectives as well as verbs and which would not require a copula in underlying structure. . . . I known of no creole where an alternative analysis of adjectives would be required.

For Atlantic creoles, analysis of what are ostensibly adjectives as stative verbs goes back further, to the work of Bailey (1966).

As we have seen, in the conservative Oceanic languages (especially EO languages), "adjectives" are stative verbs (Pawley 1973), some of which can be used to modify nouns directly. What had for decades been taken by missionary grammarians of Oceanic languages to be a copula is, instead, an SRP within the VP. It is ironic that the analytical missteps of an earlier generation of grammarians of Oceanic and an older generation of grammarians of creoles are being repeated by some analysts of Melanesian Pidgin.

Similar parallels exist between Oceanic tense-aspect markers, usually fitting into a slot in the VP between the SRP and the verb, and the tense-aspect markers of Atlantic creoles. Again, this suggests the appropriateness of analyses in terms of universal grammar, as Bickerton has proposed. But it may well have had a special historical significance. Apparently the nineteenth-century nautical pidgin used by whalers and traders in talking to "the natives" in China and the Pacific, and probably used on ships to communicate with Portuguese and Caribbean crew members, incorporated many of the core structures of the Atlantic creoles. If so, the close congruence of patterns in the prevailing nautical pidgin with patterns common to Oceanic languages would doubtless have facilitated the reanalysis and expansion of this nautical pidgin along Oceanic lines.

The structural parallels between Austronesian languages and creoles have in fact been noted before, with reference to a different part of the world—the Malay Archipelago. Collins (1980: 36–39) notes that many of the general features that are supposed to distinguish creoles (or pidgins and creoles) from natural languages—features such as "preverbal particles to express aspect and tense formation, the use of reduplication in derivatives and phrase structure, omissions of the copula"—are found in Ambonese Malay. Indeed, Collins notes in Ambonese Malay five of the twelve features described by Taylor (1971) as commonly found in European-language-based creoles: "Ambonese Malay corresponds to this list of features as well as [do] some of the well-known creoles of European origin" (Collins 1980: 39). Collins concludes that "though Ambonese Malay is not a European-based creole, it seems that the characteristics common to these creoles correspond remarkably well to Ambonese Malay features" (p. 39). This might seem to pose no problem, since there are historical grounds that could lead one to view Ambonese as a pidgin Malay that has been creolized. But Collins goes on to examine Trengganu Malay, a dialect from the Malay Peninsula historically far removed from any possible processes of pidginization and subsequent creolization, in regard to these supposedly distinctive features of (pidgins and) creoles in general, or at least of European-language-based creoles. He finds that Trengganu Malay, a natural (Austronesian) language, meets these criteria in the same ways, and almost as pervasively, as Ambonese Malay. In short, these parallels are fundamental to Austronesian grammar.

Where we find such convergences between patterns in substrate languages and in creoles, these convergences represent not historical accidents but "default" structures, that is, unmarked or underlying patterns of a universal linguistic logic. We would want to make no claims that the grammars of Oceanic (or Malay) languages represent an underlying universal grammar more directly than any other natural languages—only that in some important respects the Oceanic pattern, especially when we strip off particular systems of surface marking characteristic of individual languages or subgroups, reflects unmarked and maximally "natural" constructional patterns. Hence, to the extent that Oceanic speakers contributed to the formation of Pacific pidgin syntax, and to the extent that they did so by stripping off surface marking to find basic patterns their native languages shared, this process of excavation was taking them along universal channels as well as ones reflecting the "major syntactic choices" of Oceanic. Not surprisingly, Europeans, in producing what they imagined was a simplified form of English, based partly on the conventions of "native talk"/nautical pidgin already established in the northern hemisphere, were often following similar paths. This is partly to say, as Kay and Sankoff (1974) have done, that the more speakers simplify and the deeper they dig, the more closely languages converge on basic minimally marked and maximally natural patterns: precisely the conditions for "developmental conspiracies" on all sides.

Once more we see why, as Goodman (1985) and Mufwene (1986) have argued, substrate influence, superstrate influence, diffusion, and universals of grammar must all be seen as mutually complementary and interactive, not mutually exclusive, processes. The intersection of universal logics and faculties, language-learning strategies, and both substrate and superstrate models opens up particular paths for simplification, borrowing, and grammatical reanalysis.

Given all this, are there any grounds for inferring that substrate languages had a greater and more direct role in the formation of a Pacific pidgin than in the development of other pidgins and creoles? Why is the Pacific case special and linguistically interesting?

The picture given by Mühlhäusler and Sankoff, who have viewed Melanesian Pidgin developmentally, depicts Tok Pisin as distinctive and interesting because unlike many plantation pidgins it neither disappeared in the nineteenth century nor creolized, but progressively expanded in lexical and syntactic resources. Even when it finally began to undergo creolization in the second half of this century, for the great statistical majority of its speakers it remained a second and secondary language. Hence the processes of development—of the pronominal system, of tense-aspect marking, of causatives and a host of grammatical and lexical elaborations—provide a kind of test case of a pidgin that grows much richer than pidgins are supposed to be.

Melanesian Pidgin is indeed linguistically interesting and important, and much of this interest has precisely to do with the degree of its elaboration; in that, I am in agreement with Mühlhäusler and Sankoff. But the conventional picture, which takes Tok Pisin as the canonical dialect of Melanesian Pidgin and examines its development in the setting of New Guinea (without looking at New Hebridean and Solomons dialects), raises a series of deep linguistic paradoxes. Making these paradoxes explicit will serve to introduce the case for a degree of substrate influence beyond what the literature would lead us to expect, not hitherto fully recognized or adequately analyzed, either historically or linguistically.

The fundamental paradox with which the comparative evidence confronts us is that a whole series of key grammatical patterns that have been analyzed by Mühlhäusler and/or Sankoff as representing a progressive elaboration of New Guinea Pidgin (and are mainly considered to have taken place in this century, in many cases during the second half of it) are also found in Solomons Pidgin and the Bislama of Vanuatu. These include patterns that have some plausible relationship to patterns in Kuanua

(Tolai), taken as the "principal substrate language" of what is supposed to be a separate lineage of pidgin development,* as well as patterns that do not, and hence supposedly cannot represent substrate models.

The features common to all three daughter dialects of late 1880s southwestern Pacific pidgin include not only a very substantial core of lexical items,† but a substantial core of syntactic patterns. The following patterns are common to all three dialects:

1. The basic structure of the pronominal system, including many patterns supposed to have developed in Tok Pisin since 1900. Pronoun forms (if we view *olgeta* and *ol* as old variants of the same form) are essentially identical in all three dialects; and so is the structure of the paradigm itself (including dual and plural sets and a distinction between inclusive and exclusive nonsingular first person). So too are what have been taken to be specific historical anomalies in the Tok Pisin system, such as the use of the so-called "predicate marker" *i* to maintain reference across clauses in discourse, specific constructional patterns such as *hem i* using this predicate marker, and the use of the "they" pronoun (*ol* or *olgeta*) as a generalized plural marker.

2. The use of pronouns to embed relative clauses.

3. The systematic use of the transitive suffix *-im* to mark transitive verbs, and many of its specific uses (e.g., to create transitive verbs from statives) supposed by Mühlhäusler to have developed in the twentieth century in New Guinea. Forms utilizing the transitive suffix include a long list of specific verbs, such as *kapsaes-em* (*kaptsait-em*) 'overturn, pour out' and *kas-em* (*kis-im*) 'reach, obtain,' that have no direct semantic motivation in the superstrate lexifying language, and for many of which special developmental scenarios in New Guinea have been proposed.

4. The grammaticalization of tense/aspect markers, such as the irrealis-marking *bai* (*babae*), a phenomenon supposed to be recent in Tok Pisin.

5. The use of both periphrastic causatives using *mek-* and grammaticalized causatives using the transitive suffix *-im* (the latter supposed by Mühlhäusler to have no motivation in substrate languages, and hence to represent the application of universal faculties of language expansion by pidgin speakers).

6. A number of complementizing and relativizing constructions (using forms such as *see* and *wea* and *bulong*), some of which are supposed to be relatively late developments in Tok Pisin.

7. The use of *-fela*/*-pela* in a particular set of interconnected slots:

---

*Sankoff is less narrow than Mühlhäusler on the separateness of the Tok Pisin lineage.

†Many of which, like *mekenois*, have been treated by Mühlhäusler as representing the elaboration of Tok Pisin in this century.

a. Suffixed to quantifiers (*tu-fela, sam-fela*).
b. Suffixed to a smallish class of attributive statives, used both as stative verbs and as modifying nouns (*big-fela, gud-fela*).
c. Suffixed to demonstratives (*dis-fela, dat-fela*), used both as determiners and as pronouns.
d. Adverbially, apparently as a second, stative verb in compound-verbal constructions (*kilim strong-fela*).
e. Suffixed to pronouns or numerals, to indicate plurality of pronouns (*mifela, tufela*).

According to Mühlhäusler, the uses of *-fela* remained unstable and unsystematic until the twentieth century; yet the same pattern is represented in exactly the same form in all three dialects, and use in all five slots is documented in nineteenth-century texts. In an unpublished manuscript (Keesing n.d. 3), I show how regular the pattern established by the 1880s was, and how *-fela*, as a form probably initially introduced into the Pacific from China-coast pidgin, was expanded by Oceanic speakers in ways directly patterned on substrate languages (including verbal uses of attributive statives and adverbial uses of forms marked with *-fela* in compound verbal constructions).

8. A whole set of clause-initial phrasal interrogatives (derived from English "what name," "which way," "what time," etc.).

9. A distinctive system of marking possession, using *bilong* to conjoin nouns, and nouns with pronouns, to mark a genitive relationship metaphorically based on proximity.

10. What Sankoff and Brown (1976) characterize as "*ia* bracketing" accompanying relative clauses, a pattern found in all three daughter dialects—but not really a bracketing of relative clauses at all, since *ia* occurs in the same environments in the absence of the embedded clauses (see Jourdan 1985 for Solomons Pidgin).

A few of these may possibly represent parallel developments in Tok Pisin on the one hand and Bislama and Solomons Pidgin on the other; but if so, they could only have emerged out of a common dialect that already contained the essential materials. In the face of such massive grammatical resemblances, entailing not only the same forms but in most cases identical labels drawn from the original lexifying superstrate language,* the only reasonable inference is that these patterns were already incorporated in a Pacific pidgin of the 1880s from which all the modern dialects are derived.

In making these criticisms, I do not intend to dismiss the extremely

---

*In ways that, as with *-fela* or *bilong* or *olgeta*, are so different from the meanings in the lexifying language that they could not be parallel borrowings.

important contributions Mühlhäusler and Sankoff have made. As pioneers of what was fifteen years ago almost unknown territory, they have provided the foundations on which subsequent studies build, and the benchmark interpretations against which comparisons can be based. Beginning the serious study of Melanesian Pidgin in New Guinea was an obvious and justifiable strategy, and has had many positive and important consequences for an emerging country and for linguistic theory. What is unfortunate is that until very recently, virtually no serious work had been done on the other dialects of Melanesian Pidgin. Tok Pisin has been the canonical dialect essentially by default. Thus its special history and external relationships have remained largely hidden. Moving the focus back in time and outward in space renders Tok Pisin, as well as its sister dialects, more comprehensible.

We are inevitably led into both chronological and theoretical misinterpretations if we seek to analyze the syntactic elaboration of Melanesian Pidgin primarily as a twentieth-century phenomenon, which took place *in situ* in New Guinea. This is an illusion that has been possible only in the virtual absence of data on the Solomons and Vanuatu dialects. If all the developments supposed to have taken place since the separation of the New Guinea lineage, and inside New Guinea, were as reported, it would represent the most massive phenomenon of parallel grammatical evolution in the history of our species.

Fortunately, such an explanation is unnecessary. In fact, most of these developments had taken place or were well under way by 1890, when Tok Pisin was cut off from the rest of the zone where pidgin was developing. Where genuinely parallel development has taken place, it represents a development logically prefigured in the structures, specific labels, and lexical content already present in the pidgin of the late 1880s.

An example will illuminate this question. The postnominal demonstrative *ia*, derived from English "here," is discussed by Sankoff and Brown (1976) and Mühlhäusler (1986). Mühlhäusler's summary (p. 181) will introduce the question: "The full stress-bearing *hia* 'here' of earlier Tok Pisin, in constructions such as *dispela man hia* 'this man here,' has been changed to unstressed *ya*. This form has come to convey either emphasis or 'noun previously referred to in a text' (that is, it has moved in the direction of a definite article, as in *man ya* 'this man, the man')." Yet exactly the same unstressed *ia* is found, in identical environments and serving identical functions as those described as recent in Tok Pisin, in both Bislama and Solomons Pidgin. It is found, in the supposedly recent unstressed form, in the pidgin of old Solomon Islanders who learned it as a lingua franca on pre–World War II plantations and have been largely isolated from subsequent changes in the dialect (and, incidentally, it exactly corresponds to a postnominal demonstrative in many EO substrate languages, including those of Malaita). It is also found in the Bislama of "bush" speakers in Vanuatu (Charpentier 1979; Camden 1979).

Some might argue that these dialects have simply changed in parallel with Tok Pisin, and independently; the ancestral form was a stressed *hia*. But there is considerable evidence that "hia" is an artifact of the European scribes recording the form as "here," and that for Oceanic speakers the form has always been an unstressed *ia*. Consider the following renderings of prayers in the pidgin of Malekula (Vanuatu) from the 1890s, recorded by Pionnier (1913), virtually our only scribe of early pidgin whose phonological renderings were not distorted in the direction of English by code interference (although his own French led to some orthographic awkwardness):

Nème long Big fala masta ia God (p. 194).

Long big fala Masta ia, i stap tri fala (p. 194).

Blad ia i goud, i oach ol tigne man i mèkèm no goud (p. 195).

Around 1900, Jacomb (1914) recorded for New Hebridean Pidgin these constructions:

Man 'ere 'e long feller too much (p. 97).

Capsize 'im milk 'ere long jug (p. 94).

Much of the elaboration of Melanesian Pidgin is a late-nineteenth-century phenomenon, not a twentieth-century phenomenon. Far from providing the critically needed case where the progressive elaboration of a pidgin can be documented, Tok Pisin as recorded in New Guinea represents a very special case of the transplantation of an extensively elaborated pidgin to alien linguistic soil. It seems that, so transplanted, New Guinea Pidgin underwent considerable withering of its syntactic resources;* part of what Mühlhäusler has documented is the progressive reconstitution and reelaboration of an already elaborated pidgin, as well as its partial relexification from a new source substrate language (Kuanua, i.e. Tolai) and to lesser degree, a new superstrate language (German).

A further implication is that what are relatively clear substrate models and motivations, in terms of the languages spoken in the zones where, as we have seen, the initial expansions of Pacific pidgin took place, disappear when we look at the setting to which the New Guinea dialect was

---

*In some ways, Tok Pisin has compensated for the loss of syntactic resources by lexical expansion. Jeff Siegel, who after extensive work with Tok Pisin found himself in Vanuatu and working with Bislama, was amazed by the syntactic richness of Bislama in comparison to Tok Pisin, but at the same time, struck by the lexical poverty of Bislama.

transplanted. Many patterns pervasive in EO languages are either absent or attenuated in the Oceanic languages of the Bismarck Archipelago that constituted the new ("principal") source of substrate influence. These are strong claims. Much of the rest of the book will seek to establish grounds for them. The case for Oceanic patterns in Melanesian Pidgin needs now to be opened.

To the extent that Oceanic speakers played a creative role in the development and elaboration of a distinctive Pacific pidgin, we can expect that this would have entailed not simply discovering patterns Oceanic languages had in common, at a fairly abstract level, but a process of simplification.

It has been well known for a century, since Schuchardt's pioneering research, that pidgins and creoles have relatively simplified grammars, and that some kinds of surface markings characteristic of natural languages (e.g., case marking, articles, and the grammaticalized marking of pluralization and various kinds of agreement) are not drawn in such contact languages. Furthermore, since redundancy has to be at a maximum, and coding complexities at a minimum, we can expect that the lexicon will initially be limited, relying heavily on paraphrase and context; and that constructional complexities will be kept at the minimum. Here we need to draw on universalist perspectives regarding grammatical simplification and on pragmatic and functional-grammatical insights about optimizing intelligibility in discourse strategies. Such simplification is well illustrated in Silverstein's Chinook data, and in work on dozens of pidgins and creoles (see Mühlhäusler 1986 for a valuable summary). We will find ample evidence of it in the Pacific.

To the extent that Pacific Islanders had a strong formative influence on the grammar of a developing pidgin, and given the linguistic picture I have sketched, we could also anticipate rather different forms of simplification, which strip not all the way back to underlying universal patterns or maximally unmarked patterns, but to structures distinctive of Oceanic languages and their major syntactic "choices"—toward a kind of stripped-down Abstract Oceanic rather than a kind of universal "default grammar" of maximally unmarked constructions. In many respects, the two sorts of simplification will converge; in some, they will not.

On the other hand, we could anticipate that some constructional patterns extremely widespread in Oceanic, rather than being directly incorporated into pidgin, might be achieved periphrastically, because English as lexifying language offered no appropriate form or pattern, because the Oceanic pattern would be opaque to superstrate speakers, or because the Oceanic pattern relies too heavily on grammaticalization.

Otherwise stated, we would expect a pidgin, even where speakers of genetically related languages with an overall structural similarity had played a central part in its creation, to be considerably simpler in its surface marking and syntax than *any* natural language. However, we would also expect that a pidgin created in such circumstances would fairly quickly become considerably more complex syntactically than the contact languages Bickerton (1981, 1984) considers to be "true" pidgins, formed on a kind of ad hoc survival basis by speakers of unrelated languages forced by circumstances into radical interlingual communication.

A first telling example of these processes of simplification emerges if we examine possessive constructions in Melanesian Pidgin. Exactly how Oceanic possessive constructions evolved is a complex issue (see Lynch 1973, 1982). For our purposes, it suffices to sketch a general pattern characteristic of many EO languages, and probably derived from an early interstage OC language, if not POC. In this pattern, a series of distinctions is drawn in the relationship between possessor and possessed:

1. A relationship of inalienability, characteristically of part to whole (e.g., of the human body, or a plant or animal). Such inalienable possession is marked, in most daughter languages, by directly suffixing possessive pronouns to the noun (e.g., "hand-me").

2. A generalized relationship of alienability, such that the "possessed" entity is metaphorically cast as being in proximity to the possessor. This proximate relationship is characteristically expressed by suffixing possessive pronouns to a possessive particle, which in many daughter languages is a locative particle.

3. One or more relationships of semialienability, marked by attaching possessive pronouns to one or more special possessive particles. The most widespread special form of semialienability marks "edibles," to be eaten by the possessor; a less-common form (though possibly equally old) marks liquids that could appropriately be drunk by the possessor. (The particles marking edibility and drinkability are apparently derived from verbs meaning 'eat' and 'drink.') One or both of these kinds of distinctions of semialienability have been lost in many daughter languages. In other daughter languages, notably Nuclear Micronesian languages, such distinctions have been extensively (sometimes bewilderingly) elaborated.

Despite the near universality of the distinction of inalienable possession in Oceanic languages, it is not surprising that this distinction is neutralized in Pacific pidgins. In this case, the universal-guided path of simplification, the neutralization of a language-family specific distinction,* has

---

*Though as Charles Fillmore (1968) pointed out, this distinction is itself not devoid of underlying universal motivation.

been followed. The path of simplification here entails a "developmental conspiracy" in relation to superstrate speakers, to whom the alienable-vs.-inalienable distinction would have been unacceptable or opaque. In the hypothetical scenario proposed in the preceding chapter, where Oceanic speakers were placed into a multilingual environment without politically and ideologically dominant superstrate speakers, it is a moot point whether they would have incorporated a distinction of inalienable possession (the equivalent of "hand-me" or "eye-me," although of course it would not have been lexified from English). In the real scenario, they clearly did not. I infer that this kind of neutralization of surface distinctions and markings would be a fundamental process in the formation of pidgins even in the limiting case where those who contribute to its formation all speak related languages. This process is well illustrated by Siegel's data on Pidgin Fijian (1987).*

The use of a form that in the superstrate language is verbal, "belong," as the possessive particle is an interesting phenomenon on which Clark (1979: 16) and Mühlhäusler (1986: 160–61) have commented. Mühlhäusler notes that "belong" serves as one of the two prepositional particles in Pidgin, with a meaning of 'for, possessive or purpose.' It is worth adding to this characterization the fact that to Oceanic speakers, "belong" used as possessive particle appears to be based on a metaphor of proximity, as is the relationship of generalized alienable possession. That is, the thing possessed is metaphorically at or proximate to its possessor. (This metaphor is used in many languages as a way of characterizing possession.) This makes "belong" a kind of special or marked case of the more general prepositional particle "long," for Oceanic speakers. Indeed, I have many texts in which old Solomons Pidgin speakers occasionally use "long" where "belong" would be expected. Because of code interference, English speakers have brought the wrong intuitions to "belong," and have often used it infelicitously (or, ironically, have mocked Islanders for using it grammatically).

Melanesian Pidgin dialects have varied considerably, in time and space, in the other uses to which they have put "belong," as complementizer (to join "in order to," "by means of which to," or infinitival complements). It would take us too far afield to explore these variations and their relationships to patterns in substrate languages, but it will be a worthwhile focus of further study. Suffice it to say that the logic of these uses is a fundamentally Oceanic one, and that these extensions of "belong" fur-

*Interestingly, in Collins's analysis of Ambonese Malay (1980), he notes that this dialect, which may plausibly be viewed as creolized from a trade pidgin, does not incorporate the alienable/inalienable distinction characteristic of the substrate Austronesian languages of the area.

ther develop and rest on metaphors of proximity in ways opaque or illogical to superstrate speakers.

We can usefully look briefly at the generalized all-purpose locative "long," as representing a further example of simplification and condensation. (Like "belong," "long" has some other grammatical functions, e.g., as complementizer, which vary considerably among dialects of Melanesian Pidgin.) Oceanic languages characteristically use a range of locative particles and prepositions to express spatial/directional relationships that are collapsed semantically in Melanesian Pidgin *long*. This represents a case of both semantic and syntactic generalization. It is worth noting, however, that in dealing with spatial relationships, Melanesian Pidgin dialects (especially as used by older speakers who learned them on plantations) reveal their Oceanic roots. Particularly in EO languages, terms for spatial locations ("in front," "behind," "inside," "underneath") are morphologically nouns, treated as inalienably possessed by the following noun, and often marked with a preceding locative particle ("at the house's front," "at the canoe's underneath"). "Front," as a noun or a marker of relationship, usually has a temporal as well as a spatial meaning. Older speakers of Solomons Pidgin characteristically use English-derived spatial terms (*andanit long kiniu* or *fastaem long haos*) as if they were nouns.

To the extent that the grammar of a developing Pacific pidgin incorporated Oceanic syntactic patterns, then, it incorporated them through a kind of collapsing and simplifying process, as theories of pidginization would lead us to expect. But given the pervasive importance of substrate models and the degree of stabilization and expansion reached, even a century ago, by Melanesian Pidgin, the result is—as Bickerton (1984: 187) notes—a pidgin that incorporates such features as transitive suffixes: a pidgin thus unlike any other. It is to the transitive suffixes that we can now turn, for unmistakable evidence of the stamp of Oceanic grammar.

The form "-him" suffixed to verbs was undoubtedly brought to the Pacific as part of the European repertoire for "talking to natives." Clark (1979: 16) notes its occurrence (as "um") in American Indian English and apparently in early Nigerian Pidgin. It seems to have been used in the Pacific early in the nineteenth century, judging by Dana's fragments from Hawaiians in San Diego and by fragments from the Aboriginal Australian pidgin at the beginning of the century.*

The form "um" or "him" used by Europeans as part of their repertoire of "Kanaka talk" was sporadic and unsystematic, and probably had no fixed syntactic function. A careful look at its use in twentieth-century Melanesian Pidgin dialects and at the textual records of the nineteenth

---

*Jakelin Troy, personal communication.

century (despite the unreliability of European chroniclers) reveals the way in which speakers of Oceanic languages analyzed this form as equivalent to the transitive suffixes in their own languages, suffixes derived from POC *-i. In this process, Oceanic speakers generalized and standardized the form manifest by the mid-1840s (Fiji: "Me like um man") into an obligatory transitive suffix.

It is worth quoting the recent observations of Mufwene (1986: 143) on the marking of transitivity in Melanesian Pidgin and in Oceanic languages, as evidence of substrate influence—astute observations to which my research gives further substance and support:

> Use of a suffix to distinguish transitive and/or causative verbs from intransitive/non-causative verbs is one of the morphosyntactic features shared by most Melanesian languages. . . . Even though, according to Mühlhäusler, the use of *-im* to mark causative verbal derivatives is a recent and internal development on the model of some transitive verbs of the original pidgin, the fact is that those model uses are not predicted by the universalist blueprint and could have been devised only to meet the communicative needs of a population that generally marks transitive verbs morphologically in their native languages.

This correspondence between the transitive suffix (*-im* and its phonologically conditioned alternates) and the Oceanic transitive suffix is manifest in the relationship between transitive and intransitive verbs. In POC and conservative daughter languages, the largest class of verbs consists of verb roots that can be used either intransitively (to denote the performance of an act, without an implied or specified object, as "perform the act of X-ing") or transitively. When used transitively, these verbs are marked as such with transitive suffixes (or, in some cases, with an object pronoun suffixed to the verb—a pattern found with only a small class of verbs in POC but generalized in some daughter languages). In Melanesian Pidgin, we find exactly the same pattern. Thus Kwaio (Malaita, Southeast Solomonic):

(aga)aga	'look'
aga-si-	'see (s.t.)'
gumu	'pound, hammer'
gumu-ri-	'pound, hammer (s.t.)'
fana	'shoot'
fana-si-	'shoot (s.t.)'

Solomons Pidgin:

(luk)luk	'look'
luk-im	'see (s.t.)'

hamar	'pound, hammer'
hamar-im	'pound, hammer (s.t.)'
sut	'shoot'
sut-im	'shoot (s.t.)'

In marking relationship to a following object, Melanesian Pidgin uses exactly the same pattern we have seen to be widespread in EO languages. The morphologically unmarked form of the transitive suffix embodies an implicit third-person singular pronominal object marker. Where a direct-object NP follows, the transitive suffix (embodying this zero-marked implied object pronoun) serves to indicate the transitive relationship (canonically, agent-patient) to it. Where a non-higher-animate direct object is implied, but the following object-NP slot is empty, the transitive suffix itself embodies the (unmarked) object pronoun. Thus Solomons Pidgin:

mi no   luk-im   pikipiki bulong iu
I   NEG see-TRS pig   POSS   you
I didn't see your pig(s).

mi no   luk-im
I   NEG see-TRS
I didn't see it/them.

Kwaio uses an identical pattern, except that it preserves what seems to be the original PEO pattern, in which a pronominal clitic (-*a*) is used for this third-person singular object marking:

ku   'ame aga-si-a   boo a-mu
SRP(I) NEG   see-TRS-it pig POSS-you
I didn't see your pig(s).

ku   'ame aga-si-a
SRP(I) NEG   see-TRS-it
I didn't see it/them.

Where a following object is specified with a pronoun, it follows the transitive suffix. Compare Kwaio and Solomons Pidgin:

ku   'ame aga-si-'amo'o
SRP(I) NEG   see-TRS-you2
I didn't see the two of you.

mi no   luk-im   iutufala
I   NEG see-TRS you2
I didn't see the two of you.

In some cases, in Melanesian Pidgin dialects as in Oceanic languages, an object pronoun marked for other than third-person singular may be followed by an object NP. Compare Kwaio and Solomons Pidgin:

ku   'ame   aga-si-'aga'a   la   'Ubuni   ma   la   Sale
SRP(I) NEG   see-TRS-them2   ART   'Ubuni   and   ART   Sale
I didn't see 'Ubuni and Sale.

mi   no   luk-im   tufala   'Ubuni   ana   Sale
I   NEG see-TRS them2   'Ubuni   and   Sale
I didn't see 'Ubuni and Sale.

Recall that a second transitive suffix reconstructed for POC, and represented in many daughter languages, served in POC (according to Pawley's "standard" 1973 interpretation) to mark a residual class of instrumental and other semantic role relationships. On theoretical grounds, we would expect that this distinction would not be marked in Pacific pidgin—and it is not.

The correspondence between the Pacific pidgin transitive suffix, and pattern of marking agent-patient relationships, and the Oceanic pattern emerges again in a form used in both Solomons Pidgin and Bislama, although not in Tok Pisin. This is the prepositional verb *wet-em* (or, in some dialects, *weit-em* or *wit-em*) 'with (s.o.).' In many of the EO languages of the Solomons and Vanuatu, a prepositional verb marked with the transitive suffix (and hence morphologically identical to a transitive verb) is used to express 'with.' In these languages, this is the most commonly used of a small (and variable) array of prepositional verbs. We can surmise that *wet-em* was used (with various phonological shapes) in late-nineteenth-century Queensland Pidgin. It was recorded in the Pidgin of the New Hebrides at the beginning of the 1900s by Jacomb (1914: 102), who gives *me me go widim you* for 'I will come with you.'* But either its incorporation in Queensland Pidgin occurred after the separation of the New Guinea Pidgin lineage at the end of the 1880s or the form disappeared in New Guinea because its motivation in substrate languages no longer sustained it.[†] Other prepositional verbs, including *agens-em* and *raon-em*, corresponding to substrate forms, apparently are found in Bislama as well as Solomons Pidgin (Terry Crowley, personal communication, January 1988).

No appeal to universal grammar will, I think, provide a motivation for so idiosyncratic a pattern as *wet-em*, product of an odd development of a subclass of Austronesian verbs used in serial constructions. Certainly, no

---

*The significance of the "me me" sequence here will become apparent in Chapter 10.
†Like many constructions that have no equivalent in English, *wet-em* was not recorded by nineteenth-century travelers and recruiters.

superstrate influence can account for a pattern few European speakers of Bislama or Solomons Pidgin have even learned to use fluently.

Another telling bit of evidence on the correspondence between Oceanic and pidgin transitive suffixes is the widespread use, probably standardized by the late nineteenth century (judging by distributional evidence), of *win-im* 'surpass' in comparative constructions, where many EO languages have a corresponding construction, using a transitive verb 'surpass' marked with a transitive suffix. Again, a Kwaio/Solomons Pidgin comparison will serve to illustrate.

ku   ba'ita   riu-fi-'o
SRP(I)   be big   surpass-TTS-you
I'm bigger than you are.

mi   big-fala   win-im   iu
I   be big-ADJ   surpass-TTS   you
I'm bigger than you are.

Since my sketch of European-Islander interaction in the central Pacific prior to 1850 began on the island of Pohnpei, it is appropriate that a linguistic tidbit from Pohnpeian serve (albeit anecdotally) to illustrate how comfortably the Pacific pidgin transitive marker fits into the Oceanic grammatical pattern. I quote at some length from Rehg's description (1981: 204–5) of the Pohnpeian transitive suffix *-ih*:

> The basic difference between the intransitive and transitive verbs here [e.g., *deiad* 'embroider' and *deiad-ih* 'embroider (s.t.)'] is that the transitive verbs have a final *-ih* not present in the intransitive forms. . . . The . . . transitive suffix . . . is added to intransitive verb roots to form transitive verbs. This suffix seems to be used quite productively in Ponapean. It is suffixed to many borrowed intransitive verbs. [He illustrates with *kuk* 'cook' > *kuk-ih* 'cook (s.t.)' and *deip* 'tape' > *deip-ih* 'tape (s.t.)'.]
> One exception, however, is the verb 'to kick,' which has as its intransitive form *kik* and as its transitive form *kikim*, as in the sentence *Lahpo kikim Soulik* 'That guy kicked Soulik.' Probably . . . the *-im* of *kikim* is from the English 'him' and speakers of Ponapean incorrectly interpreted this as the transitive ending.

I have begun to sketch a complex dialectical process, in the nineteenth century, whereby speakers of EO languages created, mainly from borrowed elements—and following the simplest pathways opened by "developmental conspiracies"—a pidgin with a simplified grammatical structure that incorporated the core syntactic patterns common to their languages.

Where either English or nautical pidgin provided free forms as lexical items that could be equated with Oceanic grammatical elements, this transformation seems to have operated fairly directly (even though the English or nautical pidgin forms so borrowed were in some cases multimorphemic in the source language, as with the adoption of "by and by," recast as *babae*, as a grammaticalized irrealis or future marker).

Where neither standard English nor nautical pidgin provided a direct model, either the Oceanic grammatical pattern was not realized in the pidgin of the Labor Trade (e.g., the Oceanic "reciprocal prefix," which marks the action of verbs as reciprocal or taking place within a collectivity) or—where the gap is syntactically critical—was filled either by using the closest available circumlocution or by generalizing a pattern available in EO languages.

The formation of causatives shows examples of both processes. In the reconstructed original POC pattern, the causative prefix (POC **paka-*), attached to stative verbs or intransitive verbs, converts them to causative transitives with the experiencer of the state or actor of the intransitive verb as the surface direct object of the causative verb so created. This reconstructed pattern is preserved in many EO languages. An example from Kwaio will serve to illustrate; the causative prefix is here *fa'a-*.

| ba'ita | 'be big' > fa'a-ba'ita-a | 'enlarge (s.t.)' |
| leka | 'go'   > fa'a-leka-a | 'cause (s.o.) to go' |

By the end of the 1860s, "Sandalwood English" had incorporated the closest available equivalent derivable from English, using *mek-em* as transitive verb, with an embedded stative clause or intransitive verbal clause as its surface direct object. Thus, from the southern New Hebrides in 1869: "Plenty man come hear you make him bokis sing" (Paton 1895: 77). We glimpse a simpler pattern more directly corresponding to the Oceanic one from another 1869 text from southern Melanesia. Palmer (1871: 50) describes how he encountered on Erromanga the nephew of the "principal chief of Port Revolution," who "wanted me to catch [the perpetrator of an offense] and 'make him fast,' which, upon questioning him, I found meant hanging."

I point here to the early development of these causative patterns because of the alternative account given by Mühlhäusler (1980: 38–42), which I believe seriously underestimates the expansion of Pacific pidgin prior to the Labor Trade. Mühlhäusler (p. 38) describes a "jargon stage" in the development of Pacific pidgin, prior to 1880, with such a simple and unstabilized grammar that complex syntactic patterns such as causatives could not develop: "The fact that one is dealing with a one-word or two-word grammar at this stage means that constructions of the type *mekim* NV 'to cause N to do what is expressed by V' are automatically excluded, in spite of the fact that such periphrastic causatives were found in most if not all of the linguistic systems in contact." The Paton text shows clearly that the grammar of pidgin had reached considerable complexity more than ten years earlier than Mühlhäusler surmises.

The pattern of forming periphrastic causatives with *mek-em* would seem to represent a natural generalization from, on the one hand, the use of *mek-em* as an all-purpose transitive verb expressing agency—'do, create, make, bring into being'; and, on the other, the English pattern where "make it X" expresses causative meanings of the Oceanic variety. For the former, we have such texts as Captain Moresby's description (Moresby 1876: 112) of how, on Erromanga in 1872, a Lieutenant Smith negotiated with the "eastern chiefs" to signal that they understood his decision not to launch a punitive expedition against them by having them "'make a paper,' i.e. to affix their mark to a satisfactory paper to be drawn up by him." We may presume that for the interpreter and the Erromangans, the agreement was to *mek-em pepa*.

In the pidgin spoken in Vanuatu, the Solomons, and seaboard Papua New Guinea by older Austronesian speakers who learned the lingua franca in plantation contexts, the causative pattern is realized as a periphrastic *mek-em i strong* 'strengthen it,' *mek-em iumi stap* 'cause us to stay,' and so on. However, in some of these communities a pattern more like the Oceanic model has occasionally surfaced: *mek-strong* + NP or *mek-strong-im* + NP or *mek-im strong* (John Lynch, personal communication). Palmer's "make him fast" illustrates the last of these patterns, from almost 120 years ago. We find the first pattern in an 1890 text from German New Guinea examined in Chapter 5: "He make fire house" (Hempenstall 1978: 171). Interestingly, both one of the Melanesian-type causative patterns and the more usual one with an embedded clause were recorded in Samoa by Huebel in 1883 (reported by Schuchardt [1889] 1980: 24–25):

You make him some water he boil.

Make open that fellow beer.

Perhaps one reason the more Melanesian-type causative pattern did not become established in a developing Melanesian Pidgin is that, although constructions using reflexes of the OC causative prefix are widespread in Oceanic languages, in many of these languages the prefix has shifted considerably in grammatical function. Thus, whereas Southeast Solomonic languages such as Kwaio use the causative prefix to form causatives in the manner reconstructed for POC, in many New Hebridean languages, Fijian, and Polynesian languages, reflexes of the causative prefix are not used (or are no longer primarily used) to form causative transitive

verbs from statives and intransitive verbs, but have acquired a range of
other grammatical functions.

A quite different process whereby causative transitive verbs are formed
in Melanesian Pidgin is equally revealing. As noted earlier in discussing
transitive suffixes, many Oceanic languages also form transitive verbs
from stative roots by appending a transitive suffix. Pawley (1973: 128)
reconstructs for POC two classes of stative verbs, an A-class that forms
causatives with the causative prefix *paka-, and a B-class that forms
causatives with transitive suffixes. Pawley illustrates with Kwara'ae and
Fijian examples (in the latter "a high proportion of common transitive
verbs are derived from B-class statives"; p. 129), noting that "B-class
statives exist in each of the main genetic or regional divisions [of Oceanic]"
(p. 131). Melanesian Pidgin dialects have, in effect, broadened the B-
class of stative verbs (as Fijian has), generalizing the pattern of causative
formation which is, in Pidgin, morphologically less clumsy. Thus compare Kwaio,

fa'a-sui-a	'finish it' ("cause-be finished-it")
fa'a-mae-a	'extinguish it' ("cause-be extinguished-it")
bono-si-	'block it' (from bono 'be blocked')
mou-si-	'break it' (from mou 'be broken')

with Solomons Pidgin:

finis-im	'finish it'
dae-em	'extinguish it'*
bolok-em	'block it'
birek-em	'break it'

However, the two alternative modes of forming transitives from statives are both used in all three Melanesian Pidgin dialects, with the more
common verbs tending to follow the B-class pattern and the less common
ones tending to use the embedded clause (equivalent to the A-class pattern, but less syntactically efficient). As noted in Keesing (1984), some
statives in EO languages can form transitives by both modes; and where
different case relationships are established by each pattern, Melanesian
Pidgin dialects preserve the same contrast: again, unmistakable evidence
of the origin of these models in substrate languages. Thus, compare
Kwaio,

---

*In both Kwaio and Solomons Pidgin this transitive verb is formed from the verb 'die,
be dead,' which in Oceanic languages and in Pidgin includes senses of being comatose,
extinguished, etc.

fa'a-ma'u-nau   'frighten me' ("cause-be frightened-me")
ma'u-ni-nau   'fear me'

with Solomons Pidgin:

mek-em mi fraet   'frighten me'
fraet-em mi   'fear me'

Given the pervasiveness in EO languages of this pattern of forming transitive verbs from statives with the transitive suffix, it is surprising that Mühlhäusler (1980: 38–39) specifically excludes substrate models as a source for this alternative pattern: "In Tok Pisin . . . the transitivity marker *-im* is used to signal causativization. Whilst this is found in neither Tolai nor English, it is a widespread feature of many natural languages. Its use in Tok Pisin illustrates the principle that even second-language speakers of a pidgin have access to universal resources for its expansion."

These processes I have sketched in preliminary fashion underline how complex was the interplay of substrate influences, the availability of unbound forms and constructions in source languages (a valuable point stressed by Goodman 1985), and universal faculties of grammatical analysis deployed in the task of language creation and second-language learning.

In the next chapter, I will go on to analyze the development of the Pacific pidgin pronominal system, further illustrating and analyzing this complex dialectical process in which underlying common patterns in substrate languages, the resources of the lexifying superstrate language, and universal linguistic process and faculties reinforced one another and opened channels of possibility and strategies of simplification. To clarify my theoretical argument, it will be useful, in advance of this analysis of pronouns, to examine a phenomenon that has received attention both from Melanesian Pidgin specialists such as Mühlhäusler and Clark and from students of universal grammar such as Comrie: the use in all the contemporary Melanesian Pidgin dialects of *olgeta* (or the shorter form *ol*) as a marker of plurality and as a "they" pronoun.

Such an equivalence is drawn fairly frequently in a range of language families. It is also common in European-language-based creoles; Taylor (1971) includes it as one of the common (though far from universal) features of these creoles. Thus, even if we were to find such patterns in substrate languages, we would have to be extremely cautious about inferring that this was the source for their incorporation into a developing pidgin. Comrie (1981) takes it to be an expression of a universal syntactic principle, and I believe he is right. However, if we were to find such a pattern in substrate languages, we could, I think, at least argue that such a pattern, once established, would be congruent with usages in the native languages of (at least some) Pacific Islanders.

But which substrate languages? Comrie comments on Mühlhäusler's (1981) claim that this pattern has "no apparent motivation . . . in the indigenous languages of the area" (Comrie 1981: 223) as sustaining his appeal to universal grammatical principles. If we are going to seek possible correlates in substrate languages, should these be languages spoken in and close to New Guinea? We find this pattern of pluralizing nouns with the third-person plural pronoun in Bislama and Solomons Pidgin as well as Tok Pisin, which pushes its incorporation back at least as early as the 1880s. If there were any motivation in the substrate languages, it should be in those spoken in the key areas of the central and southwest Pacific by the Islanders we have seen to have been centrally involved in using a developing pidgin in the 1850s, 1860s, and 1870s—that is, the EO languages.

Pawley (1972: 35) reconstructs a pattern for PEO in which

human but not inanimate nouns [follow] the plural number marker (same as 3rd person plural pronoun) *ida, as in:

*ida   na   tamwane
PLU   ART   man
the men (lit. "they the man").

Pawley gives reflexes of this "human plural" marker *(k)ida, which is identical to the third-person plural pronoun, in twenty of the twenty-six EO languages of eastern Melanesia used in his sample, as in Raga (northern Vanuatu) ira vavine 'women' and Lau (Malaita in the southeastern Solomons) gera ngwane 'the men.' In some EO languages, such as Ghari (Guadalcanal, Solomons), the "they" pronoun acts as a general plural marker.

Mühlhäusler (1981, 1986) argues that in the development of Tok Pisin the form ol was originally used as a pronoun and was adopted as a plural marker first for human nouns, then eventually (and in Tok Pisin never pervasively) for inanimate nouns. His reconstruction of this sequence has been acccepted by both comparative syntactic theorists such as Comrie and comparative pidgin/creole specialists such as Janson (1984: 318), who comments:

It can be argued . . . that language users have to be able to denote plurality in all languages, so that markers would always arise spontaneously, in response to a need. . . . Mühlhäusler presents a detailed analysis of the development of plural marking in Tok Pisin from the jargon stage to the creolization stage, and argues convincingly that there was no influence from English or any other language. Rather, what happens is that the morpheme *ol* (from English *all*) takes on first, the function of a plural pronoun ("they") and then the function of a pure plural marker (which remains optional).

It is not unreasonable to suggest that the pronominal use came first, but it is certainly not clearly established in the textual evidence. It seems likely to me that what English speakers were analyzing as "all man" was coming to be analyzed as PLU *man* by Islanders; this usage is recorded for the Loyalties in 1851 (sentence 3, Chapter 3), Tanna in 1851 (sentence 4), and the Loyalties in 1859 (sentence 5). We find "altogether man" in the record by the late 1870s (sentence 29, Chapter 4). In 1885, we find *olgeta* and *ol* in variation, used by the same speaker (sentence 44). So the use as plural marker with human nouns is as early in the texts as occurrences of *olgeta* or *ol* as "they" pronoun. This use long antedates the separation of the Tok Pisin lineage. Much of Mühlhäusler's developmental interpretation, presented as confined to the Tok Pisin lineage, is hence quite irrelevant.

Even more difficult, for the postulated sequence, is the occurrence of *olgeta* and *ol* as plural markers for nonhuman nouns, in one case before the separation of the Tok Pisin lineage. In 1880, Coote (1882: 206) recorded at Kolombangara in the western Solomons "me take him altogether trade [i.e., items of trade goods]—musket, powder, tobacco, bead, plenty." This, as we have seen, was a period when Samoa, the New Hebrides, the Solomons, and Queensland formed a single, intricately interconnected speech community, even though the connections between Samoa and Queensland were mainly indirect. In the first half of the 1890s, Pionnier (1913) recorded what in his French-based orthography he wrote as *ol tigne* ("things").

I propose no scenario in which Islanders directly transferred this pattern from their indigenous languages such that when they adopted *olgeta* (and the short form *ol*) as a plural marker for human nouns, they then started using it as a third-person pronoun, or a reverse scenario in which, having adopted it as a pronoun, they started using it as a plural marker for human nouns. Either scenario, or the concurrent adoption of both forms, is plausible. But I see no strong basis for rejecting either out of hand, or selecting one over the other. Clark (1979: 47) likewise hedges his bets on this sequence, although he does not comment on the pattern in substrate languages. All we can say, I think, is that for speakers of EO languages (and particularly the New Hebrideans, who made up the bulk of plantation workers in the 1870s and 1880s), such a usage, however it came into a developing pidgin, would have been *congruent with* parallel patterns in (most of) their native languages. A push toward the regularization and stabilization of this pattern would not have come from English speakers, for whom it would have been counterintuitive (particularly since neither usage corresponds semantically to any sense of English "altogether," and both have only limited correspondence to usages of "all"). We may reasonably surmise that a strong push in this direction could have come from congruence with a pattern widespread in substrate languages of the EO zone, even if this were not its direct source.

Another important insight is that the use of a plural marker as "they" pronoun represents a further expression of a logical pattern where a quantifying or demonstrative determiner can act by itself as a pronoun. Consider the following patterns, attested from many texts of nineteenth-century Pacific pidgin (see Keesing n.d.3):

sam-fala pipol kam	> sam-fala kam
tu-fala man luk-im	> tu-fala luk-im
dat-fala siton i hevi tumas	> dat-fala i hevi tumas
olgeta waitman luk-im	> olgeta luk-im
mi-fala busuman du-im	> mi-fala du-im

The last construction is part of the same Oceanic pattern as "they people." Thus compare Kwaio (Southeast Solomonic), where the FP is used with nouns: *'e-meeru-a ta'a* 'we people' > *'e-meeru* 'we3Excl.'

The generalization of the use of the "they" pronoun with human nouns so that *olgeta* or *ol* comes to pluralize nonhuman as well as human nouns would have followed as a relatively natural regularization to fill a syntactic gap (see Janson 1984). Such a generalization is fairly widely distributed in various language families; as I have noted, it is found in some EO languages such as Ghari (Guadalcanal).

Once more we find a "developmental conspiracy" made possible by the naturalness of a pattern, on the one hand, and its congruence with substrate constructions, on the other. But it was a conspiracy from which English speakers, by reason of code interference, were partly excluded.

Failure to notice the pervasiveness of this "matching" pattern in the historically relevant substrate languages further underlines the costs and distortions that have come from the focus by so many scholars on Tok Pisin as the canonical dialect of Melanesian Pidgin. Apart from Ross Clark, scholars studying Melanesian Pidgin have not been specialists on the comparative grammar of Oceanic languages; and to the extent that they have sought possible models for pidgin patterns in substrate languages, they have tended to look in the wrong languages in the wrong places in the wrong time periods.

Before turning to a detailed analysis of the development of the Melanesian Pidgin pronominal system, it will be useful to come back briefly to the issue of the preferred order of constituents in the global syntax of Oceanic languages and Melanesian Pidgin.

I have noted that, given the congruence between the global syntax of most of the EO languages of the central and southwestern Pacific and the global syntax of English, we need not opt for substrate or superstrate (or universal) sources for the SVO pattern of Melanesian Pidgin. Clark (1977: 35) wrote, of the early form he called "South Seas Jargon": "The basic word order of the jargon normally follows English.* Subject precedes verb, which precedes object and other complements; modifiers, including possessives, generally precede nouns. Negation is indicated by *no* between subject and verb."

As we have seen, this "basic word order" is characteristic of most of the languages whose speakers engaged Europeans in the dialectical process leading to the development of pidgin. I see no reason why we should conclude that they followed either the English pattern or the Oceanic pattern. Indeed, it would seem that the SVO has a universal motivation, as a kind of basic unmarked order—and this is presumably one reason for its pervasiveness in pidgins and creoles (see Mühlhäusler 1986: 155–56). SVO seems to be a kind of default order, which requires minimal marking of the arguments of a predicate, creates minimum ambiguity, and entails the most direct connection between underlying order and surface sequence. In languages characterized by verb-initial preferred orders, including some Oceanic languages, case marking and other special syntactic devices are often employed to distinguish subject and object NPs (see Anderson and Chung 1977 for Polynesian VP-initial languages).

What matters is surely that, for parties on all sides of these encounters, a common order of constituents required very little negotiation. For the Europeans, it principally required that, as pidgin developed, they use redundant "he" pronouns after noun subjects, and "'em" after transitive verbs. For most speakers of EO languages, it required little modification in global syntax, although many special patterns had to be learned—for example, the roundabout periphrastic causative construction and the use of a future-marker preceding a noun subject rather than in the verb phrase. For some Oceanic speakers with verb-initial standard order, a subject NP could be topicalized or foregrounded by fronting, so for them an optional and marked order in their native language was standard and unmarked in

---

*Perhaps significantly, this passage is missing in the version Clark published two years later in *Te Reo*. The comments of his colleague Andrew Pawley might have intervened here, although this is pure speculation on my part.

pidgin. (Recall that even in languages with VP-initial syntax such as Fijian, an SRP obligatorily precedes the verb—so constructions in these languages are more congruent with the surface syntax of English, or pidgin, than might be apparent.)

Is there any evidence of Oceanic speakers of languages with VP-initial syntax using pidgin in a parallel fashion? I have found four possible early-1890s examples from the New Hebrides. Unfortunately, it is not certain what substrate languages were spoken where they were recorded; and we cannot discount the possible effects of superstrate models from French. The first three come from Pionnier's (1913) Malekula gospel materials:

I stop ouane hole bilong baniche.
There's a hole in the fence (p. 184).

Long big fala Masta ia, i stap tri fala.
This God has three elements [the Holy Trinity] (p. 194).

I stap onetap ouane Big fala Masta, no more.
In heaven there is only one God (p. 198).

There is a strong possibility that the missionaries were here mistakenly following the pattern of French *il y a* constructions, and that such sentences were not being used by the New Hebrideans. But it seems equally possible that the existence of such a construction in French led the missionaries to record a possible order of constituents that an English speaker would have turned around to follow English word order. The fourth example seems more solid, but its island source is not specified. Again, the text comes from a French speaker (Beaune 1894: 122):

Yu save where he stop big fellow pigeon?
Do you know where there are big pigeons?

Perhaps in the New Hebrides of the 1890s, speakers of some substrate languages were bending the syntax of pidgin even more strikingly to fit the patterns learned natively.* If so, they were carrying further a process that had already been under way for fifty years, of creating a common language almost entirely lexified from a foreign source, but incorporating a somewhat simplified model of an ancient syntactic pattern shared, in its general pattern, by speakers of hundreds of languages on scores of islands.

---

*I show in Chapter 13 that speakers of Western Solomonic languages, where the subject NP canonically follows the VP, use such constructions sporadically in speaking Solomons Pidgin.

CHAPTER 9

 The Pidgin Pronominal System

IN THE PRECEDING CHAPTER, in examining transitive suffixes in Pacific pidgin against the background of Oceanic grammar, I sketched one element in the syntactic pattern I have characterized as the "core" of sentence structures—in Oceanic languages and, I suggest, in Melanesian Pidgin. We need now to look at further elements of this core pattern.

The complex interplay between substrate and superstrate models and universal channels and strategies of language simplification we saw in the last chapter is further strikingly manifest in the development of the pronominal system in the pidgin of the southwestern Pacific. In examining this interplay against the background of the historical and linguistic evidence set out in the preceding chapters, I show in this chapter how the dialectical relationship between substrate and superstrate languages generated the pronominal system of late-nineteenth-century pidgin. I will go on in Chapter 10 to show that the simplified paradigm supposed to prevail in modern dialects of Melanesian Pidgin ignores a partly hidden side of the entire pronominal system. In explicating this hidden side, I will advance an alternative account of the "predicate marker" that has challenged and puzzled students of Melanesian Pidgin. In doing so, I will show that the core syntactic pattern of pidgin corresponds quite directly to the structure of Oceanic languages.

In looking in Chapter 4 at the texts of Pacific pidgin in the 1870s and 1880s, I suggested that a pronominal paradigm had by then begun to stabilize into a standard set of forms. It has been noted since Schuchardt's time ([1883, 1889] 1980) that the *semantic* categories of Pacific pidgin corresponded to those of Oceanic Austronesian languages, in the existence of a dual (and often trial) set as well as singular and plural, and in the distinction between inclusive and exclusive (nonsingular) first-person pronouns. This point, I think, needs no further specific underlining. But does the pronominal paradigm follow the Oceanic system in other ways?

Melanesian Pidgin pronouns are (at least according to the "standard" analysis) not case-marked, as Oceanic pronouns are: a single set is used for subject and object pronouns, and used in possessive constructions. We have seen that Proto-Oceanic and Proto-Eastern Oceanic are reconstructed as having had four sets of pronouns—focal pronouns, subject-referencing pronouns, object pronouns, and possessive pronouns—the last being clitics attached to prepositional particles, or directly to inalienably possessed nouns. Pidgin dialects use a single set of pronouns as subjects, objects, and possessives (leaving aside for the moment the so-called "predicate marker").

Such a lack of case marking of pronouns in a stable and expanded pidgin constitutes another manifestation of "simplification," the neutralization of surface agreement marking and consequent generalization, which I have illustrated. This phenomenon is consistent with, and essentially predictable from, general grammatical theory regarding pidgins/creoles, and again needs no further elaboration. But as will be seen, matters are not quite that simple, particularly when we juxtapose the question of case marking and the phenomenon of the "predicate marker."

If we are to consider seriously the possibility that speakers of diverse Oceanic languages played a major part in the creation of the grammar of Pacific pidgin, in effect excavating the common grammatical designs underlying the surface patterns in their native languages and lexifying them through English, we need to look carefully at the pronominal forms available in the superstrate language to lexify a developing pidgin.

Some of the problems of fit between English and Oceanic pronominal systems can be graphically perceived if we set out two pronominal paradigms in which case-marked English object pronouns and then case-marked English subject pronouns are arranged in an Oceanic pattern. Recall that in the prototypical Oceanic pattern there are four sets of pronouns, but that the FPs and object pronouns are morphologically similar, and the SRPs and pronominal suffixes are morphologically similar. In Table 9.1, I label the two pronominal paradigms "object" and "subject."

When we arrange the English pronouns in a Melanesian pattern, the problematic points in congruence become apparent. First of all, English provides no lexical forms with which to maintain the inclusive/exclusive distinction. If superstrate speakers (who mostly ignored this distinction or got it wrong) had been the primary agents in the creation of a Pacific

TABLE 9.1

English Pronominal System Arranged in an Oceanic Pattern

Number and person	Object pronouns	Subject pronouns
Singular		
1	me	I
2	you	you
3	him, her, it	he, she, it
Dual		
1 inclusive		
1 exclusive	* us two	* we two
2	* you two	* you two
3	* them two	* they two
Plural		
1 inclusive		
1 exclusive	us	we
2	you	you
3	them	they

pidgin, this distinction would almost certainly have been neutralized in favor of a "we" and/or "us" form. Despite 120 years of European errors and confusion, the distinction has been established and preserved.

Second, English "you" provides no distinction between singular and nonsingular (the Indo-European familiar-singular form having dropped out of general use). Some marker of singular versus nonsingular is needed to fill out a pidgin paradigm. Although English has no dual (or of course trial) pronominal sets, the addition of the morphemes "two" (and "three"), Oceanic style, easily allows this expansion of the English paradigm.

Third, English draws gender distinctions in the third-person singular slot when referring to higher-animate beings; but "he/she/it" distinctions are extraneous in an Oceanic paradigm.*

Let us now consider the case markings. In first and third person, English distinguishes between object and subject pronouns; in second person, "you" is used for both object and subject.

If we look at the fit between the two pronominal systems, in relation to the processes of simplification and neutralization of marked distinctions examined in Chapter 8, we can focus our questions more sharply. We could anticipate that the English gender distinctions in third-person singular would be neutralized, in favor of the unmarked (male) forms, "him" and/or "he," representing a congruence between the substrate pattern and universal markedness hierarchies.

---

*Although in the use of object pronouns, in particular, Oceanic languages characteristically mark nonsingular number only with reference to higher-animate nouns.

TABLE 9.2

Hypothetical Adaptation of English Pronominal System to a Developing Pidgin

Number and person	Pronoun	Number and person	Pronoun
Singular		Plural	
1	me	1 inclusive	[?]
2	you	1 exclusive	us
3	him	2	you
Dual		3	them
1 inclusive	[?]-two		
1 exclusive	us-two		
2	you-two		
3	them-two		

But would we find two case-marked pronominal sets, or would they be collapsed into a single set? On comparative and theoretical grounds, examining patterns in Atlantic and Indian Ocean creoles and hierarchies of markedness, we might expect that a developing pidgin would have adopted a single pronominal set, and that the unmarked set adopted would have been the object pronouns. In various English-based pidgins and creoles (and in English speakers' intuitions about simplification and "foreigner talk"), we characteristically find "me" and "him" and "them (dem)" forms as generalized. "Us" is more problematic; but it still is the more probable. In a hierarchy of generalizability, the subject pronouns are the marked ones; and the object pronouns will be accepted in the subject slot more readily than the reverse.

We might have expected a paradigm something like that shown in Table 9.2 (which should be preceded by a giant asterisk). This paradigm preserves a distinction between inclusive and exclusive nonsingular first-person forms. General theory and the pronominal systems of Northern Hemisphere creoles would have led us, in fact, to expect this distinction to be neutralized in a developing Oceanic pidgin, as a marked distinction unrecognized in the superstrate language; but as we have already seen, it was preserved—a striking piece of evidence that something rather different was happening in the development of a pidgin in the Pacific: a difference manifest in a domination of substrate patterns over both universal directions of simplification and superstrate patterns.

Would we then have found a complete neutralization of the case marking distinguishing object from subject pronouns? We might guess, first of all, that superstrate speakers would, in their own speech, continuously have introduced case-marked subject pronouns ("I," "we"). We could guess that to the extent that there was a bifurcation of registers, one used by Islanders who were in sustained contact with superstrate speakers when dealing with them, and the other used between Islanders, the two registers would incorporate different pronominal systems precisely on the basis of such case marking (as well as gender marking).

Indeed, there is considerable evidence across the full span of a century that pidgin speakers for whom English genuinely was a target language, or at least who, as mission workers, foremen, bosuns, and so forth were continuously interacting with Europeans, were using these English-derived pronouns in dealing with "Masters," although they were presumably fluent speakers of the prevailing pidgin in dealing with fellow Islanders. We will see that a gender distinction ("she" and "her" as pronouns) sporadically appears for a century, and exactly in these contexts of sustained Islander-European interaction (although we can guess that in many of the recorded instances, it was the scribe's misrecording or attempt to communicate pidgin to a popular audience that accounts for the "she").

I turn shortly, in Chapter 10, to the question of case marking; although prevailing wisdom would have it that Melanesian Pidgin dialects have a single pronominal paradigm (and a funny "predicate marker"), we will see that things are not that simple. But first, it will be useful to consider how the blanks in the hypothetical paradigm—a set of forms for first-person inclusive and a distinction between singular and plural in second person—were filled in.

An effective solution to the gap for first-person inclusive—a gap for Oceanic, not English, speakers—was improvised out of the "you" and "me" forms, in the form "you-me." We find it attested in such sentences as "Me save—you me go," recorded by Beaune (1894: 122) in the New Hebrides, and in the contemporaneous pronominal paradigm given by Pionnier (1913) for the New Hebrides in the early 1890s. Its occurrence in all three Melanesian Pidgin dialects, as well as early texts, places the time of its incorporation in the 1880s.

That still left a need for a marking of plurality for second-person forms. A "solution" was produced—not predictably, but not surprisingly—through a generalization on semantic grounds of the particle *-fela*, which as we have seen was by this time regularized in Pacific pidgin in a series of interlinked syntactic slots: suffixed to quantifiers, to attributive adjectives and stative verbs, and to demonstratives, as determiners and pronouns. We saw in the preceding chapter how its extension to fill out the paradigm of personal pronouns followed a more pervasive pattern of generalization (*tu-fela man* > *tufela*, *mi-fela man* > *mifela*).

This provided a distinction between "you" and "you fellows," which would have been quite intelligible to English speakers. This is attested in such passages as

By-and-by big fellow master come up, me hear him good you fellow talk (1885 court transcripts on "The Return of the New Guinea Islanders" from an Islander named Sandfly, from "Grass Island" in the Massim; Jan. 23, 1885, no. 1462).

You fella bring me fella big fella clam (recorded in the Solomons, 1908; London 1909: 360).

There is, moreover, a problem with the first-person exclusive forms, since we find no forms like "us" anywhere in the textual record. As London's sentence indicates, *-fela* also provided a distinction between "me" and "me fellows" that would similarly have been transparent to English speakers. This form is manifest in the texts in such further passages as

Altogether along shore fire gun at me fellow. . . . Barton sing out along me fellow he say, "Ted he die; me fellow pull up alongside" (court disposition recorded from a Tikopia, Solomon Islands, speaker; Queensland 1896).

You look out along me suppose they shoot me fellow (a Malaitan, recorded by a court reporter; Queensland 1896).

Me fella want copra man, me fella no want missionary (recorded on Tanna, 1896; Guiart 1956: 124).

Given the quantifier "two-fellow" (I am using the English versions of these forms for purposes of explication), we find an expectable "you-two-fellow" for dual:

By-and-by he say, "You two fellow go work along sugar-cane and I give you some tobacco you two fellow no go back in canoe" (1885 court transcripts on "The Return of the New Guinea Islanders," from Sandfly from "Grass Island"; Jan. 23, 1885, no. 1462).

Third-person nonsingular forms pose a similar problem, since we do not find "them" often in the textual record of Pacific pidgin (as we might have expected from the data on Northern Hemisphere creoles). As we will see, this third-person plural slot is the least stable part of the paradigm. One form we might have expected, once the process of marking plurality with "-fellow" had been set in motion, was its generalization in this slot as well in the form of a distinction between "him" and "him-fellow." There are signs in the early texts of a kind of collective groping to fill this awkward third-person nonsingular slot, and scattered glimpses of such forms, particularly "him-fellow" (for Oceanic speakers, *hem-fela*). Thus Layard recorded in New Caledonia at the onset of the 1880s: "Him fellow all same man-a-bush" (Schuchardt [1883] 1980).

Governor Solf of Samoa recorded in 1895: "Master, him fellow white man, he no savee speak English" (Mühlhäusler 1978a: 72). London's version of the fall from Eden includes "Him fella he make'm altogether" (1909: 359). This last, however, is suspect because London appears to have had an inadequate command of the prevailing pidgin, and to have incorrectly surmised that "him fella" was a demonstrative (elsewhere he gives "him fella Adam him want'm mary"); in both passages, it has a singular reference. The same is true of a passage from his interaction with Solomon Islanders, which otherwise tend to be more accurate pidgin than the "Eden sermon": "Pickaninny stop along him fella," meaning that a hen proffered for sale had produced eggs (recorded in the Solomon Islands in 1908; London 1909: 360).

But "him-fellow" did not in the end become established as the third-person plural form. It was outcompeted, for reasons and through processes we can only speculate about, by the pronoun derived from English "altogether" (Melanesian *olgeta*), which we examined in the preceding chapter both in its form as a plural marker and its form as a pronoun. However, the third-person nonsingular pronouns in Melanesian Pidgin dialects have been, and for some continue to be, unstable.

I have noted that by the 1880s a regular pattern in Pacific pidgin was the use of prenominal forms marked with *-fela*—the demonstratives *dis-fela* and *dat-fela*, the quantifiers *tu-fela* and *tri-fela*—as pronouns. This provided, as I have noted, both a pattern that could be generalized (*mi-fela*, *yu-fela*) and a ready-made set of forms for "they two" and "they three." I have given some examples of *tu-fela* as a pronoun. To these we can add another recorded by London (1909: 363): "So Adam Eve two fella stop along garden, and they fella have'm good time too much." The "they fella" is probably a Londonesque misrendering, but the "two fella" is more likely to be genuine, given the occurrences of this form in all three daughter dialects.

I shall not ponder further the question of how "altogether" became incorporated as the "they" pronoun. But it is important to note that once it was, the possibility of its ramifying through the pronominal paradigm (as "fellow" did) was set into motion. That entailed both the use of "altogether" with other pronominal forms to mark their plurality, and analysis into its ostensible component morphemes ("all" and "together" or simply *"gether").

One pattern that seems to have been explored in the 1880s and to have surfaced recurrently turns up in the transcripts of the 1885 Queensland inquiry on "The Return of the New Guinea Islanders" (if we can believe the transcripts, which seem most accurate when reporting the pidgin spoken by those who actually testified, as in these passages, as opposed to the court interpreters). In this pattern, *olgeta* rather than *fela* served to mark pronouns as nonsingular:

He gammon me altogether (Feb. 25, 1885, no. 5239).

Jack take me altogether (Feb. 25, 1885, no. 5298).

You altogether stop three yam [= years] (Feb. 25, 1885, no. 5320).

Knibbs (1929: 89), who was in the Solomons in 1913, records: "What name you altogether go sleep? This place he no belong you and me."

Once *olgeta* had become standardized as a plural pronoun, some New Hebrideans, treating *ol* as the equivalent of their forms derived from PEO **da*, coined *tugeta* and perhaps in some places *trigeta* (see Charpentier 1979: 310) for third-person dual and trial, to fill out the paradigm (see also Guy 1974). Indeed, Charpentier (1979: 280) surmises that the process of change went in the opposite direction:

The English adverb "together" has been used in Bislama as equivalent to the third-person dual personal pronoun of Melanesian languages, and has assumed the form *tugeta*. The syllable "to" has been assimilated to the English numeral "two." By extension, the English adverbial expression "all together" has given rise to a pronoun *olgeta* 'they' in Bislama (my translation).

In inferring that *tugeta* was the initial form from which *olgeta* is derived (by treating *-geta* as a morpheme), he is almost certainly wrong, on grounds both of the early attestations of *olgeta* and *ol* as pronouns and of the much wider distribution of *olgeta* (whereas *tugeta* is used only by some Bislama speakers). Thus in Tanna in 1877, Giles ([1877] 1968: 41) recorded: "Suppose you let him some boy go along a Queensland, we buy him altogether."

Indeed, the analysis of *tugeta* as parallel to *olgeta* seems to have prospered only in French-speaking areas of the New Hebrides: it is so incongruous to English superstrate speakers that this probably militated against its regularization in areas where they were dominant, giving a strong push toward *tufela* (on this point, cf. Camden 1979 and Charpentier 1979: 310). Once *olgeta* was accepted as the plural marker for humans, another possible generalization of the pattern, which would have been more acceptable to English speakers, is *olgeta-fela* or *ol-fela*; both are attested in the New Hebrides in the 1890s (Pionnier 1913: 187).

Pionnier, who was stationed as a priest on Malekula from 1894 to 1900, provides detailed evidence on the pidgin pronominal paradigm that was apparently becoming standardized by then. Pionnier gives an incomplete paradigm (Table 9.3), apparently in part because he did not pick up

TABLE 9.3

Pionnier's (Incomplete) Pidgin Pronominal Paradigm

Number and person	Pronoun	Number and person	Pronoun
Singular		Trial	
1	mi	1 inclusive	you mi tri fala
2	you	1 exclusive	
3	hème, i[a]	2	
Dual		3	tri fala
1 inclusive	you mi	Plural	
1 exclusive		1 inclusive	you mi olguita
2		1 exclusive	
3	tou fala	2	
		3	olguita, ol fala

[a] *i* is not recorded by Pionnier in his pronominal paradigm, but is represented in dozens of occurrences in his texts. I will return, in Chapter 10, to the question of this "predicate marker."

TABLE 9.4

Supplementation of Pionnier's Paradigm

Number and person	Pronoun	Number and person	Pronoun
Singular		Plural	
1	mi	1 inclusive	yumi [olgeta]
2	yu	1 exclusive	mifela
3	hem, i	2	yufela
Dual		3	olgeta
1 inclusive	yumi		(olgeta fela)
1 exclusive	mitufela		(ol fela)
2	yutufela		(hemfela)
3	tufela		

the inclusive/exclusive distinction (giving only an inclusive form), and did not notice the problem of marking nonsingular number in second person.*

From all this, we can reconstruct a paradigm of the dominant pronominal forms established in the pidgin broadly common across the southwestern Pacific by the early or mid-1890s, using Pionnier's orthography as the basis for our phonological approximations, and filling in the gaps in his paradigms from the attestations recorded in the preceding paragraphs (Table 9.4).

We can see from all this a gradual stabilization of the pidgin pro-

*Perhaps because of the similar ambiguity in French *vous* as in English "you" despite the availability of a *tu* form.

nominal system in the 1880s and 1890s, but a paradigm containing enough internal logical contradictions and possibilities that there were some elements of instability and variation well into the present century. Indeed, this variability continues among older speakers in bush areas of Vanuatu and the Solomons, as we will see.

Before going on, it is worth considering more explicitly the significance of the semantic structure of the Melanesian Pidgin pronominal system in relation to questions of universal grammar and substrate influence. Because the marking of an inclusive/exclusive distinction in Pacific pidgins and the marking of a dual set so clearly and obviously follow a substrate pattern and not a superstrate pattern, the theoretical importance of this congruence has often been ignored or understated—or even denied, on the basis of the supposedly late stabilization of these distinctions. But in my view, these congruences remain the most compelling single piece of evidence of the historically primary role of Pacific Islanders in shaping a developing pidgin in the Pacific. This point has been well grasped and stated by Mufwene (1986: 141–42):

> A system with an inclusive/exclusive distinction is more complex and more marked than that without this distinction. . . . Even though Mühlhäusler discards the role of substrate influence in the emergence of these distinctions in Oceanic pidgins/creoles (because they are allegedly late developments), note that they cannot in any case be internally motivated. . . .
>
> The role of the substrate languages in the development of the dual/plural and inclusive/exclusive distinctions could not be ruled out, . . . particularly on account of the fact that no other pidgin/creole in a different contact situation has ever developed similar distinctions. . . .
>
> The fact that the substrate languages are relatively homogeneous with regard to these distinctions as well as, I assume, the fact that Tok Pisin, Bislama and the like have been used for so long as second languages by essentially the Melanesians themselves can explain why the same distinctions have developed in these pidgins/creoles: they respond to certain semantic distinctions to which the users are already accustomed. The fact that they have developed late does not reduce their identity as substrate influence.

In fact, as we have seen, the inclusive/exclusive and dual/plural distinctions seem to have been well established by the 1890s, and probably—on both textual and distributional grounds—by the 1880s. Inadequacies of European scribes notwithstanding, by a century ago Pacific Islanders had left these unmistakable marks on the developing pidgin of which they were primary architects. We can go on to see a more subtle kind of marking, which has been more difficult for linguists to read.

CHAPTER 10

Subject-Referencing Pronouns and the "Predicate Marker"

I HAVE SO FAR taken as given the received wisdom that there is a single set of pronominal forms in Melanesian Pidgin, unmarked for case. I will now go on to show that this is by no means a simple matter. In the process, I will shed light on the much-debated "predicate marker" in Melanesian Pidgin.

A key source of evidence is what was recorded as "he" following noun subjects: what European grammarians call a "resumptive pronoun." Once more, we find a case in which a pidgin form was not adopted directly from either a substrate pattern or a superstrate pattern, but arose from a kind of collusion between the two: a congruence motivated not simply by historically accidental similarities between the languages involved, but by the universal grammatical patterns that underlie them. Hall (1966: 83) is essentially correct when he infers that this "he"

reflects a merger of the substandard English habit of recapitulating a subject by means of a pronoun—as in "John, he's an idiot" or "my mother, she always spanks me"—and the Melanesian-Micronesian feature of morphologically distinct pronouns that recapitulate subjects and introduce predicates, as in Marshallese *ladrik e-gerabal* 'the boy, he works.'

However, we will see that, like many other linguists who have approached Melanesian Pidgin from the direction of Tok Pisin, he errs in inferring that the "predicate marker" "cannot be considered a pronoun."

The relationship between the Oceanic SRPs and the (to an English speaker) redundant resumptive "he" after a noun subject was in fact noted by Schuchardt in his addendum to and commentary on his original 1883 paper: "The pleonastic use of the third person personal pronoun after the subject and before the object in Melanesian is better founded than I had assumed ([1889] 1980: 26).*

Writing almost a century later, Walsh (1978: 191) suggests that the Pidgin "predicate marker" *i* reflected an Oceanic Austronesian pattern, but notes that "the case for an EAN [Oceanic] derivation has not yet been adequately documented." Camden (1979) uses the evidence from the New Hebridean language Tangoan to suggest a correspondence between predicate marker and what I have called subject-referencing pronouns. But these remain isolated and relatively ad hoc suggestions of such a relationship, which has yet to be coherently argued and documented or widely recognized. Again, this partly has to do with the focus on Tok Pisin and the tendency for linguists analyzing Tok Pisin to have insufficient knowledge of the grammar of Oceanic (and particularly EO) languages. I will suggest that the *i* form is indeed historically a pronoun, although it has become a residual or vestigial one for speakers of Tok Pisin, (particularly speakers of Papuan languages which lack any substrate motivation to sustain it).

In the early stages of pidgin development in the Pacific, the collusion between English speakers' resumptive pronouns and Oceanic speakers' SRPs is recorded in such early texts as the following (the numbered texts are from Chapters 3 and 4):

Tanna man he no too much like work. . . . All man he only get one woman (1859; sentence 4).

nother day's sun he come all right (1860).

And these from the early stages of the Labor Trade:

Captain, he buy him four boy belong a me (1870; 16).

Well, master, man Makura, he no want missionary (1872; 17).

Why did a developing pidgin incorporate the equivalent of Oceanic SRPs at all (if it did), given the redundance of such short verbal pronouns in English, the variation in semantic marking in substrate languages, and the general strain toward simplification and the loss of grammatical markers in pidgins?

Or more interestingly, let us turn the question around. If Oceanic speakers were playing their part in this process of collusion by pulling pidgin syntax in an Oceanic direction, would we not expect to find a more pervasive pattern, instead of (or developing out of) the sporadic appear-

*French speakers, relatively free from code interference from English, and having access to *moi*, *je*, and other constructions closer to an Oceanic pattern, have in general been much better observers and chroniclers of Pacific pidgin pronouns than English speakers.

ance of a subject-referencing "he"?* I have argued that at the very "core" of Oceanic syntax lies a clause structure minimally comprising a VP incorporating an SRP and (in transitive clauses) an object-marking pronoun. The subject NP is an optional expansion on this VP, as is an object NP. Once subject reference is established, with an explicit noun or contextually, reference is maintained in subsequent clauses with SRPs within the VPs: there are no subject NPs in such clauses. For an Oceanic speaker to adopt a system where, as in English, pronominal anaphora is maintained by using a subject pronoun in the subject-NP slot is no minor act of simplification but a relatively drastic alteration.

If indeed what to English speakers was a "resumptive" and syntactically and semantically redundant "he" was being analyzed by Oceanic speakers as an SRP, what is crucial is in fact *not* the occurrence of this pronoun following noun subjects, but the maintenance of subject reference pronominally in subsequent clauses. We have seen that in many Oceanic languages it is precisely in the clause where a noun subject is introduced that the otherwise obligatory SRP is optionally (or as in Pohnpeian, obligatorily) deleted.†

How would such a usage, for third person, turn up in the texts? By the same "he" being used in subsequent clauses, rather than the "him" that was being used as an object pronoun (e.g., "belong him"), as in "he no fight that time them fellow take box belong him" (Queensland 1896).

That is, these third-person pronouns were distinguished by the very case marking that prevailing wisdom tells us should not have existed. Consider some of the early texts where "he" occurs as subject pronoun (sentence numbers from Chapters 3 and 4):

Suppose missionary stop here, by and by he speak (1859; sentence 4).

Look here, Tanna man he lazy, he plenty lazy, he no like work, he walk about (1867; 14).

Misse White no good he plenty fight (1877; 26).

Very good you go look chief belonga me: he like spik you . . . chief he old man. No savey walk good (1878; 25).

Mi see him overseer he bin hit him Cao first time. He been kick him long boot (1884; 43).

---

*I will have more to say about its phonological shape.
†For this reason, despite Mühlhäusler's suggestions to the contrary (Mühlhäusler n.d. 1), we cannot assess whether the pronominal pattern was becoming Oceanic or not by calculating the relative frequency of clauses with noun subjects with and without "resumptive pronouns," even leaving aside the probable virtual randomness with which English-speaking scribes wrote down what were to them redundant but stylistically quaint usages.

Suppose he work strong fellow, white fellow he no hit him;* suppose he lazy, he hit him a little fellow. Sun, he come up, he go work; sun, he go down, he go sleep (ca. 1884; 45).

We see here what I take to be a perfectly Oceanic pattern of pronominal reference, using "he" as SRP in contrast to the "him" contemporary texts show to have been serving as object pronoun (as in *bilong hem*). In the last text (sentence 45), the pattern is unmistakable in terms of the maintenance of reference in discourse. The text comes from testimony regarding a particular recruit, so the initial reference to the "he" was contextually clear. Notice, however, that as reference is changed—from the Melanesian who is the (unmarked) "he" to the white boss, and then to the sun— a subject NP is introduced, with "white fellow" and then with "sun," each time followed by a "he" referencing that newly introduced subject.

There is a further syntactic load carried by the SRPs in Oceanic languages: they serve to embed relative clauses. Kwaio (Southeast Solomonic) will serve to illustrate:

rua   wane   gala   nigi   naaboni   ta-gala   suga-a
two   man   SRP(they2) arrive   yesterday FUT-SRP(they2) buy-it
The two men who came yesterday will buy it.

boo   ku   ngari-a   mai   naaboni   ta-gala   suga-a
pig   SRP(I) bring-it   DEI   yesterday FUT-SRP(they2) buy-it
It's the pig I brought yesterday they're going to buy.

wane   ku   aga-si-a   naaboni   te-'e   suga-a
man   SRP(I) see-TRS-him   yesterday FUT-SRP(he) buy-it
The man I saw yesterday will buy it.

In the second sentence, the direct object topicalized by fronting is the object of both the embedded clause and the matrix clause. In the third, the subject of the matrix clause is the object of the embedded clause. Such sentence structures, using SRPs to embed clauses, lie at the very heart of Oceanic syntax. It is no wonder that we find in a developing Pacific pidgin as early as 1850 a sentence such as "Great fool Uea man, steal little thing he no want, big ship come and kill him" (Erskine 1853: 347).

The complexity of the embedding of clauses possible in the expanded pidgin of the 1890s, using the (to English speakers redundant and func-

---

*I take these instances of "him" to be the transitive suffix, misrecorded by English-speaking scribes. In modern Melanesian Pidgin, when the transitive suffix is not followed by a noun and the referent is human, an object pronoun can optionally be used: V-em hem. But these instances seem to represent V-em.

tionless) resumptive "he," is illustrated by a sentence from Catholic missionaries in Malekula, New Hebrides, recorded by Pionnier (1913: 194):

wen	man	i	mek-em	nogud,
when	man	SRP(he)	do-TRS	bad

If a man does wrong,

sapas	man	ia	i	ded
if	man	DEM	SRP(he)	be dead

when this man dies

bel	bilong	hem	i	kapsae	daon,
soul	POSS	him	SRP(it)	sink	down

his soul sinks

ples	i	nogud
place	SRP(it)	be bad

to a bad place.

A few years later, again from the New Hebrides, Jacomb (1914: 99) gives further clear examples of relative clauses embedded with pronouns, in the pidgin he learned as a barrister in Vila from about 1900 onward, as in "me 'ear 'im one feller man 'e talk" (I heard one man say). Jacomb illustrates the possible syntactic elaborations with a pidgin rendering of English "Go and get my pen out of the chest of drawers in my room":

"you go take 'im one feller something 'e stop along room belong me,
'e stop 'long big feller bokis close up long window.
'Im 'e belong make mark long paper: 'im 'e black: 'im 'e
small feller: all time you look 'im me make mark long paper along 'im."

Or, in a more probable phonological rendering:

yu	go	tek-em	wan-fala	samting
you	AUX	take-TTS	one-DET	thing

'You go and take something

i	stap	long	rum	bilong	mi
it	be	LOC	room	POSS	me

from my room

i	stap	long	big-fala	bokis	klosap	long	windou
it	be	LOC	big-ADJ	box	near	LOC	window

which is in a big box near the window.

hem	i	belong	mek	mak	long	pepa	hem	i	bilak	hem	i
it	it	for	make	mark	LOC	paper	it	it	black	it	it

It's for making marks on paper; it's black, it's

sumol-fala   oltaem   yu   luk-im   mi
small-ADJ   always   you   see-TTS   me
small; you often see me

mek   mak   long   pepa   long   hem
make   mark   LOC   paper   with   it
making marks on paper with it.

But many questions remain. Is there a corresponding *focal* pronoun, which in the Oceanic pattern is optionally used to emphasize the pronominal subject as topic (as in French *moi, je*)? And what about first- and second-person pronouns, singular and plural?

I infer that when we find, in the nineteenth-century texts, subject pronouns English speakers recorded as "me" and "you," these too were being used by Oceanic speakers in constructions paralleling those of their native languages: that is, where the obligatory core of (verbal) sentences consisted of a VP, with an SRP preceding the verb. Let us look again at such usages in the textual record (here I again give the numbers of sentences used in Chapters 3 and 4):

You 'fraid me se-teal. Me no se-teal, me come worship (1869; sentence 9).

You want to buy him boy, what name you give it belong a boy? Suppose you give me one fellow musket, me give you one fellow boy (1877; 27).

Me sick me stop over there no more. Me stop no more there, me want to go along big fellow house (1877; 31).

Me speak cappen belong man-o-war, suppose you no look out (1878; 24).

You see Massa, you bin tell me altogether man fool put im red longa face. Me no fool, me put im blue (1878; 29).

You no like'm me? . . . Me like'm white man. You come (ca. 1885; 40).

Of course English speakers applied a different analysis, using these pronouns in an English-like fashion in the subject-NP slot—and needing only to adopt, sporadically, a (to them redundant) "he" after noun subjects. The skeptical linguist may choose to do the same. Is there any direct evidence that these pronouns were being used as SRPs, so that sentences without explicit noun subjects consisted of VPs?

First of all, consider the "he." We have strong evidence from this period that "belong him" was being used in possessive constructions. So for the third-person singular, a distinction was apparently being drawn between subject and object pronouns. That suggests the strong possibility that there was an (implicit) parallel distinction between the "you's" of "you no look out" and of "belonga you" in text sentence 24 (1878), and between the "me's" of "me bin work long-a Maryboro" (26; 1877) and "chief belonga me" (25; 1878). But if "he" was being used as a subject pronoun, and "him" as an object pronoun, can we infer that "he" was a *subject-referencing* pronoun parallel to the SRPs in substrate languages? What we would need to find, to be sure that this follows an Oceanic pattern, is "him" used as equivalent to a *focal* pronoun. Did "him" fit into the (optional) subject-NP slot in a pidgin clause, and "he" into an obligatory slot within the VP?

Jacomb's account of 1900-vintage New Hebridean Pidgin gives "'im e go" for 'he goes' and "woman e go" for 'she goes' (1914: 92). We have seen in his texts that *hem i* constructions were being used in full clauses without noun subjects, but that *i* alone was being used to embed relative clauses. "Him he gammon boy too much" was recorded in the Solomons in 1895. But the existence of these sequences in all daughter dialects makes it almost certain that Islanders were using such constructions by the 1880s—constructions in the pattern of Oceanic grammar parallel to "cappen he" or "man Tanna he," but that, unlike these, having no correspondence with an English usage,* are likely not to have been used by English speakers or to have been recorded by them.

Having raised the question of the accuracy of recorded texts, it will be useful to expand on it. I consider that the problems of syntactic and phonological textual accuracy to which I have alluded impose such a pervasive filter between what Islanders said and what Europeans (and especially English speakers) wrote that we have to be careful and skeptical in the extreme in drawing statistical or other conclusions about the development of Pacific pidgin. The distortions were introduced both at the level of how English speakers heard and interpreted what Islanders were saying and at the level of how they chose to write it, particularly since they were mainly writing for the benefit of readers to whom pidgin as spoken by the Islanders would have been completely opaque.

Consider the pronoun English speakers haved consistently represented as "he" in the great majority of texts recorded through the 1920s, and often beyond. Given that "he" is the only English approximation in terms of which *i* could be represented, it seems very likely that most Islanders from the 1860s onwards were using *i* rather than *hi* where Europeans recorded "he." One of the most telling pieces of evidence for this is the detailed set of texts provided by Pionnier from Malekula in 1894. As a French speaker mercifully free from English code interference (though inheriting some orthographic problems), Pionnier consistently represents "him" as *hème* (or sometimes *him*), and consistently represents what

---

*But again compare French *moi je* or the less common but possible *lui il*.

English speakers were writing as "he" with *i*, as in "oumane i goud tou-meutch maman bilong him, Papa bilong hème no long graoun" (Pionnier 1913: 198). We have further confirmatory evidence from the New Hebridean Pidgin of this period. On Tanna around 1896, Macmillan recorded "You show me book and number where kava e stop" (Guiart 1956: 126).* In the pidgin of Vila in the New Hebrides learned by Jacomb around 1900, neither "him" nor "he" is recorded as having an aspirated "h" onset. Alexander (1927: 214), a British jurist who was in the New Hebrides just before World War I broke out, recorded there "By 'n by Kong Kong 'e fas 'im rope along bokis you fight 'im 'e sing out" ('The Chinese man will put a rope around the piano').

The persistent tendency of English speakers to write pidgin according to the closest English grammatical analysis emerges in the way the transitive suffix was recorded. When it precedes a noun direct object, it corresponds to no English form, and hence was usually recorded as "'m," "'im," or "'em." But when there is no noun object (and particularly when the implied object is human), the same transitive suffix was characteristically recorded as "him," sometimes in the same sentence, as in

You leave-'im bush-man, he all right. You teach-'im salt-water man. [The "salt-water men" proffered the reverse characterization.] Very good you teach-'im bush-man. He no good. You make him quiet. Salt-water man he all right, you leave him (recorded on Malaita, 1904; Young 1926: 153–54).

Canoe he no catch him! (Solomons 1912; Herr and Rood 1978: 93).

Shark he fight 'em—take him finish (Solomons 1912; *ibid.*, p. 148).

Here the same transitive suffix, phonologically *-em* or *-im*, was being recorded as "'em ('m)" or as "him," depending on its syntactic environment.

A similar pervasive problem of code interference surrounds the form English speakers have consistently written (and probably usually pronounced) as "altogether."† There is no evidence that Pacific Islanders have ever used, anywhere, the putative second syllable of "altogether": it

---

*Mühlhäusler argues that *we(a)* as relativizer appeared late in New Guinea (1970s), but comments (1986: 189) that it is used in "Bislama, Solomon Islands Pidgin English, Tok Pisin, Queensland Kanaka English, . . . Torres Straits Broken and Northern Territory Kriol." That it is recorded here prior to 1900 in the New Hebrides—and, incidentally, in Solomons Pidgin in 1910, in "all same man where he walk about" (Deck 1910)—argues for it being an old form in the region. It seems, however, to have been a form emanating more from superstrate than substrate speakers; the latter, as we have seen, characteristically use SRPs to embed relative clauses.

†In the 1960s, I encountered a number of British colonial officers who had worked in the Solomons for years and were otherwise relatively fluent in Solomons Pidgin who consistently pronounced *olgeta* as "altogether."

is, everywhere, *olgeta, olketa, oloketa*, or similar variations. In the modern creolizing urban dialect, it gets condensed downward, into *okta* or even *ota* (Jourdan 1985), but there is no evidence of it anywhere following the superstrate phonological pattern despite the repeated and consistent misproduction of this pattern for a century by superstrate speakers. Again, the only one who got it right was the French-speaking Pionnier, who represented it as *olguita*.

A further word needs to be said about statistical counts. Given the linguistic filters imposed by the chroniclers of the period, who so pervasively misheard (or misrepresented what they heard), I regard statistical counts from the texts as next to useless in assessing developmental issues (except as showing a slightly and slowly increasing sophistication on the part of the best of the chroniclers). The most extensive corpora are from the testimony recorded at various commissions of inquiry. In using them, we are at the mercy of court reporters who did the best they could, in various mixtures of pidgin and English, to convey what was said.* We also see, in a close reading of the texts, how those Islanders (such as the slippery Cago†) who had worked closely with Europeans produced a mixture of English and pidgin for the court (although this was probably a very different register than they used with fellow Islanders), in contrast with the speech recorded from those Islanders who spoke pidgin well enough to testify for themselves. We further find differences (including differences in pronominal usage) between sentences imputed by Islanders to Europeans and sentences imputed to fellow Islanders. Given all these internal variations in the corpora, as well as the overall filters of anglicization and partial comprehension through which they were differentially passed, statistical counts from them are next to (and sometimes worse than) useless.

With this as background, we can turn to the sequence hypothesized by Sankoff (1977). She reconstructs a sequence in which single "strong" subject pronouns in use in 1885 were by 1900 changing into a new pattern where a strong pronoun "him" was followed by a cliticized "pronoun copy" in some constructions. Sankoff's insights are valuable and important, but I believe she misinterprets the starting point of the sequence of cliticization. Had she recognized the Oceanic pattern of the pronominal syntax of the pidgin of the 1880s, she would, I think, have been led to a rather different interpretation.

---

*In the absence of a standard pidgin orthography, and given their aim of preserving a transcript that would be intelligible to English speakers, many of whom would not know pidgin.

†Wawn (1894: 349) speaks of "Cago, the rascally interpreter of the *Hopeful*, afterwards relied on by the Royal Commission," and speculates on how he pressured New Guineans to alter their testimony so as to present the recruiters in a favorable light.

As we have seen, in the early time period (1885 and before) when "he" was supposedly being used as a "strong" pronoun (in sentences with pronominal subjects), it was also being used following noun subjects, a pattern found in texts as early as 1850. Is the "he" following noun subjects "strong," or is it already "cliticized"? Is it a different "he" pronoun than the one used as pronominal subject? The far simpler analysis, simply on linguistic grounds, is to see *hem* as the pronoun that fits into the subject-NP slot, so that *hem i* sequences are grammatically parallel to, for example, *tana man i* in "Tanna man he lazy, he plenty lazy, he no like work" (Tanna, New Hebrides, 1867; Adams 1984: 174)—even if *hem i* does not turn up in the early texts. That is, "he" when it occurs as pronominal subject in these early texts is not, I think, a "strong" pronoun in the sense assumed by Sankoff; rather, it is what Givón (1984) would call a "de-stressed independent pronoun" that references an implied noun subject.

The pattern *hem i* supposedly emerging in a post-1890 "first wave of cliticization" occurs in all Melanesian Pidgin dialects. To assume that "him" is here replacing "he" as a strong pronoun, and at this point "he" is becoming de-stressed, forces us to assume a parallel developmental process in all three dialects of Melanesian Pidgin (and in Torres Strait Creole, where *hem i* was recorded in 1898). This is not completely implausible, given processes of pronominal shift set out by Givón (1984) and others; but it forces us to make a strong assumption of parallel evolution for which there is no direct evidence. The distributional evidence strongly suggests an alternative explanation: that by the 1880s *hem* was being used in the FP slot (i.e., the slot into which a subject NP would fit) and as the object pronoun, and *i* was being used in the SRP slot in the VP.

A second pattern, hypothesized by Sankoff to have occurred in Tok Pisin in a "second wave of cliticization," 1900–1930, manifests a generalization of the *i* with all nonsingular subjects (including first and second person). This may indeed represent an independent development in Tok Pisin. But the distributional evidence again suggests that this pattern existed in the 1880s, if only as one of several alternative patterns. The Bislama of Vanuatu (at least as spoken in some areas) incorporates an almost identical use of *i* as an all-purpose "predicate marker" for nonsingular slots (Camden 1979). Sankoff's interpretation of this "second stage" again implies that the process of "cliticization" in the two long-separated dialects has followed exactly parallel lines: not impossible, but in my view implausible.

I agree with Sankoff that the cliticization of *i*, entailing its losing its force as a third-person singular pronoun in its own right, has probably been an important process in the subsequent development of Tok Pisin. (Perhaps this is a "natural" entailment of a developmental progression in which *i* became generalized so as to lose its marking for third person; perhaps it also reflects the transplantation of a language whose major syntactic models come from EO languages to a world where Papuan languages mainly prevail.) But I believe her broader claims of cliticization represent a misreading of the early pidgin pronominal system, a misreading for which any linguist who did not know how subject pronouns operate in EO languages can be well forgiven.

I infer the existence of the following pattern for singular pronouns in the Pacific plantation pidgin of about 1890:

Person	Object/Focal	SRP
1	mi	mi
2	iu	iu
3	hem	i

Is there any direct evidence of *mi . . . mi* and *iu . . . iu* constructions? There are only a few fragments of textual evidence from the 1880s, which we will shortly glimpse. But again, the evidence from daughter dialects is in my view compelling. Sequences of *mi mi* and *iu iu* are found in Bislama, Solomons Pidgin, and regional dialects of Tok Pisin, especially among Oceanic Austronesian speakers. In some of these dialects, such sequences occur only when a particle intervenes between the paired pronouns; in other dialects, they can occur in direct sequence.

We have textual evidence from Jacomb (1914) of *mi mi* and *iu iu* being in use at the turn of the century in New Hebridean Pidgin. He comments that "A further trick of the language is to repeat the words 'Me' and 'You'" (p. 104). He gives "me me no want 'im" (p. 104) and "me me catch 'im pay belong me finish" (p. 96) in illustration. Most striking, in its Oceanic syntactic pattern, is Jacomb's "man 'ere 'e come first time, me me come behind" (p. 102). Here the contrast is drawn in a parallel construction between "man 'ere," who came first, and "me," who came second; that is, the FP in the second clause is counterposed to the noun subject of the first:

man	ia	i	kam	fastaem,	mi	mi	kam	bihaen
man	DEM	SRP(he)	come	first	FP(me)	SRP(I)	come	after

That man came first; me, I came second.

A similar construction, with the parallel subject NPs reversed, occurs in Jacomb's "Me me missionary: nother feller man 'ere 'e man belong darkness" (p. 98).

In contemporary Bislama, direct sequences of *mi mi* and *iu iu* are common in virtually all local usages. Camden (personal communication, Sept. 28, 1983) writes, "I know of no dialect of Bislama in which the forms *mi mi* and *yu yu* are not completely normal." He exemplifies with the sentence *Yu yu kam long ples ya olsem wanem?* 'And *you*, what have you come here for?' Researchers Jacques Guy, Margaret Jolly, and Darrell Tryon all confirm that sequences of *mi mi* and *yu yu* occur in the local dialects of Bislama used by speakers of the indigenous languages with which they have worked. Camden notes further that the second *yu* or *mi* is obligatory, the first is optional, and would be used where "the focus is . . . on the 'you,' in contrast with somebody else, fitting precisely the 'focal pronoun' category you use." Charpentier (1979) gives

Bae mi mi blok-im marid ya.
I will prevent this marriage (p. 299)

Babae mi mi ded.
I will be dead (p. 352)

Babae yu yu kakae.
You will eat (p. 352),

as paralleling

Em i ded finis.
He is dead (p. 352).

For Tok Pisin, such constructions appear to be common in areas where Oceanic Austronesian languages are spoken. In some local dialects, notably in New Britain (Ward Goodenough, personal communication, May 1983, with reference to Nakanai and neighboring areas), the *mi mi* and *iu iu* pronouns occur in direct sequence. In other dialects, the paired pronouns apparently occur in surface constructions only where a topicalizing, modal, aspect-marking, or other particle intervenes between them. For Manus, I have recorded (from Bernard Kaspou):

Mi bae mi go.

Mi nao mi stap.

Iu bae iu go.

Iu nao iu stap.

In Solomons Pidgin, constructions of the latter sort, where the FPs and SRPs are separated by a particle, are pervasively common. Thus, from my texts of older speakers of EO languages of Malaita and Guadalcanal who learned Solomons Pidgin in the 1920s and 1930s in plantation and police work:

Mi nao mi faet wet-em olketa nomoa.
It was I who fought with them (a Kwara'ae, Malaita, speaker).

Mi tuu mi kam mi stap weit-em.
I, too, came and stayed with him (a Lau, Malaita, speaker).

Mi nao mi kil-im.
It was I who hit him (a Tasimboko, Guadalcanal, speaker).

Mi tu mi kam dat taem.
I too came at that time (a Talise, Guadalcanal, speaker).

Den mi taem mi rid-im leta . . .
The time I read the letter . . . (a Talise speaker).

Iu bae iu mek-em.
You'll do it (a Kwaio, Malaita, speaker).

In Solomons Pidgin, the paired pronouns are used in direct sequence only when a pause intervenes, providing a clear punctuation and topical emphasis:

Oraet, mi, mi godaon longo wafu.
Well as for me, I went down to the wharf (a Kwaio speaker).

Den mi rid-im, mi, mi tink: ae, fada wande mi . . .
Then when I read it, I said to myself, 'Hey, the Father wants me . . .' (a Talise speaker).

I suspect that by the end of the 1880s, speakers of Pacific pidgin tended to avoid direct repetition of those pronouns that were not case marked to distinguish focal pronoun from SRP (i.e., *mi* and *iu*), although *hem i* probably was regularly used in direct sequence. Such a statistical pattern could then have been regularized as a rule blocking such direct repetition in some daughter dialects, and could have disappeared in others. At least, the two fragmentary records of such usage from the 1880s that may reflect such a pattern have forms intervening between the two pronouns:

Mi wantaim mi kam Samoa (from Samoa, quoted by Mühlhäusler 1978a: 107).

Me man me no all same other man, me bring your boy back (Queensland transcripts, "Return of New Guinea Natives," Feb. 14, 1885, no. 3577).

The second instance is problematic, since it is not quite clear what the structure of the sentence is. The "me" pronouns may be in different clauses, the first an equational clause "I'm a man" and the second an embedded "who isn't like other men." However, such constructions in EO languages may use FP and SRP. Compare Kwaio (Malaita, Southeast Solomonic):

nau	wane	ku	'ame	taa'ua	wane	ngaai
FP(me)	man	SRP(I)	NEG	be like	man	other

I'm not like other men.

Note that in this Kwaio sentence, the FP, not the SRP, is used to mark the subject of the equational clause. SRPs, incorporated within VPs and (among other things) marking the base that follows as verbal, can occur only in clauses with VPs as predicates. Equational clauses and/or prepositional clauses are, in Kwaio and a number of other EO languages, nonverbal; they cannot incorporate SRPs. The significance of this point for the analysis of the so-called "predicate marker" in Melanesian Pidgin will be noted shortly.

Two major questions raised by my analysis remain to be explored. One is the question of what SRPs, if any, were being used in nonsingular slots—for example, for second-person dual or first-person (exclusive) plural. The answer is complicated, as will shortly be seen; I infer that several alternative systems, none fully stabilized, were probably in use. A more manageable, and related, question is why the case distinction between "him" and "he" (*hem* and *i*) was not matched by a corresponding distinction between FP and SRP for first and second person. Why did a developing pidgin not incorporate a distinction between "me" (as object pronoun and FP) and "I" (as SRP), paralleling the distinction between "him" and "he"?

The problem was in fact perceived by Schuchardt, the first serious student of Melanesian Pidgin. He comments ([1889] 1980: 26) that "*Him* appears as an accusative, *he* as a nominative. That can really be nothing more than accidental. *He* is surely felt only as a phonetic variant of *him*; otherwise we would have *I* in addition to *me*."

The textual evidence suggests that there was a recurrent drift in the direction of a "me"-vs.-"I" distinction over many decades. We have already an early example of it, in the speech of the Gilbertese "King" Tubureimoa of Makin (MacCallum 1934: 252), who in 1889 was recorded as saying "Me, I got power." We may surmise that this drift came both from a tendency of Oceanic speakers to incorporate a distinction in pidgin represented in their native languages and from the tendency of English speakers (those who did not know pidgin well) to use "I" as subject pronoun, which gave a continuous source of an alternative pattern, contrasting "I" and "me." The clearest indication of such a pattern comes from Ray's account of the pidgin spoken in the Torres Strait Islands in 1898 (Ray 1900: 251): "'Me' and 'him' are also used preceding 'I' and 'he': *me I go*, I go; *him he go*, he goes; *him he run*, he runs." Here we have unmistakable evidence of an Oceanic Austronesian pattern where *hem* is being used as FP and *i* as SRP; and where first-person forms are following the same pattern.

Sankoff's (1977) count of usages in the 1885 Queensland Commission transcripts, which shows "I" (244 cases) predominating over "me" (124 cases) is (as she suspects) spurious because the court reporters have undoubtedly misrecorded many of the texts, "correcting" the pidgin usage. Moreover, a great many of the utterances came from a small handful of interpreters, notably Cago of "Burra Burra," whose pidgin was considerably more anglicized than that of most of those whose testimony was recorded directly with the notation "spoke English." The texts we have seen from the 1850s onward (Chapters 3 and 4) overwhelmingly incorporate "me" as subject pronoun. Yet there are enough instances of "I" to allow us to infer with considerable confidence that it was in sporadic use by Islanders as well as Europeans. Thus, as we saw earlier, Rannie recorded from Malekula in 1884: "All right, you give me ten stick tobacco and I give 'em you head belong my small fellow brother" (sentence 21). Schuchardt ([1883] 1980: 19) gives, in the texts provided by Layard, the British Consul in New Caledonia, "I no fight him" and "I make kai-kai."

Doubtless some of the occurrences of "I" in the 1885 Queensland transcripts are genuine, in such sentences (from those who themselves "spoke English", e.g. "Sandfly" of "Grass Island") as

You two fellow go work along sugar-cane and I give you some tobacco you two fellow no go back in canoe (Jan. 23, 1885, no. 1462; here, however, he is quoting a European; and in most places he is recorded as using "me").

Perhaps the regularization of *mi* as both FP and SRP, despite the sporadic use of "I" (*ae*), was partly a result of the absence of any parallel case marking of the second-person form "you" in English. There may have been a kind of pull from "him" and "he" in one direction, and of "you" in the other. If so, the simpler pattern prevailed.

Was there another kind of pull, toward neutralizing the distinction between *hem* and *i* and using *hem* in both FP and SRP slots? Here the evidence is unclear, but it is worth noting that there are two isolated recorded occurrences of "him" being used as subject pronoun in the 1880s, both from Layard in New Caledonia: "Missis! Man belong bullamacow him stop" and "You savey where man him stop?" (Schuchardt [1883] 1980: 18–19).

We can usefully bridge between this question of contrast between FP and SRP and the remaining question of forms used in nonsingular slots. English not only provided subject pronouns "he" and "I" as possible monosyllabic forms that might be used as SRPs; it also provided possible forms for two plural pronominal slots (first person "we" and third person "they") that could have been incorporated into a developing Pacific pidgin as SRPs marked for person and nonsingular number. Why did "we" and "they" not become regular SRPs? That will usefully bring us to the question of what forms were used as the obligatory pronominal constituents of sentences with nonsingular subjects, explicit or anaphorically or indexically implied.

The textual and contemporary evidence suggests that, like "I," these forms have been continuously injected into pidgin by English speakers with an inadequate command of prevailing usage, and that they have been intermittently adopted by Islanders (presumably particularly ones whose indigenous languages have SRPs marked for person and nonsingular number, and/or those in continuous close contact with superstrate speakers). Again, the texts set out earlier provide useful examples:

What for Government Agent no let boat's crew help-'em boys when altogether want go Queensland? Suppose we been have 'em good fellow Government, we full up now (1884; sentence 20).

Me think all the boy want to kill me; then me, sandfly, go back and speak we come along three moon (1885; 44).

We too close already; by and by when that fellow finish dance they fire up along you and me (recorded on Tabar, 1884; Rannie 1912: 53).

Churchill (1911) gives several instances of such usages, including "you me two fellow we" and "these two fellow they." It is hard to discern which of these instances may have been misrecorded, but some of them are probably genuine. For "they," Tom Dutton (1980: 85) recorded from Tom Lammon, a New Hebridean who had learned Pidgin in Queensland in the 1880s, "They no givem that kain a thing" ('They don't keep that kind of thing').

I recorded some interesting occurrences of "they" from old Solomon Islanders, particularly men who had served as police in the 1920s. The first was spoken by a Lau speaker from Malaita, the second by a Tasimboko, Guadalcanal, speaker:

mifala	luka	nao	ma	oloketa	busumane	dee	kamdaon
SRP(we)	look	PRF	and	PLU	bushman	SRP(they)	come down

We looked and (saw that) the bushmen were coming down.

hem	nao	i	save	haomas	pipol	wea	dee	faet
FP(him)	TOP	SRP(he)	know	how many	people	REL	SRP(they)	fight

He's the one who knows how many people (actually) fought.

I asked the Lau speaker, who had learned Solomons Pidgin in the constabulary, why he sporadically used *dee* rather than the *olgeta* he usually employed. His answer, although perhaps it cannot quite be taken at face value, suggests the possible continuing role of superstrate influence in pidgin pronominal usage:

Taem mi stap long gafaman nomoa, hem nao mi iusim disfala tok—"dee duim." Waeteman i kam long Solomon aelan nao ma i talem see "dee duim." Mifala tekem. Mifala duim weitem* oloketa, bikos olketa gifim long mifala. Steret toko, "olketa i duim." Bataa disfala toko i kamu, see "dee duim."

It was when I was with the government, that's when I used this kind of talk, "dee duim." The Europeans came to the Solomon Islands and said "dee duim." We adopted that. We did it along with them, because they gave it to us [i.e., used it with us]. The proper usage is "olketa i duim." But this usage that came was "dee duim."

This brings us back to the question of nonsingular SRPs in nineteenth-century pidgin. I will suggest that in the Pacific plantation pidgin of the 1880s, there may well have been several alternative sets of pronouns used as obligatory subject markers (and corresponding to the SRPs in substrate languages).

In discussing Sankoff's "cliticization" hypothesis, I noted that both modern Tok Pisin and modern Bislama in Vanuatu, at least in their codified "standard" forms as interpreted in the standard analyses, incorporate *i* as a generalized "predicate marker" used to maintain nonsingular reference (in first, second, and third person) once subject reference has been established with a noun or a pronoun (marked for person and number). Assuming that the reader is more or less familiar with analyses of Tok Pisin in the literature, I shall examine Camden's (1979) analysis of the pronominal system of modern Bislama. His forms are displayed in Table 10.1.

In assessing this paradigm, and whether it could have been represented in an 1880s Pacific pidgin from which both Tok Pisin and Bislama are derived, it is useful to ask how these pronouns operate in relation to the functional problem of maintaining reference in discourse. According to the standard analysis of Tok Pisin and Bislama, the original reference is established with either a noun subject or a pronoun in the subject-NP slot at the beginning of a clause, fully marked for person and number. With either a noun or a pronoun subject in this slot, an immediately following "predicate marker" (which is not marked for person and number) may optionally be included or omitted. In subsequent clauses, as long as the reference remains unchanged or is contextually clear, the unmarked

---

*The construction do + TrS with + TrS exactly follows the Lau idiom meaning 'imitate, follow the pattern of (s.o.).' For more on Lau-Pidgin calquing, see Chapter 13.

TABLE 10.1

Bislama Subject Pronouns (Camden 1979)

Number and person	Focal (FP)	Predicate marker
Singular		
1	mi	mi
2	yu	yu
3	em	i
Dual		
1 inclusive	yumitu(fala)	O, i
1 exclusive	mitufala	i
2	yutufala	i, oli
Plural		
1 inclusive	yumi	O, i, yumi
1 exclusive	mifala	i
2	yufala	i
3	olgeta	oli, i

"predicate marker" *i* suffices to maintain reference, even though it is un-marked for person and number, and hence without this context would be ambiguous. When reference is switched or otherwise becomes ambiguous, or needs periodically to be restated, the subject NP, either a noun or an FP, may be reiterated. For Bislama, Camden (1979: 88–89) notes:

In Bislama . . . in short utterances and at an informal . . . level of conversation, predicate clauses in which an implicit first-, second-, or third-person singular or third-person plural noun or pronoun subject is not explicitly named are common, number and person of the subject being indicated by the predicate marker.* In longer utterances and at a more formal level of language use, the various subjects and subject changes are indicated by the use of nouns and pronouns, subsequent reference to them being maintained by the appropriate use of predicate markers. In the first- and second-person dual, trial, and plural forms, however, the subject noun or pronoun is never omitted.

Since in first and second person, a subject can never be a noun by itself, the last part of Camden's explanation must be qualified. A noun must be conjoined with a pronoun ("we, John and I," "you, John and Bill," or in Oceanic "we John and Bill") to denote first or second person; so Camden might better have said that "a subject pronoun is never omitted."

Because for Bislama a "subject pronoun" is apparently a mandatory component of a clause with first- or second-person nonsingular reference, an alternative analysis of the Bislama system suggested itself to me several

*But potentially ambiguously so, since *i* is the "predicate marker" for all nonsingular slots as well as third-person singular.

TABLE 10.2

Bislama Subject Pronouns (Keesing 1983)

Number and person	Focal (FP)	Subject-referencing (SRP)
Singular		
1	mi	mi
2	yu	yu
3	em	i
Dual[a]		
1 inclusive	iumitufala	iumitu(fala), i
1 exclusive	mitufala	mitufala, i
2	yutufala	yutufala, i
3	tufala	tufala, i
Plural		
1 inclusive	iumi	iumi, i
1 exclusive	mifala	mifala, i
2	yufala	yufala, i
3	olgeta	ol-i, i

[a] A trial set is of course implied here, with *-tri-* in place of *-tu-*.

years ago,* prompted by my analysis of Solomons Pidgin pronominal usage. Table 10.2 displays my alternative 1983 analysis.

I see no strong grounds in the texts available to me or Camden's account that would rule out this alternative paradigm for contemporary Bislama (at least as used by older "bush" speakers, and at least in some areas). Here some of the data presented by Charpentier (1979) are particularly interesting, and show that at least there is considerable variation in pronominal usage in New Hebrides/Vanuatu.

First of all, it is clear from Charpentier's data that many New Hebrideans use sequences of *olgeta ol-i*, as in "Mebi olketa oli kakae" 'Maybe they are eating' (p. 351), and "Olketa oli wok-em wan nakamal i big-wan" 'They are making a *big* [not a small] nakamal [men's house]' (p. 365). Charpentier (p. 310) comments that "in the Bislama of South Malekula, it is not common to say *olketa* + verb, the usage given in Camden's dictionary."

Second, it is clear that some speakers of Bislama, at least in some contexts, use sequences in nonsingular first and second persons that similarly pair the longer form of SRP I hypothesize with the matching FP, as in "yu-mi-tu yu-mi-tu stap kakae" 'we're in the process of eating' (p. 351).[†]

---

*Alternative, that is, to the paradigm set out by Camden 1979.

†This Bislama construction, where *stap* is used to indicate that an action is under way (Charpentier translates with French *en train de*) is less common in Solomons Pidgin, where the perfect-marking particle *nao* indicates (ambiguously) that the action is either under way or finished (where necessary, the latter can be distinguished with *finis*).

More commonly, it would seem, where the FP and SRP are used together, the short and semantically unmarked form of SRP *i* is used. I have already noted Charpentier's recording of *tuketa* rather than *tufala*, in South Malekula.

As will be seen in Chapter 12, older speakers of Solomons Pidgin use a pronominal system very similar to this, although the *-i* canonically marks third-person reference, and is virtually never used for first- and second-person forms. Against my alternative analysis of modern Bislama rests the fact that, unlike the singular forms, sequences such as **iumi iumi*, **mifala mifala*, and **yufala yufala* seem seldom if ever to occur. Otherwise, if I read Camden correctly, *i* can serve to mark pronominal reference in third person, whether singular or nonsingular; but *i* cannot do so (by itself, as SRP) in first- and third-person nonsingular, where a form of pronoun marked for person and number must be used, as we saw in Camden's explanation that "in the first and second person dual, trial and plural forms . . . the subject . . . pronoun is never omitted." That is,

o yu-fela i kranki be bae yu-mi tes kakae wanem wetem kakae nao ya
'Oh, you're crazy, but what are we going to eat with this [vegetable] food now?'
(Charpentier: 374),

contains an FP (*yu-fela*) and an SRP (*i*) in the first clause, and an SRP (or an FP?*) in the second.

Charpentier's data show a close calquing of the Bislama pronouns onto the local languages (mainly those of South Malekula) he knows well. Recall that New Hebridean languages vary considerably in the coding of semantic information in SRPs, from those languages in which the full set of person/number distinctions reconstructed for Proto-Eastern Oceanic is preserved to those that (like Mota) have lost virtually all of this marking. We may guess that pronominal usage by speakers of Bislama, given the range of choices presented, varies accordingly. Charpentier (1979: 311) articulates a similar argument:

We have noted numerous differences among authors in regard to their analyses of the pronominal system of Bislama. Beyond the variations resulting from the fact that Bislama is a language still in the formative process, and thus not fully stabilized, these differences seem to us to correspond to the divergent systems within the Melanesian substrate. . . . In fact, these differences do not prevent mutual intelligibility (my translation).

---

*This question seems undecidable. Perhaps here, as we find in widely distributed substrate languages, we have an FP that is used in the slot where syntactically one would expect an SRP.

But what about the pidgin of the 1880s? Did pronominal usage follow the pattern Camden infers for modern Bislama, where *i* serves to maintain pronominal reference, once established, at least in third-person singular and in nonsingular? The texts from the late nineteenth century and early twentieth century show nonsingular subject pronouns being used in a way that seems to parallel the use of singular subject pronouns, and might be taken as evidence (if the general thrust of my interpretation equating Melanesian Pidgin pronouns with Oceanic SRPs can be sustained) of the use of such forms as *olgeta* and *mifala* and *iumitufala* as SRPs:

What for Government Agent no let boat's crew help-'em boys when altogether want go Queensland? (1884; sentence 20).

By and by me fellow buy'em gun along man-we-we (ca. 1885; 37).

Me save—you me go (Beaune 1894: 122).

So Adam Eve two fella stop along garden (London 1909: 363).

My reading of the textual evidence of the late nineteenth century suggests that several alternative pronominal patterns were in use, as Charpentier suggests is presently the case in Bislama. I will set these out in a series of paradigm tabulations. They differ primarily in the forms used for first- and second-person nonsingular; the third-person forms were apparently more stable (despite the sporadic use of a "they" form). I shall set out several possible sets, illustrating (where I have not already done so) their attestation in texts of the period. Version 1, below, illustrates a paradigm in which no semantic distinctions are drawn for person, with the generalized SRP *i* serving as an all-purpose predicate marker (for third-person singular and all nonsingular persons).

Plural		FP	SRP
1	inclusive	iumi	i
1	exclusive	mifala	i
2		iufala	i
3		olgeta	i

I have noted that the SVO order of constituents characteristic of most EO languages of the central and southwestern Pacific makes the marking of person and number on subject pronouns functionally less crucial than it would seem to be in languages where a VP introduces the clause. And I have noted that in many of the languages of the central and northern New Hebrides, characterized by such SVO order of constituents, the marking of person and/or nonsingular number on SRPs is attenuated or completely absent. The extreme form of this lack of marking, as in the Banks Islands language of Mota, entails the use of a single unmarked form

for all pronominal slots, singular and plural (hence a more drastic simplification than the paradigm I suggest here for pidgin, where singular
forms in first- and second-person—not, of course, shown here—would
have distinctive SRPs). Unfortunately, we have very little evidence on
how pronominal reference is maintained across clauses in such languages.
However, we might guess that speakers of languages such as Mota where
semantic marking on the SRP is minimal may well have used pidgin in
this way (older speakers probably still do).

Some New Hebridean languages (I have used Maewo to illustrate)
have two sets of SRPs, one used to establish or change subject reference
and a second and simpler unmarked set to maintain pronominal reference
once established. The pidgin of the 1880s may well have allowed such an
alternative pattern of pronominal usage, something like the following:

Plural		FP	SRP	
			|A|	|B| or B
1	inclusive	iumi	iumi	i
1	exclusive	mifala	mifala	i
2		iufala	iufala	i
3		olgeta	oli	i i

That is, the short *i* form may have been used by some speakers only for
third person, singular or nonsingular. I will show in Chapter 12 that just
such a system of pronominal usage was being used by Solomon Islanders
in the 1920s and 1930s; the data provide no means to determine whether
it existed, as an alternative possibility, in the pidgin of the 1880s or
1890s. An important point is that such alternative analyses, by speakers
with different pronominal patterns in their native languages, yield identical or very similar surface strings.

But is this all analytical nonsense? Are such problems simply an artifact of a stubborn assumption that pidgin grammar follows an Oceanic
pattern? If instead we analyze pidgin grammar in terms of subject pronouns and predicate markers, as conventional wisdom would have it, do
we not avoid such sophistry? I have argued in Chapter 7, looking at
Silverstein's analysis of Chinook Jargon, that such alternative analyses are
precisely what we should expect under conditions of interlingual contact,
on theoretical and comparative grounds. The situation in the southwestern Pacific was rather different from the situation on the northwestern
coast of North America, in that the relevant substrate languages were all
genetically related, many of them relatively closely—and also, as we have
seen, in that the surface structures of substrate and superstrate languages
are much more alike than they might have been. But as we have seen,
their differences allowed considerable variability in the grammatical analy-

ses used by various participants in this sustained multilingual encounter, and in their discourse strategies in using a developing lingua franca.

Another set of data not only will serve to confirm the existence of yet another possible pronominal paradigm in use in the late nineteenth and early twentieth centuries; but would seemingly also confirm that the line of analysis I have taken, in distinguishing FPs and SRPs and in proposing alternative paradigms, is correct. In this pattern, quite congruent with the Oceanic system, nonsingular SRPs are marked for person; but they assume the same form as the corresponding singular forms. That is, the pattern set out below represents a generalization of the pattern in the tabulation on p. 163.

Plural	FP	SRP
1 inclusive	iumi	(iumi ?)
1 exclusive	mifala	mi
2	iufala	iu
3	olgeta	i

Consider, in illustration, the following fragment. We find three times in the sentences in London's version of Adam and Eve (1909: 363) "me fellow me" (*mifala mi*), as in "Me fella me savvee talk along white man." Here, if London is correct (and not mistaking "me fella" as a demonstrative, or "fella" as a noun), we find an FP fully marked for both person and nonsingular number paired with a short pronoun marked for person but *not* for number. The same pattern seems to be represented in a fragment of the (Queensland-derived) pidgin of the Papuan coast, apparently recorded in 1907. A Papuan preacher is here haranguing local villagers:

You New-Ginn man, you no look out that Fellow Man along-top. Suppose you no look out, you too much sick. Suppose you look out along Him, He look out along you (Chignell 1909: 96).*

This would seem to represent one (never regularized) outcome of a recurrent search for pronominal forms equivalent to the Oceanic SRPs, shorter than the FPs and carrying just enough semantic information to maintain reference. Indeed, there is some further evidence of such usages in first- and second-person nonsingular, in the post-1900 New Hebrides— usages where the SRP assumes the form used in singular, with the nonsingular reference established indexically or within the subject NP. From Alexander (1927: 214), who was in the New Hebrides before 1914, we find:

---

*However, in the context of a sermon, one cannot be certain that "New-Ginn man" is used with a plural reference; the preacher could be speaking individually to each of his listeners.

Master 'e speak, "Now *you sickis feller you* go along big feller boat, altogether catch 'im [they have] one bokkis you fight 'im 'e sing out [i.e., a piano]." *Me feller me* go along boat. Bokkis 'e stop along hole belong boat [the hold]. By 'n by Kong Kong [Chinese] 'e fas 'im rope along bokis you fight 'im 'e sing out. Now one big feller machine 'e got long feller 'and too much [a crane], 'e put 'im along worf.

The patterns in italic type are so patently Oceanic that I find in them quite strong confirmation that Islanders acquiring pidgin as adults, in the late nineteenth and early twentieth centuries, used the pronominal system in an Oceanic manner, with a set of FPs and a set of SRPs. And I find in them strong confirmation that alternative analyses were being used. We get yet further confirmation of both points if we recall the patterns, illustrated earlier, where English-derived subject pronouns were being used as SRPs in first- and third-person plural: *mifala wi* and *olgeta de*.

The data on Solomons Pidgin I analyze in Chapters 11–13 strongly suggest that variant analyses reflected variant patterns in the substrate languages. Pidgin, as it had developed by the onset of the Labor Trade, had a strongly Oceanic character that allowed of such analyses in terms of substrate languages.

The data suggest to me that, for New Hebrideans in the Labor Trade at least, the stabilization in the pronominal forms used as objects/possessives and as free (i.e., focal) subject pronouns was not matched by a corresponding stabilization of a set of pronouns used within VPs (and equivalent syntactically to the Oceanic SRPs) as the obligatory subject markers within clauses. The variation in the amount and nature of semantic marking of the SRPs in the Oceanic languages of the New Hebrides allows us, I think, to understand why such stabilization was slow and incomplete, and how and why alternative and relatively unstable paradigms emerged and persisted there well into this century (and why, as Charpentier argues, alternative patterns still exist in the Bislama of older speakers in rural areas).

To sum up: I see in the textual record of the late nineteenth century and in daughter dialects strong evidence that pidgin was developing a pronominal system paralleling the systems of Oceanic languages in its general structure, although its lexical forms came (with considerable bending) from English. In this system, subject pronouns fitted into two grammatical slots. One set, identical to the object/possessive pronouns, was used in the subject-NP slot. The singular forms (at least) were optional, and served to topicalize or emphasize pronominal reference. A second set of subject pronouns fitted into the verb phrase; at least for singular forms, these were the obligatory subject pronouns of a clause or sentence. The plural forms were much less stable than the singular forms: I have presented several alternative paradigms that seem to be represented in the texts or implied by usage in daughter dialects.

If my analysis is correct, the so-called "predicate marker" that has so intrigued analysts of Tok Pisin is nothing more, and nothing less, than a short, unmarked form of subject-referencing pronoun, used (in some versions of pidgin) as a generalized nonsingular pronoun (and in other versions as a third-person pronoun unmarked for number). When used as a generalized nonsingular pronoun, it is the cousin—indeed we might note that it is an almost identical twin—of the SRP in Mota: *i.*

Why, then, call it a "predicate marker" and not a pronoun? It maintains reference anaphorically. Does it mark predicates? Since in Oceanic languages, SRPs have a secondary syntactic role of marking the bases that follow as verbs, and marking the phrases in which they occur as VPs, we might imaginably call them (among other things) "verbal predicate markers." However, as I have illustrated for Pohnpeian and Kwaio, where in an Oceanic language some predicates (equational predicates, prepositional phrases) are nonverbal, the subject pronouns used with them must be the FPs, not the SRPs. In other Oceanic languages, equational sentences are treated as if they were verbal (in "Manu is a curer," the SRP is used, and the noun "curer" is used, on the model of stative verbs, as if it were the stative verb 'be a curer'). Similarly, prepositional phrases are made into verbal constructions with verbs meaning 'be located at' or 'be with.'

Once we perceive that what are ostensibly adjectives in Melanesian Pidgin are being used as stative verbs, when they follow the "predicate marker"—and recall that such a realization for Indian Ocean creoles came belatedly and recently from the work of Corne (1981) on Ile de France Creole—then we perceive why the "predicate marker" marks verbal predicates: it is not a copula. In *hem i big-fala*, the predicate is the VP 'it be big.' But are there verbless sentences in Melanesian Pidgin dialects? We have very limited data on these points for local dialects of Melanesian Pidgin; moreover, if we were led to ask questions about substrate languages and how speakers of particular Oceanic languages use pidgin, we would confront the fact that there are very few Oceanic languages of Melanesia for which we have good evidence on these points.

My own data from the Solomons indicate that the substrate languages vary a good deal in their treatment of equational sentences and locative and other prepositional sentences; and they indicate the way in which patterns in substrate languages shape pidgin usage. I showed in Chapter 6 how in Kwaio, prepositional sentences ("He is at the seacoast," "He is with his brother") are nonverbal. The FP, rather than the SRP, must be used. Kwaio speakers of Solomons Pidgin correspondingly use *hem long*

solowata or *hem weit-em barata bulong hem.* They also could use the verb
stap 'be located, exist' in such constructions. Speakers of the nearby
To'abaita language of northern Malaita have an intransitive verb exactly
corresponding to *stap* in their language; we may guess that they use verbal
constructions in Solomons Pidgin. My data suggest parallel patterns with
equational sentences, which can be treated as verbal (with the coordinate
noun treated as if it were a stative verb, which as I noted is a common
Oceanic pattern) or as nonverbal.

The pervasiveness of nonverbal constructions, both in equational sentences and in locative sentences, in Solomons Pidgin is illustrated at several points in this short passage recorded in 1986 from a middle-aged Fa-
taleka (Malaita) speaker who had learned Pidgin on prewar plantations:

olsem	tu-fala	waeteman	mifala	go	wak	fo	tufala
so	two-ADJ	European	SRPweE	AUX	work	for	them2

The two Europeans we went and worked for

long	dea	long	Bugotu,	tu-fala	hafkas	nomoa,	ia?
LOC	there	LOC	Bugotu,	two-ADJ	half-caste	only	RHET

there at Bugotu were just half-castes.

faata	bulong	tufala	long	araikwao,	maata	bulong	tufala,
father	POSS	them2	LOC	European	mother	POSS	them2

Their father was European, their mother

—	boe	nomoa.	Tufala	ia,	wan-fala	Sedrik,	'anaa	wan-fala
—	native	only	FPthey2	DEM	one-ADJ	Cedric,	and	one-ADJ

— only a native. One of the two was Cedric and the other

Eriki.	Hem	nao	tufala	araikwao	mitufala	go	waka	long
Eric	FP(it)	TOP	two-ADJ	European	SRPwe2E	AUX	work	LOC

Eric. Those are the two Europeans the two of us went to work

olketa	nao	ia,	taem	olketa	istap	long	Kosaruru	ia,	long
them	PRF	DEI	when	SRPthey	stay	LOC	Gojaruru	DEI	LOC

for, when they were there at Gojaruru, on

Bugotu.	Nao	mifala	go	waka	mifala	go	istap	longo
Bugotu	Then	SRPweE	AUX	work	SRPweE	AUX	stay	LOC

Isabel. So we went and worked, we stayed on

aelan	ia
island	DEI

that island

olketa	kol-em	long	Fera,	destaem	eafiri	long	hem	nao.
FPthey	call-TRS	LOC	Fera	now	airfield	LOC	it	PRF

they call Fera, which has an airfield on it now.

The first three sentences here are equational, lacking verbs and "predicate markers";* the final clause is locative, and it, too, is nonverbal. Exactly seventy years earlier, the entomologist W. H. Mann (1948: 482) had recorded, in the speech of a Choiseulese police sergeant, what seems to be a verbless equational clause followed by verbal clauses (including a stative clause and two prepositional clauses): "Him big fellow master, he 'nother kind; he no catch'm coconut, he no belong sekool, he no belong gov'ment."†

Is there evidence of such nonverbal constructions in nineteenth-century pidgin? Consider the following sentences in the 1890s New Hebridean pidgin recorded by Pionnier (1913: 194): "Nème long Big fala Masta ia God." This *ia* is a demonstrative, from English "here"; there is no "predicate marker" in this equational sentence, or in "Nème bilong San bilong God, Jesus" (p. 195). With a prepositional phrase as predicate, Pionnier (p. 196) gives us: "Ouata bilong you ouat plece?" and "Oumane i goud toumeutch maman bilong him, Papa bilong hème no long graoun ('The father and mother of the very good woman are not on earth')."

Here we have exactly the same pattern found in Kwaio, and in the way Kwaio speakers use Solomons Pidgin, but occurring in the New Hebrides pidgin of the 1890s. This constitutes strong though not conclusive evidence that verbless sentences occurred in the Bichelamar of Malekula, at least, and that they contained no "predicate marker." In these sentences there are no third-person singular subject pronouns at all, however, so the case is far from certain. But we find further confirmatory evidence elsewhere in Pionnier's data. As translation for *celles-ci*, he gives "olguita oumane hème ia" (1914: 188), which probably represents a prepositional relative clause:

olgeta wuman hem   ia
PLU   woman FP(him)   DEM
the women who are here. . . .

The pattern is characteristically Oceanic; compare Kwaio:

wane bobola'a ngai   lo'oo
man   black   FP(him)   DEM
this Melanesian man (lit. "black man who is here").

---

*Except for the embedded relative clause in the first sentence. The first two sentences have no subject pronouns at all; the third has a focal pronoun, clearly distinguishable as such by the following deictic.

†Here, as always, we are at the mercy of our scribe; in a few other places Mann uses "him" where "he" was almost certainly actually used.

What is most significant in this fragment from Pionnier is the use of what I take to be the FP *hem*, rather than the SRP *i*.

Another fragment, from a less reliable scribe, is an utterance recorded on Tanna in the early 1880s: "This big fellow man belong a ——, some place with an unpronounceable name" (Thomas 1886: 260).

A tidbit of evidence on this point, from the Queensland Pidgin old Solomons Islanders (who would have learned pidgin as young men in the 1880s and 1890s) were using in Mackay, northern Queensland, in the early 1930s, comes from Noel Fatnowna (n.d.). Fatnowna, grandson of a Malaitan, grew up speaking pidgin in Mackay. He was instructed in Malaita customs by old men who had experienced nineteenth-century blood feuding among the Kanakas. He describes in his autobiographical account how he and other young boys were warned not to sleep against the thatched walls of the men's houses. The elders warned that an enemy might creep up to the wall, identify who was sleeping next to it—saying to himself *hem ia nao* 'here he is'—and spear his victim through the thatch. Here we have (in this recalled Queensland Pidgin) the FP rather than the SRP used in a verbless locative sentence—exactly as in Solomons Pidgin as used by Malaitans.

The data on these points for contemporary local dialects of Melanesian Pidgin (and Melanesian Oceanic languages) are unfortunately incomplete. But they suggest that if, in labeling the "predicate markers" of Melanesian Pidgin, we chose to emphasize their syntactic function in marking what follows, rather than their discourse-strategic function of referencing the subject anaphorically, they would turn out to be "verbal predicate markers," again functioning in the same way as the SRPs of Oceanic languages. I see nothing to be gained in regarding them as other than pronouns, however limited their semantic content in particular Melanesian Pidgin dialects.

The Oceanic structures of Melanesian Pidgin dialects, and the continuing bending of these structures in the direction of substrate languages in this century, by adults learning pidgin in plantation contexts, become even more clear when we narrow our view to Solomons Pidgin: the least known, least well-documented dialect of Melanesian Pidgin, but one that embodies crucial clues to its underlying structures and historical dynamics.

The Development of Solomons Pidgin

THE PROCESSES through which Solomons Pidgin ac-
quired patterns somewhat different from those of the antecedent pidgin of
Queensland, and from the Bislama of Vanuatu, further illuminate the
mechanisms of language change I have sketched. In this chapter and the
two that follow, I shall first examine the general process of change, arguing that the Malaita languages have had a particularly strong impact on
the development of pidgin in the Solomons since separation of the Solomons and New Hebrides pidgin speech communities, and showing some
clear markers of that impact. In Chapter 12, I look again in detail at pronouns. I will show that Solomon Islanders reanalyzed the pronominal system of Queensland Pidgin (or at least, seized on one of its alternative possibilities) so as to encode distinctions (and hence preserve discourse
strategies) in substrate languages. The result is that, with further minor
bending, speakers of Malaita languages can use Solomons Pidgin in ways
directly congruent with, and calqued on, the syntactic patterns of these
native languages—and still produce acceptable linguistic coin in the
plantation settings and other multilingual situations in which pidgin has,
until recently, been mainly used. In Chapter 13, focusing on Kwaio (a
Malaita language) but illustrating with data from speakers of other Solomons languages, I illustrate how closely and pervasively this calquing
operates—hence coming back to the puzzle with which I began the first
chapter. This calquing is further illustrated in the Appendix.

Whereas Mühlhäusler (1981, 1986) has argued that substrate models
will have an impact on a developing pidgin only at certain crucial points
in its development, the data I have set out so far suggest that as long as
speakers of relatively closely related languages are the numerically pre-

ponderant (if politically subordinate) participants within a multilingual pidgin-using community, the process of bending a lingua franca in the direction of substrate languages can be continuous, through the period in which the pidgin remains a secondary language acquired in adulthood. Mufwene (1986: 142) has anticipated exactly these continuities in the development of Pacific pidgin dialects:

> Their long pre-creole stages do not affect the fact that they can still be making their structural selections from the substrate or superstrate languages. . . .
> The fact that [particular patterns modeled on substrate languages] have developed late does not reduce their identity as substrate influence as long as they have contributed, or are contributing, to the formation of the structures of these languages, making them more responsive to the communicative needs of their speakers.

In the Solomons, this process of bending in the direction of the dominant substrate languages continued until the mid-1960s, when Solomons Pidgin increasingly became the primary language of an expanding urban speech community (Jourdan 1985).

Although Solomons Pidgin in its contemporary urban forms and the urban Bislama of Vanuatu differ markedly in some respects, the apparent gulf between them is misleading. First, in each country rural speakers use pidgin in the phonological patterns of their native languages, and the relatively arbitrary choice of different orthographic conventions for the two dialects creates a spurious impression of uniformity for each dialect and of contrast between them. As Charpentier (1979) has shown convincingly for Bislama, the establishment of a supposedly standard form disguises the marked regional variations in lexical content and grammatical usages (even though these latter variations may to a substantial degree represent choices among the alternative syntactic pathways available in a more or less common language; the variation is almost certainly greater in Bislama than in Solomons Pidgin, partly because for many speakers the dominant superstrate language in this century has been French; their Bislama incorporates a substantial French-derived lexicon).

Not surprisingly, the further we go back in time, the more similar the two dialects are. Solomon Islanders and Ni-Vanuatu (New Hebrideans) who acquired their pidgin dialects as young adults in the internal plantation systems of the 1920s and 1930s were, after all, learning dialects that had only been separated for some twenty years. The contrasts between them fell well within the range of variation, phonological and grammatical, among the versions of pidgin spoken in the New Hebrides or Solomons, or at an earlier period in Queensland. That is, the contrast between the pidgin of a speaker from Tanna or Aneityum in the southern

New Hebrides and Ambae (Aoba) or Maewo in the northern New Hebrides, as of 1920 or 1930, or between a speaker from Malaita and a speaker
from Santa Cruz or Choiseul, was probably greater than the contrast between the pidgin of the Maewo speaker and that of the Malaitan.

In the chapters that follow, I will focus on Solomons Pidgin as it is
spoken by older men from rural areas who acquired their command of the
language before World War II, in traditional contexts of plantation work,
and who have been relatively isolated from the further linguistic changes
under way since the 1960s. In 1984, Christine Jourdan showed a film
taken by the anthropologist Bud Jackson on Santo, northern Vanuatu, in
which "bush" speakers enacted episodes in the Labor Trade, to older
speakers of Malaita "bush" pidgin. Jourdan wanted to test the degree to
which the Malaita pidgin speakers could understand the "bush" pidgin
from Santo, and to record their comments about the Bislama used on the
film. The result confirmed what had been transparent to me in seeing the
film several years before, and in listening to tapes: that these dialects are
so close as to permit a very high degree of intelligibility. I have no doubt
that if a dozen men in their sixties and seventies from more remote village
areas of northern Vanuatu were transplanted now to bush settlements on
Malaita, they could communicate without difficulty with their Solomons
contemporaries in a pidgin that had diverged only minimally in the two
plantation communities by the 1930s. The changes consisted more in reanalysis and minor rearrangement of forms common to the two diverging
pidgin dialects than in the innovation of new forms.

But what reanalyses and rearrangements? And if substrate languages
played an important part, which languages could they plausibly have been?

I shall show that in the latter stages of the Queensland Labor Trade,
when Solomon Islanders became the numerically dominant element in
the labor force, they were mainly speakers of Southeast Solomonic languages. I will show that of these Southeast Solomonic speakers, the numerically dominant component were speakers of Malaita languages, themselves closely related.

I will go on to show that when the pidgin speech communities of the
southwestern Pacific were separated at the beginning of this century, and
an internal plantation system was established in the Solomons, the predominant component of the labor force again consisted of speakers of
Southeast Solomonic languages; and among these, Malaitans were again
the dominant component.

Price and Baker (1976) usefully summarize the statistical evidence on
the island sources of Queensland recruits by five-year periods. We can examine their data from several directions. A first is to set out the percentage of Islanders from the entire Solomons group in relation to the total

TABLE 11.1

Solomon Islanders and Southeast Solomonic Speakers as Percentage of All Recruits
to Queensland, by Five-Year Periods, 1868–1904

Period	Solomon Islanders	Southeast Solomonic speakers	Period	Solomon Islanders	Southeast Solomonic speakers
1868–1872	2.2%	1.5%	1888–1892	43.2%	41.9%
1873–1877	10.3	9.1	1893–1897	51.5	50.5
1878–1882	14.9	13.7	1898–1904	62.1	60.0
1883–1887	22.7	17.9			

SOURCE: Price and Baker (1976).

TABLE 11.2

Southeast Solomonic Speakers as Percentage of All Solomons Recruits to Queensland,
by Five-Year Periods, 1868–1904

Period	Southeast Solomonic	Other Oceanic	Non-Austronesian
1868–1872	70.7%	29.3%	—
1873–1877	90.0	1.8	8.2%
1878–1882	92.4	3.9	3.7
1883–1887	86.7	6.2	7.0
1888–1892	96.9	—	3.1
1893–1897	98.1	—	1.8
1898–1904	98.9	—	1.1

SOURCE: Same as Table 11.1.
NOTE: Rows do not necessarily total 100 because of rounding.

number of recruits who went to Queensland (Table 11.1). We can re-
calculate these figures, taking as our target group speakers of Southeast
Solomonic languages as a percentage of the total number of recruits to
Queensland. Some of the islands (e.g., Isabel) have speakers of both
Southeast Solomonic and other Oceanic languages; I have erred on the
low side in calculating percentages of Southeast Solomonic speakers. A
comparison of the figures will show that throughout the Labor Trade to
Queensland, it was speakers of these languages who were the preponderant Solomons component of the Queensland labor force.

We can calculate the percentages of speakers of (1) Southeast Solomonic; (2) other Oceanic Austronesian; and (3) non-Austronesian languages in relation to the total number of Solomon Islanders recruited to
Queensland in these five-year periods (Table 11.2).

Most Solomons recruits came from Malaita, Guadalcanal, Makira (San
Cristobal), Gela, and smaller islands where Southeast Solomonic languages are spoken. Throughout the period, only a tiny trickle of recruits

came from other islands in the Solomons group (e.g., New Georgia, Choiseul, Shortlands, and Santa Cruz). Similar percentages turn up, not surprisingly, in Siegel's (1987) calculation of labor recruiting for Fiji, although this is less salient for the development of pidgin. Listed below are the percentages of Southeast Solomonic speakers recruited to Fiji as a proportion of the total labor force recruited from the Solomons, as reconstructed from Siegel.

Period	Southeast Solomonic	Other Oceanic	Non-Austronesian
1876–1887	95.5%	4.2%	0.3%
1888–1899	98.6	1.2	—
1900–1911	98.8	0.9	0.1

Which Southeast Solomonic languages were represented in these totals? The total Solomons labor force in Queensland can be divided to show the percentages of islanders originating in the four main island groups where Southeast Solomonic is spoken (in Table 11.3, I count Ulawa with Malaita and Ao Raha, Ao Riki, and Uki with Makira, a grouping based on linguistic connections).

A comparison of Table 11.1 with Table 11.3 shows that in the period when Solomon Islanders began to be statistically predominant in the Queensland Labor Trade, speakers of Malaita languages were becoming increasingly preponderant within this Solomons component of the labor force. Siegel's Fiji data show the same trend toward Malaita dominance; the percentage of Solomon Islanders who were speakers of Malaita languages rose from 61.0 percent in 1876–87 to 76.2 percent in 1888–89 and to 88.3 percent in 1900–1911 (Siegel 1987).

The numerical dominance of Malaitans in the Solomons labor force,

TABLE 11.3

Origins of Southeast Solomonic Speakers in the Queensland Labor Force, by Five-Year Periods, 1868–1904

Period	Number	Percentage from:				
		Malaita	Guadalcanal	Makira	Gela	Other
1868–1882	82	8.5%	14.6%	11.0%	36.6%	29.3%
1873–1877	910	48.6	20.4	12.2	8.8	10.0
1878–1882	1,688	31.6	35.4	10.2	15.2	7.6
1883–1887	2,891	43.2	26.9	4.4	12.2	13.3
1888–1892	3,588	47.3	29.0	1.9	18.7	8.8
1893–1897	3,084	58.6	24.6	3.3	11.6	1.9
1898–1904	5,081	70.9	16.0	5.7	6.3	1.1

SOURCE: Reconstructed from Siegel (1987).

with Guadalcanal speakers as a second but much smaller component, continued with the development of an internal plantation system. Figures from the 1920s show Malaitans accounting for 65–70 percent of the Solomons labor force (Keesing 1986). Speakers of Southeast Solomonic languages probably remained a more or less constant 85–90 percent of the total Solomons labor force, plantation and domestic, until World War II.

It should not be surprising that substrate influences on Solomons Pidgin, if any, contributing to its differentiation from Bislama should have come from Southeast Solomonic languages. And although the major grammatical patterns of Southeast Solomonic languages are quite similar, we should not be surprised if Malaita languages had left some special grammatical and lexical impress on a distinctive Solomons Pidgin.

In this and the next two chapters, especially Chapter 13, I will bring us back to the puzzle with which I began the book: that a speaker of a Malaita language has for decades been able to acquire fluency in a "bush" dialect of Solomons Pidgin through the grammatical mold of his own language, learning new lexical and grammatical labels as equivalents to forms in his native language and following most of the syntactic patterns and discourse strategies of that native language. The range of syntactic constructions used in Solomons Pidgin is very similar to that in Southeast Solomonic languages; and many of the pidgin lexical items are already present as loanwords in the indigenous languages of the Solomons. Scant wonder that fluency in Solomons Pidgin as a plantation lingua franca has been acquired very quickly, often in a matter of a few weeks.

Yet the pidgin so acquired—by a Malaita speaker, or with scarcely more difficulty, a Guadalcanal speaker—has been essentially fully intelligible to other participants in the Solomons plantation speech community, despite phonological differences and some variations in constructional choices. I am not talking about strange local dialects of Solomons Pidgin (like some New Guinea Highlands versions of Tok Pisin), the result of calquing, which are virtually intelligible to "mainstream" speakers; I am talking about the dialect that was common coin of Solomons plantation speech communities for sixty years, and is still used by Pidgin speakers from rural villages who have not participated in the new urban speech community.

The close correspondence between Solomons Pidgin and Southeast Solomonic languages represents in part the bending of Queensland Pidgin in a Southeast Solomonic direction, in some quite specific ways that will be examined in the pages to follow. But such bending could in turn have been possible only if the Queensland Pidgin of the 1890s already had a very strong Oceanic Austronesian cast. I have shown in the preceding three chapters that Queensland Pidgin already embodied a global syntactic pattern, a mechanism for marking agent-object relationships through a transitive suffix, possessive and causative constructions, and a pronominal system, all of which corresponded to fundamental Oceanic structures—structures clearly and directly represented in Southeast Solomonic languages.

I shall attempt no systematic comparison between Bislama and Solomons Pidgin. Our data on both dialects are insufficient, both in regard to texts and in regard to regional variations, to permit effective comparison.* I shall here examine, in advance of the analysis of pronouns, three specific shifts in Solomons Pidgin that can be documented with some confidence. Before turning to these patterns, however, it is worth illustrating the problem of lack of evidence.

Charpentier (1979: 179), one of our principal authorities on New Hebrides Bislama, comments that students who have had sustained contact with Tok Pisin or Solomons Pidgin have introduced into Bislama a regularization of the transitive suffix *-im*. He illustrates with *luk-im* 'see someone' in place of the older Bislama *lukluk*, and *lukaot-em* 'supervise, watch over someone' (French *surveiller quelqu'un*) in place of the original *lukaot*.

Both *luk-im* and *lukaot-em* are standard in Solomons Pidgin. Moreover, they correspond directly to forms widespread in Malaita (and other Southeast Solomonic) languages: the transitive suffix marks the contrast between an intransitive verb and its transitive counterpart, as in Kwaio:

> (aga)aga   'look'
> aga-si-   'see (s.t.)'

Does this then mean that Solomons Pidgin generalized the transitive suffix beyond the range of its use in Queensland Pidgin, following patterns in substrate languages? Does it mean that Bislama lost the marking of transitive suffixes on some verbs because of usages in substrate languages? Or does it mean that Bislama speakers in the particular historically French-dominated region Charpentier knows best do not use these forms although they are used elsewhere in Vanuatu? (The supposedly borrowed forms are represented in Jacques Guy's [1974] and Camden's [1977] dictionaries.) Any attempt to do a systematic comparison of the two dia-

---

*Christine Jourdan, whose Ph.D. thesis (1985) and field data do much to fill the gap in documentation of Solomons Pidgin, was unfortunately allowed—because her period of research coincided with an almost complete ban on research by expatriates—to work only on Guadalcanal, and hence could not document extensively variations in Pidgin usage in rural communities. For Vanuatu, ongoing research by Darrell Tryon and Jean-Michel Charpentier on regional differences in Bislama should do much to clarify the range and nature of dialectal variation.

lects, or to reconstruct the process of divergence in detail, immediately runs afoul of so many problems of this sort that the exercise quickly becomes relatively arbitrary. However, some inferences can be made with confidence.

There is clear evidence in the nineteenth-century texts that *bin* was being used in the southwestern Pacific to indicate that a described event or state occurred or existed in the past, or that it had been completed. This form is widely distributed in Northern Hemisphere creoles, and we may assume that it was one of the elements in a nautical pidgin carried to the Pacific by early whalers and traders. Since it is standard in Tok Pisin and Bislama, we can on distributional as well as textual grounds place its standardization in Pacific pidgin prior to 1890. *Bin* occurs in sentences (20), (26), and (29) in Chapter 4, recorded 1877–78 and 1884 in widely spread parts of the southwestern Pacific (the New Hebrides, the Ile des Pins, and the Bismarcks). While this form turns up sporadically in the early Solomons texts, it has virtually disappeared in the pidgin of older Solomon Islanders who learned it as a plantation language before World War II.

In place of *bin*, these Solomon Islanders use a device exactly corresponding to one universal in the Malaita languages: the perfect marker *nao*, in the VP following the verb (but occasionally in clause-final position). In the texts set out in the next two chapters, and in the Appendix, the ways in which this perfect marker is used will be abundantly illustrated. As I have explicated in my *Kwaio Grammar* (1985), the corresponding perfect-marking particles in the Malaita languages articulate a state at a reference time (the time of the speech event) to an earlier state or event to indicate that the two are essentially and inseparably connected, and to focus attention on the present state. Thus, they can indicate that the action of a verb has taken place in the past, or that it is presently under way. With stative verbs, they indicate that a state (of becoming hot, of growing, of breaking, and so on) has finished coming into being or being realized. *Nao* in Solomons Pidgin has exactly the same grammatical and semantic force (scant wonder that very few European speakers of Pidgin use it "properly"). Thus compare Solomons Pidgin *nao* in *hem-i go nao long sitoa* 'He already went to the store' or 'He's on his way to the store' with Kwaio *no'o* in *ngai e leka no'o naa sitoa* 'He already went to the store' or 'He's on his way to the store.'

Interestingly, and probably not coincidentally, the perfect-marking particles in all the Malaita languages consist of n(VV) (with the two vowels sometimes separated by a glottal stop). Moreover, as Linda Simons (1985) has pointed out, the same particle (sometimes slightly modified) serves in the Malaita languages as a topicalizer. Following a noun or pronoun in the slot preceding the VP (usually a subject NP), n(VV) as topicalizer serves to emphasize the noun as topic. Thus, compare Solomons Pidgin *hem nao i wak-em* 'He's the one who did it' with Kwaio *ngai ne-'e age-a* 'He's the one who did it' (here *ne-'e* is a contraction of *no'o* + SRP) and *gila no'o la age-a* 'They're the ones who did it.'

Solomon Islanders also use another resource for marking the completion of an action, the form *finis* as the second verb in compound verbal constructions. This form is manifest in all three major Melanesian Pidgin dialects, and is attested in late-nineteenth-century texts.

The form *nao* is used in some more limited contexts in Bislama, to indicate that an action is under way, or that a state has come into existence, as in these sentences given by Charpentier: "*mi mi slip nao* 'maintenant, moi je dors'" (now I'm going to sleep) and "*em i big-man finis nao*" 'he has now become an important leader.' *Nao* must have been part of the grammatical repertoire available in Queensland Pidgin at the end of the nineteenth century. We find it in Pionnier's data from Malekula in the 1890s. For French *maintenant* he gives "naouia," which transparently is *nao ia* (1913: 192); and he gives sentences such as "you fraïlle naou ol taïme 'vous avez peur maintenant' [you're now in a state of fear]" (p. 196).

As might be expected, *bin* is by no means completely absent in the early Solomons texts, although I have found relatively few attestations:

The natives on the beach me been see take one fellow box, they carry him away along scrub; "boy" been have dat box he run away too (a court recorder's version of testimony by a Tikopian; Queensland, 1896).

My word, I no savey which way I no been kill that white man. He no carry him musket—he carry nothing. One time altogether man belong me he stop all round doctor—he one fellow. I got cartridge along my musket, and I went to shoot him. I try but I can't (Deck 1910).*

Me savvy, he all the same where man no gottem leg because dockiter been cut him off finish. Now he catchem new one along timber. New feller tooth he all the same. Me savvy (an Isabel speaker, 1913; Knibbs 1929: 76).

Me been try him B. P. and Lever [Burns, Philp and Lever's, major plantation enterprises]. This time me try him another place. . . . Me been try him Faisi two time and Rubiana two time. Altogether place belong one kind he one kind. No matter, me try him Lever this time (*Planter's Gazette*, Dec. 1922: 18).

In these citations, as always, the sources are unreliable; but cumulatively, they provide evidence that—not surprisingly—*bin* was in at least sporadic use into the 1920s.

*Much of the rendering of the Pidgin here is fanciful, so the "been" is suspect.

Our evidence for the use of *nao* in this period is similarly limited. Predictably we find it recorded only in those contexts where the use of English "now" would be semantically appropriate. Thus:

The day before he die he tell-'im altogether heathen people about Jesus, he tell-'im "Me go now; me no fright, Jesus He come for me" (1910; Young 1926: 207).

Me Suinau. Me good fellow now (1916; Mann 1948: 294).

This last is a particularly nice example because the man's name, recorded as "Suinau," is in fact constructed out of the stative verb *sui* 'be finished' plus a northern Malaita version of the perfect-marking particle: the name, rendered in Solomons Pidgin, would be "Finis-Nao."

But judging by the speech of the oldest speakers from whom I have recorded extensive texts—men who learned Solomons Pidgin in the early 1920s and have had limited contact with it since—the perfect-marking *nao* had effectively replaced *bin* by this stage in the development of Solomons Pidgin. The excerpts in the next chapter, which illustrate developments in the pronominal system, also compellingly show this change.

However, once more we should not be surprised to find parallel shifts in parts of Vanuatu. Charpentier (1979: 353) comments that in "the region of the capital, Port Vila, and among the young people educated in British schools, a past durative *bin* is in use [my translation]." Charpentier gives as an example *mi bin stap long aeland ya.* "Never," he says, "do the old Melanesians of South Malekula utter such a phrase. This aspect marker *bin* is not part of the lexicon of the pidgin they use. No such aspect marker exists in the vernacular languages of this region" (p. 353). The hypothesis implied by Charpentier's comment, that *bin* is the new and intrusive form, is doubtful in view of the extensive attestations of *bin* in nineteenth-century pidgin in the New Hebrides, and across a wide region of the southwestern Pacific, and in view of the presence of *bin* in Tok Pisin.

The virtual disappearance of *bin* must count as one of the diagnostic points of divergence between Solomons Pidgin and other dialects of Melanesian Pidgin. (This must be qualified for the contemporary period, since *bin* has been reintroduced through contacts with Tok Pisin, and is becoming common in the Solomon Islands Broadcasting Company version of Pidgin and is being used in some urban registers.) In view of the preponderant presence of Malaitans in the labor force since the turn of the century, it should hardly surprise us that the direction of change has been one that has brought Solomons Pidgin into close parallel with the Malaita languages.

A second line of development takes us back to the "prepositional verbs." Recall from Chapter 8 that Bislama and Solomons Pidgin incorporate a prepositional verb *wet-em* 'with (s.o.).'* For Bislama, Charpentier (1979: 374) gives as an extract from a story:

o	yu-fela	i	kranki	be	bae	yu-mi	tes	kakae	wanem
oh	youPl	SRP	be crazy	but	FUT	we(Incl)	ASP	eat	what

Oh! You're crazy, but what are we going to eat

wet-em	kakae	nao	ya?
with-TTS	food	now	RHET

with this [vegetable] food?

Jacomb (1914: 102) gives "me me go widim you" from the New Hebridean Pidgin of about 1900.

Solomons Pidgin has developed a further set of forms used as prepositional verbs.† In Chapter 6, I set out some Kwaio prepositional verbs including 'with,' 'against,' 'around,' 'about,' and 'away from.' In Kwaio, the relationship of these prepositional verbs to their objects is, as with transitive verbs, marked either with transitive suffix + pronominal clitic or by the clitic alone. Solomons Pidgin incorporates a similar set, marked with transitive suffixes but used as prepositions:

wet-em	'with'
agens-em	'against'
abaot-em	'about'
raon-em	'around' (also used as intransitive verb)

Other forms less commonly recorded include *koros-im* and *antap-em*, as in

hem-i	tas	go	koros-im
SRP(he)	ASP	go	across-TTS

He just went across (it),

given by Fifi'i as equivalent to Kwaio (Malaita):

me-'e	bi'i	leka	folo-si-a
and-SRP(he)	ASP	go	across-TTS-it

And he just went across (it).

and in the following, from a Simbo (western Solomons) speaker:

dee	diamp	antap-em	evri	pipol	ia
SRP(they)	jump	on-TTS	all	people	DEM

They jumped on all those people.

---

*The phonological shape varies, and may be *weit-em* or *wit-im*.
†Terry Crowley advises me (January 1988) that some Bislama speakers use further prepositional verbs, including *agens-em*, *raon-em*, and *kas-em*, so this development may well antedate the separation of New Hebridean and Solomons dialects.

These forms fit into exactly the same slot as their equivalent forms in Southeast Solomonic languages:

mitufala	stori	nao	wet-em	Dione	ana	Diake
we2E	converse	PRF	with-TRS	Dione	and	Diake

The two of us had a yarn with Dione and Diake.

mifala	put-um	pis	tri	ia	agens-em	doa
weE	put-TRS	piece	tree	DEM	against-TRS	door

We put that log against the door.

Compare Kwaio:

mele	faafata	no'o	fe'e-ni-a	la	Dione	ma	la	Diake
SRP(we2E)	converse	PRF	with-TRS-it	ART	Dione	and	ART	Diake

The two of us had a yarn with Dione and Diake.

meru	aru-a	mee	'ai	no'ona	fono-si-a	sinamaa
SRP(weE)	put-it	piece	tree	DEM	against-TRS-it	door

We put that log against the door.

A third direction of change in Solomons Pidgin is one I have analyzed in some detail elsewhere (Keesing 1986), and which I will outline very briefly here: the grammaticalization of *(bae)bae* as irrealis/future-marker. A more detailed analysis would require reference to the pronominal system, with SRPs fully marked for person and number, which will be our focus in the next chapter.

This marker of irrealis/future is theoretically important because, in the literature, the transformation of what was until recent decades a temporal adverb in sentence- (or clause-)initial position to a grammaticalized pre-verbal particle is supposed to reflect a late phase in Melanesian Pidgin development, particularly associated with incipient creolization (Sankoff and Laberge 1973).

For English speakers, as the source of lexification and the initial input to the process of pidgin formation, "by and by" is a sentence-initial adverbial. Throughout the whole history of pidgin in the Pacific, English speakers have used it this way, and this superstrate usage has provided a kind of anchor holding "by and by" in sentence- (or clause-)initial position. In this constructional pattern, "by and by" precedes a noun subject.

In the substrate languages of the Solomons and Vanuatu, irrealis/future/nonaccomplished mode is characteristically marked with preverbal particles. The most common position for such a particle is suffixed to the SRP; but in a number of these languages, particularly those of the Guadalcanal-Gela subgroup of Southeast Solomonic (see Keesing 1986), this particle precedes or is prefixed to the SRP.

In contrast, the sentence- or clause-initial position in which English speakers invariably place "by and by" is a slot in the substrate languages that can be filled with various temporals and temporal phrases ("today," "next-moon," "last time"), and by modals ("maybe") fronted (from a position in the VP) for emphasis. The pidgin form (*babae, bambae,* or some phonological variant) adopted to establish a future time-frame became regularized in this slot in the nineteenth century. This use of *bambae* as what has been called a "temporal adverb" is not surprising, given the general pattern in pidgins (and creoles) from other parts of the world of not grammaticalizing such elements; and given the continuing pull from superstrate speakers to keep "by and by" in this position.

But here an interesting possibility of a "developmental conspiracy" involving complementary but very different analyses by Oceanic and English speakers opens up, in constructions where the subject is pronominal. In a construction with a noun subject, "by and by" comes either before the noun or after it. But this is not the case in clauses with pronominal subjects, if I am right in my analysis of the late-nineteenth-century use by Oceanic speakers of "he" and "me" as equivalent to the SRPs in substrate languages. Consider the following texts:

You see all Lifu man can't swim, by and bye me drowned (Clark 1979: 37).

Suppose missionary stop here, by and by he speak (Tanna, 1859; McFarlane 1873: 106).

By and by me fellow buy'em gun along man-we-we (1884?; Cromar 1935: 117–18).

By-and-by he like-'im plenty, he come all the time (1886; Young 1926: 47).

Notice that the contrast between the grammars of English speakers and Oceanic speakers with regard to subject pronouns allows three possible alternative analyses of such constructions. In one (which English speakers would use) "by and by" would be a temporal phrase preceding a subject NP, filled by a pronoun. A similar analysis is possible for Oceanic speakers, analyzing "by and by" as a temporal (like "yesterday" or "next-moon") preceding the VP, with its SRP, which is the essential core of the sentence (the subject-NP slot here being empty). But Oceanic speakers could also analyze such sequences as incorporating a tense-marking (or mode-marking) grammatical element *within* the VP, and preceding the SRP.

In sentences where the subject-NP slot is filled with a noun subject, there is much less room for alternative grammatical analyses. English speakers of course will put "by and by" before the noun, and in clause-initial position. Apparently Oceanic speakers in the nineteenth century usually did the same (so that for them, at least up until the 1880s, *bambae* was being used as a temporal equivalent to "next-moon," or possibly as a fronted modal equivalent to "maybe"). But one sentence recorded by Layard in New Caledonia about 1880 (Schuchardt [1883] 1980) indicates that the analysis of *bambae* as a grammatical tense marker in the verb phrase occurred (although it seems not to have been standardized) more than a century ago: "Brother belong-a-me by and by he dead." For an English speaker, the sentence represents an odd topicalization of the noun subject by fronting, but it is quite intelligible coin of the linguistic realm.

The two alternative analyses by Oceanic speakers also, as will be seen, produce different constructions when the subject-NP slot is filled with a focal pronoun. In such constructions, *bambae* either precedes both the FP and the SRP or (if it is being analyzed as a grammatical element in the VP) is interposed between them.

The two analyses seem to have coexisted in the nineteenth century, perhaps with a strong pull from English speakers toward a clause-initial position and a weaker but persistent pull from Oceanic speakers toward the grammaticalization of *bambae* as a future marker within the VP. Because in so many sentences the two analyses produce equivalent strings, and because English speakers can clearly interpret sentences with *bambae* following the subject-NP slot (by mentally rearranging them), such coexistence is not surprising.

Apparently, the two patterns remain possible in contemporary Bislama, but the canonical position of *bambae* is clause-initial, preceding a subject NP. This sequence is clearly visible where both a focal pronoun and an SRP are used. Canonically, in Bislama, the future marker precedes both pronouns. Thus:

bae mi mi blok-im marid ya
I will prevent this marriage.

And:

bambae mi mi ded
I'll be dead (Charpentier 1979: 299, 352).

The *bae mi mi* sequence also turns up in a text from an old Santo speaker (provided to me by Jacques Guy).

Note, however, that the two alternative grammars produce indistinguishable constructions in the many sentences with a single pronominal subject (an SRP). *Bambae* preceding this single subject-pronoun may be there as the initial element of the VP or as the initial element of the clause, separated from the VP by an empty subject-NP slot.

In Solomons Pidgin, the two patterns also remain possible (see Jourdan 1986 for an analysis of *bae* in the Pidgin of Honiara speakers, both adults and children). But for the older speakers whose pronominal patterns I have illustrated, the canonical position for *bambae* (or its shortened form *bae*) is in the VP, preceding an SRP. They sometimes use it preceding a noun subject; however, when they do, it appears still to be used as a grammatical element, fronted for emphasis following the pattern of "might." Some fragments from these older speakers will serve to illustrate. First, from the Kwaio speaker Tome Kwalafane'ia:

Diapani	baebae	hem-i	kam	tudee,	ia
Japan	FUT	SRP(he)	come	today	RHET*

The Japanese are going to come today.

And again,

evriting	olsem	baebae	hem-i	kas-em	iu
everything	like that	FUT	SRP(it)	hit-TRS	you

All those sorts of things could hit you

long	Ruga	bae	iu	dae,	ia
LOC	Lunga	FUT	SRP(you)	die	RHET

and you'd die, right?

From Fifi'i, another Kwaio speaker, we have:

dis-fala	masisi	ia,	nomata	siton,	safosi	thei
DEM-ADJ	matches	DEM	even	stone	if	SRP(they)

These matches

sikras-em	long	hemu,	baebae	hem-i	save	laeti	nomoa
scrape-TRS	LOC	it	FUT	SRP(it)	MOD	ignite	only

will ignite even if you strike one on a stone.

And, speaking of a feral pig,

googo	hem-i	tink-im	ples	wea	hem-i	bon
then	SRP(it)	remember-TRS	place	where	SRP(it)	be born

And then it remembers the place where it was born

long	hem	anaa	big-fala	long	hem,	hem	baebae	i
LOC	it	and	be big-ADJ	LOC	it	FP(him)	FUT	SRP(he)

and grew up, and then

kambaek,	ia
return	RHET

it comes back.

From another Kwaio speaker in his sixties, Maa'eobi, we find the future marker interposed between FP and SRP:

*My analysis of *hem-i* as an SRP is explicated in Chapter 12.

iu	bae	iu	goap	wattaem
FP(you)	FUT	SRP(you)	ascend	when

When will you go up (the hill)?

The Talise (Guadalcanal) speaker Domenico Alebua uses *baebae* within the VP, following a noun subject, even though he here exercises the option of dropping the (here redundant) SRP:

ou,	lotu	ia	baebae	kam,	i	spoel-em
oh	church	DEM	FUT	come	SRP(it)	destroy-TTS

Oh, if this church comes, it will destroy

devol	blong	iumi
ancestor	POSS	us

our ancestors.

From David Koku, a speaker of Gela, I recorded a sentence where the irrealis-marking function of *baebae* is clear:

olketa	sev-em	mifala,	bikosi	mifala	rememba,
SRP(they)	save-TTS	us(Ex)	because	SRP(weEx)	remember

They saved us; because we can recall how

ating	Diapan	baebae	hem-i	spoel-em	mifala
maybe	Japanese	FUT	SRP(he)	destroy-TTS	us(Ex)

it seemed that the Japanese were going to destroy us.

However, placement of the future marker in a slot preceding a noun subject or an FP remains an option: one that apparently serves to emphasize the time-framing or irrealis nature of the verb phrase that follows. Thus from Kwalafane'ia:

nao	mi	tanlaon	nao,	mi	see,	kokonate	long	Rifa	ia,
then	SRP(I)	turn	PRF	SRP(I)	say	coconut	POSS	Lever	DEM

So I turned and said, "These Lever's coconuts—

fosi	mifala	kaikai-em	baebae	olketa	masta	long	Rifa
if	SRP(weE)	eat-TTS	FUT	PLU	master	LOC	Lever

if we ate them, all the Lever's bosses

i	tokotoko	long	mifala,	ia
SRP(3p)	quarrel	LOC	us	RHET

would get angry with us, wouldn't they?"

Jourdan's data on urban speakers (1985, 1986) show both the stabilization of the grammaticalization of the irrealis marker and a shortening of the form reported earlier by Sankoff (Sankoff and Laberge 1973) for Tok Pisin. Although my data show a general drift toward the grammaticalization of the irrealis marker, a process apparently well established by the 1920s, they also suggest that, given the options, it is speakers of those languages where the irrealis marker precedes the SRP (including Kwaio and most of the Guadalcanal languages) who use this option most pervasively. We will examine these processes of bending a common pidgin to fit particular substrate patterns more closely in Chapter 13.

The Solomons data, conjoined with Layard's "brother belong-a-me by and by he dead," suggest that this pattern of the grammaticalization of *bambae* as an irrealis marker within the VP is, at least as a structural possibility, a century old, and long antedates creolization. Whether used in the canonical New Hebridean pattern preceding a noun subject, or the canonical Solomonic pattern in the verb phrase, *bambae* seems by the late nineteenth century to be a grammaticalized form, not simply an adverb temporally framing the clause. Evidence for this comes from the semantic force as well as syntactic placement of *bambae*. If it had been simply a marker of a future time of the clause that followed, it would not, I think, have carried the irrealis implication that it evidently did, even in the nineteenth century. Consider Pionnier's text (1914: 196) from Malekula in the 1890s: "Suppose you ded bambaïll, bèle bilong you i go onetap plece i goud tou meutch." Consider as well another irrealis-marked sentence from the Solomons in the 1870s (Raabe 1927: 119):

"Givum along too much big fella kingum," the Captain ordered the interpreter.
"Too much big kinkum fella sick. Bymby he catchum rum he fella no sick."
['Lots of the chiefs are sick, but if they got rum, they wouldn't be.']

Although speakers of Southeast Solomonic languages, and Malaita speakers in particular, seem to have bent the pidgin of late-nineteenth-century Queensland in the direction of their native languages, we need to qualify this picture in three important respects.

1. Apart from an incipient regional differentiation of pidgin dialects in the southwestern Pacific in the late nineteenth century (Queensland vs. Samoa vs. Fiji vs. New Caledonia), there would have been considerable diversity in pidgin usage (in, e.g., Queensland), partly reflecting differences between substrate languages. That is, the Tannese and the Malaitans in Queensland in the 1880s must have been using pidgin in different ways that reflected syntactic as well as phonological diversity in their native languages. They produced relatively intelligible linguistic transactions out of relatively uniform linguistic coinage. If both *bin* and *nao* were acceptable coin, we may guess that users opted for one or the other even in the nineteenth century according to patterns of aspect marking in their indigenous languages. European chroniclers were likely to use, and re-

cord, whatever pidgin forms best fit into an English (or French or German) linguistic pattern—in this case, "been" to refer to events in the
past, "now" to refer to events or states in the present.

2. As Charpentier's comments suggest, the Bislama of Vanuatu is far
from uniform. Quite apart from the effects of two competing superstrate
languages, English and French, Charpentier (1979) convincingly documents regional variations in pronominal usage, aspect marking, and other
key grammatical phenomena. His argument that this diversity reflects
bending in the direction of substrate languages, parts of which I quoted in
the preceding chapter in relation to pronominal patterns, exactly parallels mine. Some of these regional patterns of usage, as I have noted, seemingly converge with those that have taken place in the Solomons. Such
convergence is not surprising when we consider that the substrate languages involved are apparently fairly closely related genetically. Moreover, as my sketch of Oceanic grammar has indicated, those grammatical
respects in which pidgin dialects have come to converge parallel patterns
common to the substrate languages of the two areas that appear to represent shared retentions of patterns in PEO or POC. They are patterns that
lie squarely in what I have described as the "core" of Oceanic syntax.

3. Despite the preponderant influence of Malaita and Guadalcanal
speakers on a developing Solomons Pidgin, speakers of other Solomons
languages—including Polynesian languages—themselves bend pidgin to
fit patterns of substrate grammar. I will illustrate this phenomenon in
Chapter 13. Charpentier's and Jourdan's data, although limited in regional coverage, confirm that we err if we take a standard Bislama and a
standard Solomons Pidgin as uniform dialects, and contrast their idealized
forms without taking account of the diversity of each and its probable
sources.

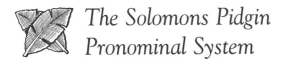 *The Solomons Pidgin Pronominal System*

FOCUSING NOW on the pronominal system of Solomons Pidgin against the background of the analysis in Chapters 9 and 10, I shall show that the changes in Solomons Pidgin partly entailed a reanalysis of or selection among existing patterns so as to approximate more closely to the patterns of substrate languages. This, as I will show, entailed the stabilization of a pattern in which FPs and SRPs are both used, in complementary ways, and in which SRPs are fully marked semantically, as in the dominant substrate languages, for person and number.

I argued in Chapter 9 that textual evidence and distributions in daughter dialects suggest that different speakers of late-nineteenth-century Pacific pidgin were using alternative pronominal paradigms. Hence, although Solomon Islanders may have pushed the plantation pidgin of the turn of the century in a particular direction, one that was further developed and stabilized in the Solomons in ensuing decades, we need not assume that this represented an innovation and reanalysis. A pronominal pattern congruent with Southeast Solomonic languages may already have been present in the plantation communities of the southwestern Pacific by the time Solomon Islanders became a dominant element (or, which amounts to the same thing, surface constructions that allowed of such an analysis may have been acceptable coin in these speech communities).

A major element in the variability of pronominal usage would seem to have been the variable use of SRPs to maintain reference across clauses— seemingly ranging from, at one extreme, a generalized "predicate marker" for third person and for other nonsingular reference, and at the other, a full set of SRPs marked semantically for person and number. The *i* pronoun following a noun subject, given that the corresponding third-person singular SRP is optional or absent in many of the substrate languages and redundant for superstrate speakers, was presumably differentially used by Islanders according to the options and strategies available in their first languages. Judging by both the textual and the distributional evidence, we would err in inferring from an increasingly complete and stable paradigm of subject pronouns that patterns and strategies of pronominal reference in discourse were more uniform in pidgin than in the native languages of Islanders participating in this speech community.

However, as I have shown, the languages of the northern and central New Hebrides are characterized by simplification, in varying degrees, of the semantic marking of person and number on SRPs reconstructed for Proto-Eastern Oceanic. In contrast, the languages of the southeastern Solomons are marked by virtually complete retention of this semantic marking. If my hypotheses that in the latter stages of the Labor Trade speakers used available pronominal forms in patterns closely following those of their native languages, the probable outcome, once the New Hebrides and Solomons speech communities were separated, would have been a drift of the two dialects in the direction of a simpler paradigm in the New Hebrides and a more complex one, fully marked semantically, in the Solomons.

My reading of the evidence is that this is exactly what happened. Speakers of Southeast Solomonic languages appear to have selected from and analyzed the pronominal forms available in the pidgin of the 1890s so as to create by the early decades of the twentieth century a system that preserved the semantic distinctions, and hence allowed the discourse strategies, of their native languages.

To understand why Solomon Islanders would have opted for pronominal patterns in which the pronouns used as obligatory subject markers (SRPs) were fully marked for person and number, we need to glimpse the manifestations of the Oceanic pronominal pattern in Southeast Solomonic languages. The Kwaio subject-pronominal paradigm was set out in Chapter 6. In Table 12.1, I give the corresponding systems for one other Malaita language, To'aba'ita, and for one Guadalcanal language, Ghaimuta.

For Ghaimuta, G. Simons (1977: 12) notes that "the verbal pronouns [i.e., SRPs] occur in the verb phrase and are used to indicate the person and number of the subject of the verb." Ghaimuta provides the option, in sentences with pronominal subjects, of using the FP without the following paired SRP, of using the SRP alone, or of using both in sequence. In general, however, in the Southeast Solomonic languages for which data are available, it is the SRP that is the obligatory subject-marking constituent of a verbal clause; and a noun subject or an FP is an optional

TABLE 12.1

Pronominal Paradigms in To'aba'ita (Malaita) and Ghaimuta (Guadalcanal)

Number and person	To'aba'ita		Ghaimuta	
	Focal pronoun (FP)	Subject-referencing pronoun (SRP)	Focal pronoun (FP)	Subject-referencing pronoun (SRP)
Singular				
1	nau	ku	(i)nau	ku, u
2	'oe	'o	(i)ghoe	ko, o
3	nia	'e	ia	e
Dual				
1 inclusive	koro	koro	(i)kogita	koko
1 exclusive	kamare'a	mera	(i)kogami	amiko
2	kamaro'a	moro	(i)kogamu	kamuko
3	keero'a	kero	(i)koira	arako
Trial				
1 inclusive			(i)lugita	kalu
1 exclusive			(i)lugami	amilu
2			(i)lugamu	kamulu
3			(i)luira	aralu
Plural				
1 inclusive	kulu	kulu	(i)gita	ka
1 exclusive	kamili'a	mili	(i)gami	ami
2	kamalu'a	mulu	(i)gamu	kamu
3	kera	kera	ira	ara

SOURCES: *To'aba'ita*, Lichtenberk (1984); *Ghaimuta*, G. Simons (1977).

expansion. In many of these languages, the third-person SRP can optionally be dropped where a noun subject is explicit.

It would not be surprising if speakers of these languages, in which SRPs
are fully marked for person and number, used pidgin pronouns in a way
that mirrored as closely as posible the semantic marking and reference-
maintaining discourse functions of their own pronominal systems. Nor
would it be surprising, given that in many cases nonsingular forms of
SRPs in these substrate languages are either identical or phonologically
similar to the corresponding FPs, if in doing so they used nonsingular
SRPs identical or closely corresponding to FPs. I will show that they did
both.

What is most interesting about the pronominal system that I believe
speakers of Solomons Pidgin used in the 1920s and 1930s (and still sur-
vives among older "bush" speakers who learned Solomons Pidgin before
World War II in plantation contexts) is that its evolution appears to require that, in the early stages of this process, Solomon Islanders were surrounded by speakers using a different pronominal paradigm. That is, it
seems unlikely that the forms of SRPs being used by these Solomon Is-

landers (which for third-person forms incorporate a clitic *-i*) could have developed other than in a context where other pidgin speakers were using an FP with a following *i*, unmarked for person and number, as SRP. Analyzing these surface strings (*hem i*, *tufala i*, *olgeta i*) in a different way, as themselves constituting SRPs (*hem-i*, *tufala-i*, *olgeta-i*), Southeast Solomonic speakers seem to have in effect recaptured from their linguistic environment the semantic marking needed to preserve discourse strategies in their native languages, while at the same time producing surface strings acceptable to others in the speech community. If my inferences are correct, such a process would most probably have begun in Queensland before the separation of the New Hebridean and Solomons speech communities in 1905. These Southeast Solomonic speakers continued to have the option of using *i* as a third-person singular SRP (so that in this slot, *hem-i* and *i* were essentially interchangeable, with the short form tending to be used after noun subjects). This short third-person form, although it carried the unmarked implication of first-person reference, could optionally be used across clauses, once reference had been established, to maintain a contextually clear nonsingular reference. The paradigm I infer is shown in Table 12.2.

As I noted in Chapter 9, Solomons Pidgin is subject to a blocking rule such that where FPs and SRPs are identical (or differ only in the suffixed clitic *-i*), they are not used in direct sequence unless separated by a clear pause. However, the paired pronouns are used in sequence when a particle (marking topicalization or other emphasis, deixis, mode, tense, etc.) intervenes between them.

TABLE 12.2

Subject Pronouns in 1920s–1930s Solomons Pidgin

Number and person	FP	SRP
Singular		
1	mi	mi
2	iu	iu
3	hem	hem-i, i
Dual		
1 inclusive	iumi(tufala)	iumi(tufala)
1 exclusive	mitufala	mitufala
2	iutufala	iutufala
3	tufala	tufala(-i), i
Plural		
1 inclusive	iumi	iumi
1 exclusive	mifala	mifala
2	iufala	iufala
3	olgeta	olgeta(-i), i

Most of the evidence of this pattern comes from elderly speakers of Solomons Pidgin who learned the language as adolescents or young adults in plantation, police, or mission work, in the 1920s and 1930s. However, although Europeans were prone to misrecord or miss such sequences (the "extra" pronouns being redundant from their point of view), we do find glimpses of contemporaneous textual evidence from the period prior to the 1920s. It is clear that Mühlhäusler is simply wrong in his assertion (n.d. 1) that the regularization of "he"/*i* following noun subjects and of the use of paired FPs and SRPs has taken place entirely since the 1930s. Let us first examine the use of "he"/*i* following noun subjects. Mühlhäusler claims that "whilst there are some early examples of resumptive he from the 1880s onward, they become dominant only after 1920" (n.d. 1). Elsewhere (Mühlhäusler n.d. 2), he claims that a sudden "Malaitanization" of the grammar of Solomons Pidgin "around 1920" "coincides with a political movement (Malaita for the Malaitans) which stressed indigenous values to the exclusion of European ones." This is a movement previously unreported in the literature. Perhaps Mühlhäusler is thinking of the post–World War II Maasina Rule movement, which surfaced in 1944 and reached its height in 1947 (Keesing 1978).

A set of texts, which are by no means selected to prejudice the case, will serve to show that the use of *i* following noun subjects was well established in the Solomons, as it was elsewhere in the Pacific, by the beginning of the twentieth century.

Suppose man-of-war he come fight me, he make plenty noise, but he all same woman—he no savee fight (from Kolombangara, 1880; Coote 1882: 206).

Plenty fish he stop (from Gela, 1880s; Cromar 1935: 235).

Devil he kai-kai first; all man he kai-kai behind (from Guadalcanal, 1887; Woodford 1890: 27).

Government he fire and George Hicks he fire, no fire plenty time. Barton sing out along me fellow he say, "Ted he die" (a Tikopia speaker, 1896; Queensland 1896).

From the first decade of the twentieth century, we have:

White man he go along Queensland, he take-'im country belong black-fellow (from Malaita, 1904; Young 1926: 152).

God He been talk along my heart. He been say, "You go along 'Daphne,' look out Miss Young" (from Malaita, 1904; Young 1926: 153).

This fellow he belong me—piccaninny belong me (ca. 1905; Abbott 1908: 59).

Young fellow mary, he belong me too (ca. 1905; Abbott 1908: 61).

You fella bring me fella big fella clam—kaikai he no stop (1908; London 1909: 359).

That fella boom he walk about too much (1908; London 1909: 359).

Me like him 2 rifle, me savvee look out along boat, some place me go man he no good, he kai-kai along me (written by a "native trader" at Santa Anna, 1908; London 1909: 360).

Me speak along him, say bokkis he stop that fella he cross along me (from Malaita, 1908; London 1909: 360).

Wind he no stop, all same man he die (from Simbo, 1908; Hocart 1922: 83).

S'pose he make him, I think he die; I think by and by devil he cross, he die (from Simbo, 1908; Hocart 1922: 105).*

"How much this fellow white man belong here he pay you b'long copra?" "Fellow white man he pay ten cocoa-nut one stick tobacco." "All right, me pay you two stick. That fellow white man he cheat—me b'long mission, me look b'long you, me no savvy cheat, suppose you sell me copra all same b'long Lord" (reported conversation between missionary trader and Islander at Roviana, 1909–10; Burnett 1910: 100).

From the second decade of the twentieth century, we have:

My word this schooner quick fellow—all same man-o-war. Canoe he no catch him! (1912; Herr and Rood 1978: 93).

Shark he come up and look 'em man—spose he sorry him good fella man, he say all right; he go away. Suppos he come up and look 'em man—he bad fella; he steal along other boy; he make 'em fight; he gammon too much he altogether no good; shark he fight 'em—take him finish (1912; Herr and Rood 1978: 148).

Willee he no kaikai yam. . . . Willee he hear about countryman belong him die finish—so now he no kai kai yam (1912: Herr and Rood 1978: 167).

This fellow musket he strong too much (1913; Knibbs 1926: 65).

What name you altogether go sleep. This place he no belong you me (1913; Knibbs 1926: 89).

No matter, suppos plant he die, me puttem this something along him and now he grow srong (1913; Knibbs 1926: 247).

Ramagooa and Muskoa he relation of Ramafuna. . . . Mara he poison father belong Filia (from Malaita, 1916; Mann 1948: 290).

Boy belong my place he got'm fright along kai-kai you (from Malaita, 1916; Mann 1948: 195).

*The frozen form *ating* 'maybe,' occurs in all three major dialects of Melanesian Pidgin and must predate 1890.

Him big fellow master, he 'nother kind; he no catch'm coconut, he no belong sekool, he no belong gov'ment. Suppose you find some small fellow along bush he no good belong kaikai you bring-m he come, him pay you along tambac (a Choiseulese speaker on Malaita, 1916; Mann 1946: 282–83).

In relatively reliable texts from the period 1900–1920, we find that speakers have the option of omitting the SRP after a noun when it occurs in a simple clause pattern (although this is by far the less commonly chosen option). In most of the substrate languages, speakers have exactly the same option. But the SRP is, as in the substrate languages, indispensable for embedding relative clauses. Consider the embedded relative clauses (marked with brackets) in one of these sentences, an utterance recorded in the ship's log of J. E. Phillips (Herr and Rood 1978: 148), as written in a Solomons Pidgin orthography.

Sapos i kamap anaa luk-im man [i bad-fala], [i stil long nara boe], [i mek-em faet], [i gaman tumas], [i olgeta* nogut], sak i faet-em, tek-em finis.

Mühlhäusler may wish to claim that "he" was the less commonly used option before 1920 (although it certainly was not in the wide array of Solomons texts, published and unpublished, I have gone through). Fortunately, we have a reasonably substantial corpus of Solomons Pidgin sentences recorded from Simbo in the western Solomons in 1908 by A. M. Hocart, who has been described as "a linguistic genius" and whose texts must, although written in an English-based orthography, be otherwise taken as quite accurate (although sometimes somewhat anglicized, since these were elicited from the best available interpreters, who were supposedly "English-speaking"). Hocart's Pidgin texts, in his various published accounts, field notes, and manuscript dictionary (Hocart 1922, 1925, 1931, 1937; Lanyon-Orgill 1969) include twenty-four clauses with noun subjects. In twenty of these clauses, the noun subject is followed by "he"; in four cases, it is followed by zero. I give a few more of Hocart's examples:

Long fellow he speak, he *varavara* [long form of prayer]; s'pose he short fellow, he *pito*. *Varavara* long fellow, plenty thing he stop (1925: 234).

Erovo no speak yet; spose Nimu he dead, Erovo he talk (1922: 77).

Mühlhäusler (n.d. 1) further claims that even in texts from the 1920s, such as Collinson's (1926), where "he" following noun subjects predominates, "what is not found . . . are examples of pronouns followed by

---

*This is probably incorrectly recorded; it seems extraneous, although it conceivably could be "completely."

'he.'" Now doubled pronouns are considerably more redundant to Europeans than a resumptive pronoun following a noun is, and it is not surprising that even if Solomon Islanders were using them in the early part of this century—as New Hebrideans were recorded to have been doing (e.g. by Jacomb around 1900 and by Alexander in 1914 [1926])—they turn up rarely in the records. But they do indeed turn up.* Thus we have:

Him he want to make new leaf (1908; Hocart manuscript dictionary; Lanyon-Orgill 1969: 147).

Some fellow he think 'long woman (where sam-fala is a pronoun [albeit not a personal pronoun] incorrectly represented as a noun; 1908; Hocart 1922: 77).

Oh, altogether, altogether go along river. Me waitem along hot water (1913; Knibbs 1929: 242).

Altogether he look him and say, "Eye belong devil-devil belong Jack here. He lookem out you and me" (*Planter's Gazette*, December 1922: 10).

Oh him-he look-em strong fella too much long boy (1927; Mytinger 1942: 26).

No, him-he boy belong Malaita (1927; Mytinger 1942: 105).

Mytinger in fact recorded as well the first clear cases of the incorporation of the cliticized -*i* to *hem* to form a fully marked third-person singular SRP (a pattern we will see extensively in the texts from speakers who learned Pidgin in this period):

Boy him-he no savvy (1927; 1942: 166)

Mastah! Mastah! Alligator-him-he stop!" (p. 254).

This pattern is quite clear if we look at texts from two old Malaita men who learned Solomons Pidgin in the constabulary in the 1920s and had their careers (and their sustained contact with Solomons Pidgin) cut off when they survived the 1927 massacre of two colonial officers and their party (Keesing and Corris 1980), one with shattered body and the other with tarnished reputation. From Tolo'au of Kwara'ae I recorded:

Mista Lilisi   i   kerap   wantaem   nao
Mr   Lillies   srp(he)   spring   at once   PRF
Mr Lillies jumped up and

i   go   insaet   haos   takisi
srp(he)   go   inside   house   tax
went into the tax house.

---

*I have just (February 1988) found a text recorded in the Solomons in 1895 by E. G. Rason, commander of HMS *Royalist*: "They [the chiefs] describe a trader they do not trust as 'him he gammon boy too much'" (Pacific Manuscripts Bureau 153, 1971, Appendix V).

ko   insaet   haos,   olketa   kiikil-im   insaet   haos,
go   inside   house   SRP(they)   attack-TTS   inside   house
[He] went into the house and they killed him in the house,

mi   no   luk-im   nao
SRP(I)   NEG   see-TTS   PRF
I didn't see it.

mi   aotsaet   wet-em   olketa   busumane   nao
FP(me)   outside   with-TTS   PLU   bushman   PRF
I was outside with all the bushmen.

mifala   faafaete   aotsaete
SRP(weE)   fight(RED)   outside
We fought outside.

Mista   Belo,   Mista   Lilisi,   tufala-i   dae   nao
Mr   Bell   Mr   Lillies   SRP(they2)   be dead   PRF
Mr. Bell and Mr. Lillies were both dead by then.

mi   nao   mi   faet   wet-em   olketa   nomoa
FP(me)   TOP   SRP(I)   fight   with-TTS   them   only
As for me, all I could do was fight with them.

mi   aotsaet   wet-em   olketa   nomoa
FP(me)   outside   with-TTS   them   only
I was just there outside with them.

Notice here how Tolo'au uses *mi . . . mi* and how he uses *tufala-i* to reference a third-person dual subject, just as he would in Kwara'ae. I am assuming that when he uses *mi* before a prepositional phrase, it is the FP
rather than the SRP. In Kwara'ae (Alec Rukia, personal communication,
April 22, 1986), one would here use the FP *nau(a)* rather than the corresponding SRP *ku*:

naua   'i   maa   fa'i-ni-a   toa   tolo
FP(me)   LOC   outside   with-TTS-it   people   bush
I was outside with the bush people.

However, one would need a much larger corpus to be certain; and this
point is not crucial to my analysis.

   The second text comes from a Lau (Malaita) speaker, Usuli Tefu'i:

oraet,   samting   hem-i   laek-em,   na   waswe   hem-i
so   thing   SRP(he)   want-TTS   then   why   SRP(he)
So if there was anything he wanted, then if he

ask-em   mi,   mi   nao   mi   du-im   deskaen   samting
ask-TTS   me   FP(me)   TOP   SRP(I)   do-TTS   this kind   thing
asked me, I'd do whatever it was.

Here again, we find both *hem-i* following a noun subject and *mi . . . mi* separated by a particle. As L. Simons (1986) notes, and as we saw in the last chapter, this topicalizing particle in Solomons Pidgin exactly corresponds to the topicalizing particle (*na, no'o*, etc.) in Malaita languages. In Solomons Pidgin, as in the substrate languages, this topicalizer has the same form as the perfect marker.

Kwalafane'ia, a Kwaio (Malaita) speaker who learned Solomons Pidgin on plantations in the mid-1930s, provides further striking evidence of this pronominal system, and how it serves to maintain pronominal reference—in exactly the same way as in his native language (on this point, see the texts in the Appendix). As in the Malaita languages, SRPs are the obligatory pronominal constituents of verbal sentences, with FPs optionally serving for emphasis or (p)reiteration:

ou,	let-im	hem-i	kam,	iumi	bae-em	raasen	fo	iumi
oh	allow-TRS	SRP(he)	come	SRP(weI)	buy-TRS	ration	for	us(I)

Oh, let him come, so we can buy ourselves rations.

foromu	masta	hem-i	no	gif-im	laaseni	longo	iumi
because	master	SRP(he)	NEG	give-TRS	ration	LOC	us(I)

Because our master didn't give us rations.

nao	mifala	redi	nao,	ia
then	SRP(weE)	be ready	PRF	RHET

Then we got ready.

mifala	rukurukudaon	long	wafu
SRP(weE)	look(RED)down	LOC	wharf

We looked down toward the wharf.

oraet,	mi,	mi	godaon	longo	wafu
so	FP(me)	SRP(I)	descend	LOC	wharf

So me, I went down to the wharf.

Later in Kwalafane'ia's text, we get an even more striking illustration of this pronominal system.

waswe	iufala	fosi	iufala	hangri	tumas	nao,
why	FP(youPLU)	if	SRP(youPLU)	be hungry	very	PRF

Why, if you were very hungry,

iufala	no	kalaemap	kokonate,	iufala	kaikai-em	kokonate
SRP(youPl)	NEG	climb	coconut	SRP(youPl)	eat-TRS	coconut

didn't you climb the coconut palms, and eat coconuts?

Elsewhere, Kwalafane'ia's text illustrates a *iumi . . . iumi* sequence, with the first pronoun, an FP, in the subject-NP slot (and reiterated by a second subject NP):

nao	hem-i	see,	iumi	finistaem,	olketa	finistaem,
then	SRP(he)	say	us(Incl.)	repatriate	PLU	repatriate

Then he said, "All of us who have finished our contracts,

iumi		go	narasaeti
SRP(weIncl.)		go	opposite

let's go to the opposite shore."

Another sentence from Kwalafane'ia's text further illustrates how SRPs marked for person and number serve to maintain reference across a complex sequence of clauses—exactly as in his native Kwaio (Keesing 1985):

nao	mifala	mi	'anaa	barata	bulong	mi
then	FP(weE)	FP(I)	and	brother	POSS	me

Then we, my brother and I,

hem-i	dae	nao,	ia,	barata	long	Maakona,
SRP(he)	be dead	PRF	RHET	brother	LOC	Maakona

one who is dead now, right, Maakona's brother,

nem	bulong	hem	Baba'aniaboo,	mitufala	kam	insaet	long
name	POSS	him	Baba'aniaboo,	SRP(we2E)	come	inside	LOC

named Baba'aniaboo, the two of us came in

Kurumalau	nao,	saet	long	Sitanmoa
Kurumalau	PRF	side	LOC	Stanmore

the Kurumalau, from Stanmore.

Note that the equational clause glossed as "named Baba'aniaboo" has no SRP; as in Kwaio, it is verbless.

Two passages from speakers of other Solomons languages who learned Solomons Pidgin in the constabulary in the same period further illuminate pronominal usage, and compellingly show that it was not only Malaitans who used this dialect. The first text comes from Vuza, a police sergeant in the 1920s and a much-decorated World War II hero, who is a speaker of Tasimboko, a Guadalcanal language. Vuza himself then appears in the cast of characters of the second text, from a Simbo (western Solomons) speaker who served in the constabulary on Malaita in the 1920s. From Vuza:

mi	luk-im	wan	man	nomoa	long	Toabaita	hem-i	kil-im
SRP(I)	see-TRS	one	man	only	LOC	To'aba'ita	SRP(he)	hit-TRS

I saw one To'aba'ita man who killed

mane	wea	hem-i	hambaka-im	waef	blong	hem
man	REL	SRP(he)	fuck-TRS	wife	POSS	him

a man who had sex with his wife.

hem-i	kil-im	finis,	kam	long	Aoke	nao,	fo	kam	ripot
SRP(he)	hit-TTS	COMP	come	LOC	Auki	PRF	INF	AUX	report

He killed him, then came to Auki to report:

mi	nao	mi	kil-im
FP(me)	TOP	SRP(I)	hit-TTS

"I'm the one who killed him."

hem	nao	hem-i	kil-im	des-fala	mane	wea
FP(him)	TOP	SRP(he)	hit-TTS	DEM-ADJ	man	REL

He's the one who killed that man who

hem-i	hambaka	long	wuman	blong	hem
SRP(he)	fuck	LOC	woman	POSS	him

had sex with his wife.

Here, in addition to the sequences of noun + *hem-i* and *mi . . . mi* we have already seen, we find *hem . . . hem-i* separated by a topicalizing particle. Compare Kwaio (Malaita):

ngai	ne-'e	kwa'i-a
FP(him)	TOP-SRP(he)	hit-him

He's the one who killed (him) . . .

gila	no'o	la	kwa'i-a
FP(them)	TOP	SRP(they)	hit-him

They're the ones who killed (him) . . .

From the Simbo (western Solomons) speaker Alik, who served with Vuza in Bell's constabulary (and who, in the western Solomons, has not used Pidgin extensively in the intervening years), we can examine some further fragments of a long text dealing with the prelude to the assassination of Bell.

oraet	Basiana	standap.	Mi—	mi	nao	mi
then	Basiana	stand	FP(me)	FP(me)	TOP	SRP(I)

Then Basiana stood. "Me, I'm

fal-om	toko	bulong	iu—	iu	nao	masta	bulong	mi
follow-TTS	talk	POSS	you	FP(you)	TOP	master	POSS	me

following your orders—you're my chief.

posi	iu	see	mi	du-im,	mi	du-im.
If	SRP(you)	say	SRP(I)	do-TTS	SRP(I)	do-TTS

If you tell me to do it, I'll do it."

oraet,	kokoko	nao,	okta	turuu	nao
then	gogogo	PRF	SRP(they)	true	PRF

Then after a while, they (Kwaio people said) "It's true."

te*   luk-im sipi   ia   hem-i   goraon long Malaita,
SRP(they) see-TTS ship   DEM   SRP(it) circle LOC   Malaita
They saw that the ship was going around Malaita,

aot long   Aoke   Oraet, istate long Fiu,   mifala   istat
out LOC   Auki   OK   start   LOC   Fiu   SRP(weE)   start
leaving Auki. OK, from Fiu, we started

long Fiu—   tek-im   takis   nao.   Oraet, hem,   Mista   Belo,
LOC   Fiu   take-TTS tax   PRF   then   FP(he)   Mr   Bell
from Fiu—collecting tax. Then he, Mr Bell,

see,   ou,   iufala   standbae.   Iu   mekelaen
say   oh   SRP(youPl)   wait   SRP(youS)   line up
said "Oh, you wait. Line up

long   mifala long   aotsaet nao   mi   mi   standap
LOC   us(E)   LOC   outside then   FP(me)   SRP(I) stand
for us outside." So then I stood

wet-em   olketa oraet—   iu   bulong   Wesiten,   ia?
with-TTS them   then   FP(you)   POSS   W. Sols   RHET
with them. Then [he said] "You're from the Western Solomons, right?

waswe,   iu   laek-em   fo   kam—   wet-em   mi?
QUERY   SRP(youS)   like-TTS INF   come   with-TTS   me
Do you want to come—with me?"

nao   Saasen Vusa   i   see   no   des-wan   kolsap   taem
then Sgt   Vuza   SRP(he)   say   no   this-one   almost   time
Then Sgt Vuza said, "No, this one is almost ready

fo   finis—   wan-wik   nomoa   blong hem   fo   stap   fo   finishi
INF   finish   one-week   only   POSS   him   INF   stay   INF   finish
to finish, he has only a week left to finish (as policeman)."

nao   Mista Belo   see   oraet, iu   istap—
then Mr   Bell   say   OK   SRP(youS)   stay
So then Mr Bell said, "OK, you stay—

iu   lukat-em   piles—   long   Aoke   iu   stap
SRP(youS)   look after-TTS   place   LOC   Auki   SRP(youS)   stay
you look after the place at Auki. You stay

longo   ples   Vusa   ana   Stifin   Maekali   anaa   Stifin   Marodo   anaa
LOC   place   Vuza   and   Stifin   Maekali   and   Stifin   Marodo   and
there." Vuza and Stephen Maekali and Stephen Marodo and

*I will shortly discuss these short SRPs using variants of English "they," which occur scattered through the texts.

Diki	Marika—	olketa	Saasen	ia	bulong	Mista	Bel—	anaa
Diki	Marika	PLUS	Sgt	DEM	POSS	Mr	Bell	and

Dick America—Mr. Bell's Sergeants—and

mi	mi	stap.	Oraet,	mi	stap,
FP(me)	SRP(I)	stay	OK	SRP(I)	stay,

I, I (we) stayed. All right, I stayed,

olketa	evri	Saasen	ia	olketa-i	stap	wet-em	mi	nomoa
PLU	every	Sgt	DEM	SRP(they)	stay	with-TTS	me	only

and all those Sergeants just stayed with me.

Here we find clear instances of *hem-i* and *olketa-i* being used as SRPs, and
clear examples of *mi . . . mi* separated by a pause or a particle. The way
pronouns can be used to maintain complex semantic reference is neatly
illustrated, elsewhere in Alik's account, by:

waswe,	iufala	laek-em	dis-fala	Basiana
INT	SRP(youPl)	want-TTS	this-DEM	Basiana

How about it, do you want this man Basiana

toko	bulong	mifala	fol-om?
talk	POSS	us	follow-TTS

to follow our talk?

And, in another passage:

oraete,	mifala	kamdaon	long	ples—	nao,	tu,	tri-fala	nomoa
then	SRP(weE)	descend	LOC	place	now	two	three-NUM	only

Then we came down there—and then only two or three

olketa	polis	i	stap	wet-em	mi	long	steisin,	long
PLU	police	SRP(he)	stay	with-TTS	me	LOC	station	LOC

police were staying with me at the station,

'eria	long	Aoke	oraet,	sipi	i	sut	kam
area	LOC	Auki	OK	ship	SRP(it)	sail	DEI

around Auki. OK, the ship was coming toward us.

fo-fala	polis	'anaa	mi,	mifala	faev-fala
four-NUM	police	and	me	FP(weE)	five-NUM

Four policemen and I, there were five of us,

mifala	go	stanbae	long	wafu
SRP(weE)	AUX	stand by	LOC	wharf

went and waited at the wharf.

But was this only a pidgin of the constabulary serving on Malaita and
working with Malaitans, whatever their islands of origin? A further illus-

tration of this pronominal system, and how it is used (exactly as in substrate languages) to maintain reference in discourse, comes from a text recorded by Jourdan from Domenico Alebua, a Talise (Guadalcanal) speaker who learned Solomons Pidgin as a church leader in his remote community:

den	taem	olketa	muvu	kam	long	hia,	padre	Buyon	and
then	when	SRP(they)	move	DEI	LOC	here	father	Bouillon	and

Then when they moved here, Father Bouillon and

padre	Koako	tufala-i	stap	long	hia	long	Avuavu	fastaem
father	Koako	SRP(they2)	stay	LOC	here	LOC	Avuavu	at first

Father Koako stayed here at Avuavu at first.

den	tu-fala	bikiman	long	longgu	tufala	send-em	nius
then	two-NUM	big man	LOC	Longgu	SRP(they2)	send-TRS	news

Then the two leaders from Longgu sent word

po	olketa	pipol	long	bush	po	kom	kil-im	olketa	pristi	ia
for	PLU	people	LOC	bush	INF	AUX	hit-TRS	PLU	priest	DEM

for the bush people to come and kill these priests.

bikos	gavman	hem-i	des	kam	nomoa,	ia
because	gov't	SRP(it)	ASP	come	only	RHET

Because the government had just come, right?

bet	gavman	taem	i	kam,	hem	olsem
but	gov't	when	SRP(it)	come	FP(it)	as though

But when the government came, it

hem-i	no	strong	olsem	tude
SRP(it)	NEG	be strong	like	today

wasn't strong, as it is nowadays.

Here Alebua uses *tufala-i* and *tufala* to reference a noun subject with dual number, exactly as he would in his native language. He also uses *hem . . . hem-i*, separated by a particle, to emphasize the subject reference—again, exactly as he would use an FP and SRP in his native language. Note how he also, and alternatively, can use the unmarked *i* to reference a noun subject. Another fragment of text from Alebua further illustrates how SRPs marked for person and number (here *olketa* as FP and *olketa-i* as SRP) are used to maintain reference across clauses in quite complex constructions.

den	olketa	mane	po	devodevolo	ia,	olketa	bipo	i
the	PLU	man	for	ancestor	DEM	FP(them)	before	SRP(it)

At that time, all the pagans, before it [the church] had

kam,	olketa-i	no	wande	her-emu,	ia,	bikosi	olketa-i	tink
come	SRP(they)	NEG	want	hear-TTS	RHET	because	SRP(they)	think

come, didn't want to hear it, because they thought

ou,	lotu	ia	baebae	kam,	i	spoel-em
oh	church	DEM	IRR	come	SRP(it)	destroy-TTS

"Oh, if this church comes, it will destroy

devol	blong	iumi
ancestor	POSS	us(Incl)

our ancestors."

Here we see how third-person SRPs marked for number serve to maintain reference across clauses that would otherwise be ambiguous. For the pagans, Alebua uses "they" pronouns; for the church and missionaries, he uses "it" pronouns. After the noun subject *lotu*, reference is clear, and Alebua omits the SRP, as he optionally could in his native language. The device of embedding a temporal clause (here *bipo i kam*) between FP and SRP is characteristically Oceanic, and common in Southeast Solomonic languages.

Finally, two short fragments—from Kazikana, a Ghanongga speaker from the western Solomons who learned Pidgin as a cook for an Adventist missionary and then served with the Coast Watcher Donald Kennedy in World War II—show this pronominal system once more. In the first segment, however, we see in one clause something closer to the New Hebridean use of pronouns, both in the direct pairing of FP and SRP and in the placement of the irrealis marker before the FP:

Amerikan	her-em	datkaen	tok	hem-i	see
American	hear-TTS	that-kind	talk	SRP(he)	say

The Americans heard that kind of talk [from the Japanese] and replied—

oraet—	iu	gogofest,	bae	mi
OK	SRP(youS)	go-first	FUT	FP(me)

"OK—you, you go first, and then me,

mi	kam	bihaen	long	iu	hem-i	see	long	hem
SRP(I)	come	behind	LOC	you	SRP(he)	say	LOC	him

I'm coming after you." That's what he (the American) said.

tokotoko	nao	hem-i	olsem
talk	TOP	SRP(it)	be thus

The conversation was like that. . . .

wan-fala	nomoa	hem-i	save	tok	Ingles	so hem	nomoa
one-NUM	only	SRP(he)	MOD	talk	English	so FP(him)	only

Only one (Japanese) could speak English. So only he

hem-i	save	toko	longo	Mista	Kenedi,	hem-i	save	raet-em
SRP(he)	MOD	talk	LOC	Mr	Kennedy	SRP(he)	MOD	write-TTS

was able to talk to Mr. Kennedy, was able to write

leta	samting	olketa	laek-em	nao,	hem	nao
letter	something	SRP(they)	want-TTS	PRF	FP(him)	TOP

letters. If there was something they wanted then he

hem-i	save	toko	wet-em	olketa	nao
SRP(he)	MOD	talk	with-TTS	them	PRF

could talk with them.

Recall how, in northern Malaita dialects such as To'aba'ita and Lau, the SRPs are optionally, and frequently, omitted in discourse when the referent is contextually clear across clauses. A fragment of text from a Lau man in his sixties, Maenuu, illustrates both the syntactic complexity that can be achieved through the SRPs (including, as in Lau, the embedding of relative clauses without special marking) and the way clauses may have no pronominal elements when reference is contextually clear (in this case, because the subject reference is maintained without change through the last three VPs). This sequence also illustrates (with *goheti lukat-em*) the use of serial verb constructions in Solomons Pidgin, exactly parallel-ing those in Lau and other Malaita languages:

oraet,	des-fala	hem-i	hetman	ia,	Ramoagalo,	'anaa
OK	DEM-ADJ	SRP(he)	headman	DEM	Ramoagalo	and

So then that one who was the Headman, Ramoagalo, and

olketa	pikanin	blong	him	nomoa,	Tome Wate	'anaa
PLU	child	POSS	him	only	Tome Wate	and

his children, and Tome Wate and

gurup	bulong	him,	hem	nao	olketa	doin	wet-im
group	POSS	him	FP(it)	TOP	SRP(they)	join	with-TTS

his group, it's they who joined with

olketa	Ingglan,	wet-im	olketa	'ami	ia
PLU	British	with-TTS	PLU	police	DEM

the British and with those police

olketa	raus-em*	mifala.
SRP(they)	chase-TTS	us

who pursued us.

taem	ia,	mifala	no	istapkwaet,	ia?
time	DEM	SRP(weE)	NEG	stay-put	right?

In those days, we weren't staying in one place, you know.

---

*In Solomons Pidgin, a rarely used loanword from Tok Pisin.

olketa   gele   nomoa,   wuman   nomoa,   olketa-i   stap
PLU   girl   only   woman   only   SRP(they) stay
Only the girls and women stayed

long   olketa   aelan
LOC   PLU   island
on the islands.

mifala   go   haeti   long   busi,   olketa-i   goheti   lukat-em
SRP(weE) go   hide   LOC   bush   SRP(they) proceed   hunt-TRS
We went and hid in the bush, and they went and searched for

mifala   olketa   sipi   ia,   'age   nomoa   long   olketa   basis   ia
us   PLU   ship   DEM   anchor   just   LOC   PLU   passage   DEM
us. All those ships just anchored in the passages.

olketa   lukat-em   mifala,   goo-go   olketa   kas-em   sam-fala
SRP(they)   hunt-TRS   us   go-go   SRP(they)   catch-TRS   some-ADJ
They searched for us, and eventually captured some people,

hol-em   sam-fala,   kamu   goo-go,   put-um   olketa   long   sipi,
hold-TRS   some-ADJ   come   go-go   put-TRS   them   LOC   ship
detained some, and eventually put them on a ship

tek-em   olketa   go   long   Aoke
take-TRS   them   DEI   LOC   Auki
and took them to Auki.

And later in Maenuu's narrative we find:

olketa   Merika   olketa   gif-im   tabeka   gif-im   naef
PLU   American   SRP(they)   give-TRS   tobacco   give-TRS   knife
The Americans gave tobacco, gave knives,

kaleko   bulanket   sitibeti,   olketa   gif-im   long   mifala
clothes   blanket   cot   SRP(they)   give-TRS   LOC   us
clothes, blankets, cots, they gave to us.

olketa   Ingglan   kamu,   taem   mifala   redi   fo   go   long   Malaita,
PLU   British   come   when   SRP(weE)   ready   INF   go   LOC   Malaita
The British came, when we were ready to go to Malaita,

oraete   olketa   kamu   nao   olketa   kamu   ofen-em   olketa   bokis
OK   SRP(they)   come   PRF   SRP(they)   come   open-TRS   PLU   box
they came and opened the boxes,

infikis,   tekaot   evri   kaleko   ia,   goo-go   i   finisi
check   remove   all   clothes   DEM   go-go   SRP(it)   be finished
checked, took out all the clothes, and when that was done

olketa	go	torou-em	long	faea
SRP(they)	go	throw-TTS	LOC	fire

they went and threw them in the fire.

Where pronominal reference is changed in discourse, as in this quite complex fragment from Maenuu's text, the pronouns mark the changes carefully and clearly:

wan-fala	mane	olsem	hem-i	gar-em	wan-fala	seksin—
one-ADJ	man	as if	SRP(he)	got-TTS	one-ADJ	section

One man who had a unit—

olsem	hem-i	saajen	nao,	ia?,	forom	hem-i	luku	hafta
as if	SRP(he)	sgt.	PRF	RHET	because	SRP(he)	look	after

who was like a sergeant, because he looked after

olketa	pipol	ia,	fo	wan	gurup	fo	waka—
PLU	people	DEM	for	one	group	for	work

all those people, for a whole group's work—

hem	nao,	olketa	Merika	gif-im	dis-fala	sote	ia,
FP(he)	TOP	PLU	American	give-TTS	DEM-ADJ	shirt	DEM

he's the one to whom the Americans gave a shirt,

gif-im	fo	man	ia	hem-i	bos—	baebae	hem-i	haf-em
give-TTS	to	man	DEM	SRP(he)	in charge	IRR	SRP(he)	have-TTS

that man who was boss—a shirt that had

satraef	blongo	hem,	hem-i	stap	long	sote	ia	tuu—	goo-go
stripe	POSS	him	SRP(it)	be	LOC	shirt	DEM	too	go-go

his stripes—until

olketa	Biritisi	luk-im,	olketa	tek-em	baeke
PLU	British	see-TTS	SRP(they)	take-TTS	back

the British saw it, and took it away.

In Chapter 6, I illustrated how the Oceanic system of marking person and number on an SRP can operate so as to include speaker or addressee —*along with* the person(s) described in a subject NP ("John and George we went," "Joe and Jack you do it"—meaning Joe, Jack, and the person spoken to). The following fragment from Fifi'i, a Kwaio speaker in his sixties, shows how exactly the same system is used in "bush" Solomons Pidgin:

ee,	wanemu	nao	faata	bilongo	iu	iutufala	sut-imu?
hey	what	TOP	father	POSS	you	SRP(you2)	shoot-TTS

"Hey, what did you and your father shoot?"

mi	see,	oo,	mitufala	sut-im	pijin	nomoa,	ia
SRP(I)	say	oh	SRP(we2E)	shoot-TTS	bird	only	RHET

I said, "Oh, we only shot a bird, OK?"

Here, it is worth stepping back to make two general theoretical points that tie this analysis back into earlier discussions of change in pronominal systems, particularly in Chapter 10. First of all, the process that appears to be implied by these texts parallels the one discussed by Givón (1984: 361) as a likely outcome of a cycling process through which pronouns progressively lose their semantic marking: "Phonological attrition eventually plays havoc with the code efficiency of pronouns, so that a depleted system of grammatical agreement is eventually replaced by a new generation of de-stressed independent pronouns."

In the case of Pacific pidgin pronouns, the process was complicated by a dialectical relationship between substrate languages and lingua franca, of a sort discussed by Silverstein (1972). The pronominal system that had developed by the late nineteenth century through this dialectical process, examined in Chapters 9 and 10, followed (in its marking of SRPs) the pronominal systems of those indigenous languages that have "depleted system[s] of grammatical agreement." This system appears to have been reanalyzed by speakers of those indigenous languages that have fully marked "systems of grammatical agreement" so as to develop a "new generation of de-stressed independent pronouns" incorporating the semantic information of pronouns in their native languages.

This leads to a second point, related to Sankoff's (1980) hypothesis of "cliticization" in pidgin. What seems to have happened in the emergence of *hem-i* as a third-person SRP in Solomons Pidgin is essentially the same phenomenon to which her analysis is addressed; and I agree with her that it represents a result of "cliticization" in which *i* partly lost its independent force as a third-person singular pronoun. As *i* became generalized to nonsingular third-person slots, it less clearly served as a "de-stressed independent pronoun" to mark singular third-person subjects (probably human subjects in particular); a cliticized form of *-i* became suffixed as third-person marker, with *hem-*, *tufala-*, and *olgeta-* as morphemes marking number. My disagreement with Sankoff, whose contribution I regard as extremely important, lies in what I see as her failure to perceive the Oceanic structure that was the starting point of this process, and hence to misread the early evidence: for Oceanic speakers, I think, *i* was (in the third-person singular) from the outset a "de-stressed independent pronoun," but one that was the obligatory pronominal constituent of verbal clauses.

The continuous pull in the direction of substrate grammars illustrated with the perfect marker, irrealis marker, pronominal system, and such specific patterns as the semantics of transitive and causative constructions and prepositional verbs, which I have illustrated in this and the preceding chapters, has had the cumulative result that the grammar of Solomons Pidgin strikingly resembles the grammars of Southeast Solomonic languages in global syntax, in many close details of phrase structure and even morphology, and in semantics. I will go on now to show the striking degree of calquing this makes possible.

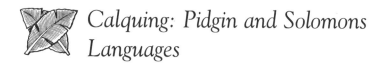 *Calquing: Pidgin and Solomons Languages*

AT THIS STAGE, it is useful to shift attention from these apparent modifications of late-nineteenth-century pidgin so as to fit more closely the grammatical pattern of substrate languages; and to see how Solomons Pidgin is actually used by speakers of Southeast Solomonic languages in discourse, and how closely it follows patterns of substrate languages and allows calquing onto them.

Looking in particular at the Kwaio language of central Malaita against a background of other Malaita languages, I shall show how and why speakers of these languages acquiring Solomons Pidgin in the first half of this century could calque pervasively and systematically onto their native languages; and how, in doing so, they could communicate with speakers of other Southeast Solomonic languages. The striking correspondence, very often morpheme by morpheme, between Kwaio (or any other Malaita language) and "bush" (in contrast to modern urban) Pidgin may be particularly evident to an ethnographer who was fluent in a Malaita language before learning Pidgin; but it can hardly escape attention once the two are arrayed together.* I will introduce as well some fragmentary data from the western Solomons that suggest a bending in the direction of rather different, though still Oceanic, substrate languages.

My own observations of monolingual Kwaio speakers arriving in settings where Pidgin is spoken, and their extraordinarily rapid acquisition of relative fluency in it (a matter of a few weeks for most) initially suggested to me that the language-learning task they faced was of a different

---

*Bickerton, in response to a corpus of paired Kwaio and Solomons Pidgin sentences I sent him in 1983, wrote that "I think you are very probably right about the nature and degree of calquing."

order than might have been expected. These observations have been confirmed by similar data gathered in Honiara by Jourdan (1985), in studying Pidgin acquisition by Malaita adults and children arriving there.

My own acquisition of Solomons Pidgin in fact had followed a path parallel to that of these Kwaio speakers. In 1964, when I first began to learn and use Pidgin extensively, I had already acquired relative fluency in Kwaio (after some twelve months of fieldwork). I found myself learning Pidgin through Kwaio, despite its English-derived lexical labels.

My intuitions were that monolingual Kwaio speakers (and, I presumed, speakers of any other Malaita language, at least) acquiring Pidgin faced mainly a task of learning a substantial new set of lexical items and grammatical forms corresponding to the categories of their native languages. Some Pidgin constructions and forms had no direct counterparts in Kwaio, and vice versa—not surprisingly. But it seemed from my informal observations, prior to 1983–84, that the striking parallels in syntax between Kwaio and Solomons Pidgin (not to mention in semantic categories), the frequent morpheme-by-morpheme correspondences between constructions in the two languages, would allow Kwaio speakers to use formulas of morpheme equivalence to learn Pidgin and to use it. Given the close relationships and grammatical commonalities among their languages, I guessed that the same would be true of speakers of any other Malaita language (and, perhaps to less striking degree, speakers of any other Southeast Solomonic language).

Several lines of research suggested themselves. One would be to do systematic studies of the parallels and contrasts between substrate languages and Solomons Pidgin (and to see if differences in the use of Pidgin corresponded to grammatical differences in substrate languages). This would entail looking closely at what I had surmised were important points in the grammar of Solomons Pidgin (e.g., future-marking, pronominal patterns, equational and prepositional sentences, prepositional verbs, transitive-marking) in relation to these patterns in particular substrate languages (most of which were poorly documented). A second line of research would be to look closely at how Pidgin is used by Kwaio speakers in terms of constructions and discourse strategies, and to use whatever means proved possible to test how closely, if at all, they were calquing on corresponding Kwaio patterns in using Pidgin (and were in effect using Kwaio grammar and semantics with new labels). A third and critically important line of research would be to study how speakers of diverse Solomons languages actually used Pidgin in communicating with one another (particularly older men who had learned Pidgin as young adults on plantations or in other work situations). To the extent individual speakers were calquing on their native languages, we might expect that they would adopt different discourse strategies when using Pidgin depending on the languages natively spoken by those with whom they were interacting. We might guess that a Kwaio speaker would and could use more complex Pidgin syntax when interacting with fellow Malaitans speaking languages closely related to his own than when speaking to a Gilbertese or Polynesian or western Solomons speaker of Pidgin. And conversely, a Roviana or Simboese (western Solomons) speaker of Pidgin might use more complex syntactic patterns in speaking with a Ghanongga speaker than with a Malaitan. Either the Malaitan or the Simboese would be likely to simplify his syntax considerably in speaking to a European. (Having through the years heard Malaitans simplify their Pidgin in trying to communicate with Europeans, very few of whom had an adequate command of the language, I had long suspected that many of the nineteenth-century texts in Pacific pidgin reflected a distortion in the direction of simplification, as well as recording errors: Pacific Islanders fully fluent in pidgin were using "foreigner talk" in communicating with Europeans who had a defective command of it.) How well did Pidgin speakers (especially speakers of "bush" varieties rather than urbanites) actually understand one another, on plantations or in other work contexts, if they were using partly different grammars, calquing on their native languages?

Unfortunately, my interest in these questions coincided with an almost total ban on field research by expatriates in the Solomons (unless they happened to be missionaries).* I have been able to spend only a few weeks in the Solomons since 1979, most of this time in the urban milieu of Honiara and in the provincial capital of Gizo, both settings where contemporary Pidgin contrasts sharply with variants spoken in the more isolated and conservative areas (notably parts of "bush" Malaita) that still provide the bulk of plantation labor. Not being permitted to do any active research in the Solomons, I have had to work at a distance and in unsystematic encounters and informal conversations in 1984 and 1986.

One strategy I devised was to have a colleague in the Solomons work with a Kwaio speaker, having him listen to a cassette on which I had uttered some 400 Kwaio sentences[†] that I had taken from texts. These Kwaio sentences were used to elicit Pidgin equivalents from my old friend Simone Maa'eobi, a man in his sixties who had learned Pidgin on plantations in the 1930s. Later, when I was able to visit Honiara briefly, I elicited Pidgin versions of the same sentences from Jonathan Fifi'i, another Kwaio man in his sixties with whom I had worked for years. Since Pidgin

---

*The terms "expatriate" and "European" are used in the postcolonial Pacific to refer to white foreigners, even though neither term is particularly apt.

[†]The illustrative text sentences from my Kwaio grammar (1985).

sentences were elicited through the medium of Kwaio sentences, this created a situation that might encourage parallel syntactic constructions where they were possible. But getting two versions helped to control for this; and my own knowledge of Pidgin assured me that the sentences were with rare exceptions quite typical and acceptable Pidgin.

A second strategy I was able to pursue when I was in Honiara briefly was to record stories in Kwaio from Fifi'i and from another Kwaio speaker of the same age, Kwalafane'ia, of events in childhood or on pre–World War II plantations. Having elicited stories in Kwaio, I asked each man to come back after a week; and when he did, I asked him to tell me the same stories in Pidgin. From each, I in fact elicited several renderings of the same story, in both Kwaio and Pidgin, over a period of three weeks, but leaving maximal gaps between Kwaio and Pidgin versions. Comparison of these texts provides many clues with regard to the calquing hypothesis and discourse strategies in the two languages.

Limited to working with Kwaio friends in the context of my own house, I could not obtain data on the Pidgin used by speakers of other languages, in relation to patterns in these substrate languages, or to study the use of Pidgin in discourse in multilingual plantation settings. During a short visit in 1986, I was not able to do any systematic research, but managed to record some conversations with elderly speakers of other Malaita languages and several speakers of western Solomons languages, which provide further comparative evidence. Hopefully, a gradual lifting of obstacles to research will allow further investigations in the near future.

The data I have been able to glean, though incomplete and perhaps distorted in some respects, nonetheless strikingly illuminate parallels between Solomons Pidgin and the Malaita languages, and the hypothesis of pervasive calquing. Elsewhere (Keesing 1987) I have approached the calquing hypothesis from an experimental direction. Taking a long account in Kwaio by Kwalafane'ia of episodes immediately prior to World War II, and during the initial Japanese attack, and using a set of correspondence formulas and lexical equivalences between Kwaio forms and their putative Pidgin equivalents, I have computer-generated a Pidgin version of the same discourse as predicted by the calquing hypothesis. I comment at length on the similarities and differences between the two grammars, as revealed by the paired sentences, actual and predicted. I then give a Pidgin account of the same events as recounted by Kwalafane'ia several weeks after his original Kwaio account. I conclude that the hypothesis of pervasive calquing is strongly supported by the data; and show from the exercise some of the ways in which Pidgin grammar is simplified.

Here I shall take a different tack, examining first the corpus of Kwaio sentences from my Kwaio grammar (1985) and the Pidgin sentences given as equivalent by Maa'eobi and Fifi'i. A useful place to begin is with the use of verbal particles, particularly markers of mode, tense, and aspect, in Kwaio and in the Solomons Pidgin spoken by these older Kwaio speakers. I will focus, to begin, on two verbal particles that mark the temporal frame of the verb: the Kwaio future marker *ta-* (or its longer form *ta'a-*, and allomorphs *te-* and *to-*) and the particle *bi'i*, usually translatable by English "just," and indicating (when the particle is used by itself) that the action of the verb has just taken place. For these Maa'eobi (SM) and Fifi'i (JF) use *bae* or *baebae* and *das* (or some phonological variant, *des* or *tes*) in Pidgin.

gila   ta-la   leka (Kwaio)
FP(them)   FUT-SRP(they)   go
They will go.

olketa   bae   i   go (SM)
FP(them)   FUT   SRP(3p)   go
They will go.

olketa   baebae   olketa-i   go (JF)
FP(them)   FUT   SRP(they)   go
They will go.

This pattern is consistent throughout the corpus. For *bi'i*, which in Kwaio occurs between the SRP and the verb, both speakers use *das* (or a pho-nological variant):

ngai   e   bi'i   aga-si-a (Kwaio)
FP(him)   SRP(he)   just   see-TRS-it
He just saw it.

hem   i   tes   luk-im (JF)
FP(him)   SRP(he)   just   see-TRS
He just saw it.

Of course, this usage parallels English "just"; is there any evidence that Kwaio speakers are calquing here? In Kwaio, the future marker can be conjoined with *bi'i*, with a semantic import not predictable from the two forms used separately. It indicates that the action of the verb will take place in a short time. Both Kwaio speakers use *baebae* and *das* together to express these meanings:

ta-goru   bi'i   aga-si-a (Kwaio)
FUT-SRP(weIncl)   just   see-TRS-it
We'll see it in a while.

bae   iumi   das   luk-im (SM)
FUT   SRP(weIncl)   just   see-TTS

baebae   iumi   des   luk-im (JF)
FUT   SRP(weIncl)   just   see-TTS

Such detailed correspondences make it inescapably clear that Kwaio speakers use these aspect markers in ways that directly follow the grammar of their native language. Yet at the same time, the resources for doing so constitute part of the pidgin linguistic system going back to the nineteenth century. The *tes* form, for example, is found in some early texts and in New Hebridean Pidgin. In Vanuatu as in the Solomons, such forms allow of calquing on substrate languages, as witness Charpentier's (1979: 353) example from Vetmbao (South Malekula):

naji   nga-mandrxa   mun
FP(him)   SRP(he)-ASP   drink
He just drank.

em   i   tes   trink
FP(him)   SRP(he)   ASP   drink

It is useful to remember that this pattern of marking aspect with particles interposed between SRP and verb is one reconstructed by Pawley (1972, 1973) for Proto-Oceanic and Proto-Eastern Oceanic. Incorporation into nineteenth-century pidgin of a form derived from English "just" as an aspect marker, in exactly this slot, and its deployment by Melanesian speakers of pidgin in ways congruent with their native languages, are entirely consistent with the historical scenario I have reconstructed. But here again we have a pattern that easily accommodates superstrate speakers, and that follows a pattern widespread in Atlantic creoles.

The evidence that Kwaio speakers are calquing on their native language in using Solomons Pidgin goes further. In fact, the entire set of Kwaio particles marking the time-frame of the verb, some of which are preverbal and some postverbal, correspond in their Solomons Pidgin usage to a set of particles derived from English but carrying exactly the same import as the Kwaio particles, and placed in exactly the same slots. We glimpsed this pattern in Chapter 11 in regard to the virtual disappearance of *bin* as a marker of past events in Solomons Pidgin. Linda Simons (1986) has discussed this phenomenon in regard to the perfect marker that follows the verb, taking To'aba'ita (northern Malaita) as her point of comparison and showing that the perfect marker—which in all the Malaita languages assumes the form $n(VV)$*—exactly corresponds to

*The vowels here vary: North Malaita *na, naa,* Kwaio *no'o.*

Solomons Pidgin *nao*. I shall instead look at two more interesting forms in Kwaio that are morphologically verbal and act as, in effect, modal auxiliaries within the VP. In Kwaio, *kee* usually serves in narrative to indicate the sequential relationship between acts described in successive clauses. *Kee* before an active verb indicates that the act described in the previous clause preceded the act marked with the auxiliary. Throughout the corpus, Maa'eobi uses *go* as equivalent to *kee*, and Fifi'i uses *go* or *gogo*.

e	kee	nigi	lo-lo'o	me-'e		bi'i	leka	folo-si-a (Kwaio)
SRP(he)	AUX	arrive	on top	and-SRP(he)		just	go	across-TRS-it

Then he arrived up there and went across (it).

hem-i	gogo	kas-im	antafu	ana	hem-i	tas	go	koros-im (JF)
SRP(he)	AUX	reach-TRS	on top	and	SRP(he)	just	go	across-TRS

Note the pervasive pattern of calquing here, in which virtually every morpheme in the two sentences directly corresponds (including the final prepositional verb). The only difference between the two sentences is the use of *kas-im* 'reach' as a transitive verb in Solomons Pidgin, where Kwaio uses an intransitive 'arrive.' An interesting pair of sentences was elicited from Maa'eobi and Fifi'i when each chose an alternative reading of an unintentionally ambiguous Kwaio sentence I had intended to be interpreted with *ta'a* 'people' as its noun subject. Maa'eobi selected this reading; Fifi'i interpreted *ta'a* as the relatively uncommon full form of the future marker.

ta'a	la		kee	kwai-ri	la'u	a-i (Kwaio)
people	SRP(they)		AUX	report	more	LOC-it

Then the people reported about that as well.
(Or, with *ta'a* as future marker, 'then they'll report'.)

olketa	pipol	olketa-i	go	taleaot	long	hem	moa (SM)
PLU	people	SRP(they)	AUX	report	LOC	it	more

Then the people reported about that as well.

baebae	olketa	go	stori	long	hem (JF)
FUT	SRP(they)	AUX	report	LOC	it

And then they'll report about that.

And, as a final example:

alata	gila	leka	mola,	gila	kee a'a-ri-a	'inoi (Kwaio)
time	SRP(they)	go	PRF	SRP(they)	AUX carry-TRS-it	taro-shoots

When they set off, they were carrying taro shoots.

taem	olketa-i	go	olketa-i	go	kar-em	taro (SM)
time	SRP(they)	go	SRP(they)	AUX	carry-TRS	taro

taem	olketa		go	nao	olketa		go	kar-em
time	SRP(they)		go	PRF	SRP(they)		AUX	carry-TRS

'inoi	long	taro (JF)
shoot	GEN	taro

The Kwaio form *me'e*, preceding an active verb, again operates as a verbal auxiliary in narrative, to convey meanings that in English would be expressed by "went ahead and." Throughout the corpus, both Maa'eobi and Fifi'i use *kam* as an auxiliary corresponding to *me'e*.

gila	me'e	fane	naa	'ue	la'akau (Kwaio)
SRP(they)	AUX	ascend	LOC	vine	DEM

And then they went ahead and climbed that rattan vine.

olketa-i	kam	goap	long	loiakeni (SM)
SRP(they)	AUX	ascend	LOC	rattan vine

ana	olketa	kam	koafu	long	des-fala	robu (JF)
and	SRP(they)	AUX	ascend	LOC	DEM-ADJ	vine

Or again,

rua	solodia	gala	me'e	ula	i	suri-a (Kwaio)
two	police	SRP(they2)	AUX	stand	LOC	beside-him

Two policemen would then stand flanking him.

tu-fala	solodia	tufala		kam	sten	weit-em (SM)
two-ADJ	police	SRP(they2)		AUX	stand	with-TRS

ana	tu-fala	solodia	tufala-i	kam	standafu	weit-em	hem (JF)
and	two-ADJ	police	SRP(they2)	AUX	stand	with-TRS	him

The use of the Solomons Pidgin prepositional verb *weit-em* 'with (him)' as corresponding to the Kwaio prepositional verb *suri-a* 'alongside (him)' by both speakers is striking. The two Solomons Pidgin renderings usefully illustrate how the transitive suffix in Solomons Pidgin incorporates an un-marked third-person ending. When the object of a transitive verb or, as here, prepositional verb is a higher-animate being, the third-person object pronoun *hem* is optionally used. Note also in these sentences that the marking of nonsingular third-person SRPs with -*i* is quite optional.

The same parallelism is manifest throughout the set of sentences elic-ited from Maa'eobi and Fifi'i—even though they often select alternative lexical equivalents, as in:

la	'ubuni	bala	te-'e		ori	mai	gani (Kwaio)
ART	'Ubuni	maybe	FUT-SRP(he)		return	DEI	tomorrow

Maybe 'Ubuni will come back tomorrow.

'ubuni	ating	baebae	i		kambek	tumora (SM)
'Ubuni	maybe	FUT	SRP(he)		return	tomorrow

'ubuni	maet	hem-i	kambek	tumora (JF)
'Ubuni	maybe	SRP(he)	return	tomorrow

Even their alternative strategies of paraphrasing when Kwaio terms with specific cultural content have no direct Solomons Pidgin equivalents are revealing; the similarities between the sentences given by Maa'eobi and Fifi'i are much more striking than their contrasts. Compare:

rua	wane	no'ona	gala		'akwa	no'o	fa-ni	lafea
two	man	DEM	SRP(they2)		run away	PRF	to-LOC	interior

Those two men ran away into the interior

na'a	nga	ta'a	i	asi	la		lofe-ga
so	ART	people	LOC	coast	SRP(they)		hunt-them

so the coastal people hunted them,

ma	ka	'ato (Kwaio)
but	SRP(it)	be difficult

but it was impossible.

tufala	ia	i		ranawe	go	long	lafea
FP(they2)	DEM	SRP(3p)		run away	DEI	LOC	interior

so	olketa	long	solowata	olketa-i		trae-em	enemi	long	oloketa
so	people	LOC	sea	SRP(they)		try-TRS	attack	LOC	them

bat	i		had	tumas (SM)
but	SRP(it)		be hard	be excessive

tu-fala	mane	ia	tufala-i		ranawe	fo	wan-fala	biles
two-ADJ	man	DEM	SRP(they2)		run away	LOC	one-ADJ	place

longo	lafea	hem	nao	dastawe	olketa	longo	solowata
LOC	interior	FP(it)	TOP	why	people	LOC	coast

trae	fo	kil-im	bataa	i		hat	tumas (JF)
try	INF	kill-TRS	but	SRP(it)		be hard	be excessive

The corpus shows striking regularities between the two speakers (whose sentences were recorded a year apart) even when they are producing Solomons Pidgin equivalents of syntactic patterns quite distinctive of or idiomatic in Kwaio for which Solomons Pidgin has no direct counterpart. Compare:

ngai	e	siri-a	'a-gala-i		aga	'oo-fi-a (Kwaio)
FP(him)	SRP(he)	want-it	for-SRP(they2)		look	search-TRS-it

He wants the two of them to look for it.

hem-i	laek-em	mek-em	tufala	lukat-em (SM)
SRP(he)	want-TRS	CAUS-TRS	SRP(they2)	search-TRS

hem-i	wand-em	mek-em	tufala-i	luk	fo	hem (JF)
SRP(he)	want-TRS	CAUS-TRS	SRP(they2)	look	for	it

Elsewhere, Maa'eobi and Fifi'i alternate this constructional pattern with another, using *fo* to mark the clause that is the object of "want":

mele	siri-a	'a-le'i	naana'i	mama-ni-'ame'e (Kwaio)
SRP(we2E)	want-it	for-SRP(them)	stay	wait-TRS-us2(E)

We two wanted them to wait for us.

mitufala	laek-em	mek-em	olketa-i	stap	weit-em	mitufala (SM)
SRP(we2E)	want-TRS	CAUS-TRS	SRP(them)	stay	wait-TRS	us2(E)

mitufala	laek-em	fo	oloketa-i	weit-em	mitufala (JF)
SRP(we2E)	want-TRS	for	SRP(they)	wait-TRS	us2(Ex)

Interrogative constructions show striking parallels that make clear that Maa'eobi and Fifi'i are using a formula of equivalences between the "wh-" forms in Kwaio and Pidgin. But again, the constructional patterns where Kwaio gives an idiosyncratic twist are more revealing of the relationships between the two languages than those where parallels are exact. In "which X . . . ?" constructions, Kwaio uses the FP following a fronted noun to embed an equational clause with the interrogative *taa* 'what'— "X it what . . . ?" Solomons Pidgin provides no corresponding pattern, but Maa'eobi and Fifi'i use exactly the same Pidgin equivalent:

omea	ngai	taa	'oo	to'o	dari-a	a-i? (Kwaio)
feast	FP(it)	what	SRP(you)	look	find-it	LOC-it

At which mortuary feast did you find it?

watkaen	fist	nao	iu	faend-em	long	hem? (SM)
which	feast	TOP	SRP(you)	find-TRS	LOC	it

watakaeni	karaafule	nao	iu	luk-im	hem	long	hem? (JF)
which	feast	TOP	SRP(you)	see-TRS	it	LOC	it

Kwaio also offers the possibility of simply using *omea taa* 'which feast' to introduce such a sentence; either way, the interrogative topicalizes the fronted object of a preposition, which is referenced by the trace pronoun *-i* at the end of the clause—a topicalization marked with *nao* in Solomons Pidgin.

Some final examples of embedded clauses will serve further to illustrate the fit between Kwaio syntactic patterns and those used in Pidgin by Maa'eobi and Fifi'i. Here, for the sake of brevity, I use the equivalences given by Fifi'i:

la	kwate-a	'ota	fa-na	ta'a	geni	la	a'ari (Kwaio)
SRP(they)	give-TRS	areca	for-it	people	female	SRP(they)	carry

They gave areca (nuts) to the women who did the carrying.

olketa-i	gif-im	biralnate	fo	olketa	wuman	olketa-i	kare (JF)
SRP(they)	give-TRS	areca	for	PLU	woman	SRP(they)	carry

sui	ma	la	ori	i	fanua	naa	ta'a	geni
finish	and	SRP(they)	return	LOC	place	POSS	people	female

Then they went back to the village of the women

la	a'ari (Kwaio)
SRP(they)	carry

who did the carrying.

finis	olketa-i	gobeke	longo	piles	bilongo	olketa	wuman
finish	SRP(they)	return	LOC	place	POSS	PLU	woman

i	kare (JF)
SRP(3p)	carry

ta'a	geni	la	a'ari-a	go'u	fa-na	ta'a
people	female	SRP(they)	carry-it	taro	for-it	people

The women carried taro for the people

la	ori	mai	naaboni (Kwaio)
SRP(they)	return	DEI	yesterday

who came back yesterday.

oloketa	wuman	olketa-i	kar-em	taro	fo	olketa	pipol
PLU	woman	SRP(they)	carry-TRS	taro	for	PLU	people

i	kambek	longo	astade (JF)
SRP(3p)	return	LOC	yesterday

(SM gives . . . i kambek astade)

la	sufa-a	wane	ta'a	geni
SRP(they)	accuse-him	man	people	female

They accused the man the women

la	aga-si-a	i	tarusi (Kwaio)
SRP(they)	see-TRS-him	LOC	water

saw at the stream.

olketa-i	go	ask-em	wan-fala	mane	olketa	mere
SRP(they)	AUX	accuse-TRS	one-ADJ	man	PLU	woman

i	ruk-imu	longo	wota (JF)
SRP(3p)	see-TRS	LOC	water

Note in these sentences the way third-person pronouns, marked and un-marked for number, are used to maintain reference. In sentences with embedded relative clauses, as elsewhere in discourse, the speaker has a choice of using a third-person pronoun marked for number (*olketa-i, tufala-i*) or the unmarked form *i* alone. Where there is any constructional or semantic ambiguity, the speaker marks number on the pronoun; where there is not, the unmarked form is likely to be used. The assumption is that the unmarked *i* references an immediately preceding noun. Note that marking the pronoun for number can actually create a semantic am-biguity that is avoided by using the short "default" form. If one used, for the last sentence, *olketa-i go ask-em wan-fala mane olketa mere* olketa-i *ruk-imu longo wota*, there can actually be no reading of "They accused the man they saw at the stream," because that would leave *olketa mere* unin-terpretable. But the confusing suggestion of coreferentiality between the "they" at the beginning and the "they" of the embedded clause is avoided by using the unmarked form of the pronoun, which can only refer to the immediately preceding *olketa mere*.

It is not possible to compare so directly the Kwaio narratives given by Kwalafane'ia and Fifi'i with the Pidgin versions of the same events they recorded a week or more later. Not surprisingly, the two men usually—in these extended narratives—gave a more detailed account of particular episodes in one language than, on a different occasion, they gave in the other. In some cases, however, they dwelled at some length on the same events. I have set out some extended sections of these parallel accounts in the Appendix, in such a way that the two accounts, on facing pages, can be compared.

This evidence further confirms that syntactically Kwaio and Solomons Pidgin are remarkably close (and that the mapping of semantic categories between the two languages is also extremely close and systematic, if we allow for the much greater lexical elaboration of Kwaio). I have no doubt that a comparison of any Malaita language with the Pidgin used by its speakers would show similar close parallels and systematic calquing. Some evidence recently collected from a Lau speaker provides substance for the argument.

In 1986, I recorded a text from a Lau speaker named Maenuu, a man in his sixties obdurately resisting Christianity despite long residence in the western Solomons, that clearly illustrates calquing on a different Malaita language. Although Maenuu's Pidgin would be quite comprehensible to a Kwaio speaker (despite the Lau-derived phonology), many of the con-structions are rather different from those a Kwaio speaker would use. Ellison Suri, a Lau speaker and amateur linguist, has reconstructed for me what he takes to be the Lau sentences Maenuu would use to express the same meanings. Some fragments juxtaposing Maenuu's Pidgin and the corresponding Lau will serve to illustrate:

bat	taem	Masing	Rul	ia,	taem	hem-i	waka,
but	time	Maasina	Rule	DEM	time	SRP(it)	work

But at the time of Maasina Rule, when it was still going on,

fosi	wan	gurufu	hem-i	kamu,	kamu	longo	wan-fala	man,
if	one	group	SRP(it)	come	come	LOC	one-ADJ	man,

if a group had come to (visit) just one person,

oraet,	saet	bulong	Masinga	Rul	'anaa	sifi	longo	biles	nao
CONN	side	POSS	Maasina	Rule	and	chief	LOC	place	TOP

then the Maasina Rule leaders and the chief of that place

baebae	kalakasini	fo	haomas	pipol	kamu (Maenuu)
IRR	gather(rations)	for	how-many?	people	come

would collect food for however many people had come.

ma	si	kada-manga	Masina	Rul	na,	kada-manga	nia	rao
but	ART	time	Maasina	Rule	DEM	time	it	work

But at the time of Maasina Rule, when it was still going on,

lea-so	tee	ogu'ua	nia	lea-mai,	lea-mai	sia-na	tee	wane	go
if	one	group	it	come	come	to-it	one	man	only

if one group had come, come to (visit) just one person,

aia,	bali	nia	na	Masina	Rul	fai-ni-a	wane	baita
CONN	side	it	POSS	Maasina	Rule	with-TRS-it	man	big

then the Maasina Rule leaders and the chief

'ana	mafera	na
POSS	community	DEM

of that place

tara'ena	koni-a	fua-na	fita	tooa	lea-mai (Lau)
today	gather-it	for-it	how-many?	people	come

would collect food for however many people had come.

The closeness of the syntactic parallelism scarcely needs to be underlined. Particularly striking is the use of the interrogative "how many" to render "however many," an idiomatic pattern distinctive of Lau that would not, for instance, be used by a Kwaio speaker. In this fragment, Maenuu uses 'and' in Solomons Pidgin where in Lau Suri uses the prepositional verb *fai-ni-a*. However, Maenuu could equally have used the directly corresponding *wet-em* in Pidgin here, as he does at several points in the text (including a passage set out earlier in this chapter). Notice also Maenuu's use of *baebae* in Pidgin as an irrealis-mode marker, where for Lau Suri uses 'today' to render the same hypothetical meaning. Like other northern Malaita languages, Lau has forms of the SRPs marked for nonaccomplished mode (and usually indicating events expected to take place in the future); but these do not have the force to mark an irrealis mode as clearly as Pidgin *baebae*.

A second fragment from Maenuu and Suri's Lau equivalent will illustrate further syntactic parallelism.

fosi	Masinga	Rul,	fosi	osem	fosi	i	stap
if	Maasina	Rule	if	as if	if	SRP(it)	remain

Supposing that Maasina Rule still was going on

longo	Malaita	goo-go	kas-em	destaem
LOC	Malaita	go-go	reach-TTS	present-time

on Malaita, up to the present time,

olsem	iufala,	olketa	Iuropin	nao,	fosi	iufala	kas-em
as if	FP(youPl)	PLU	Whites	TOP	if	SRP(youPl)	reach-TTS

and let's say that it was you Europeans who came

longo	Malaita—	olsem	Masinga	Rul	hem-i	stap	iet—
LOC	Malaita	as if	Maasina	Rule	SRP(it)	remain	still

to Malaita—that is, if Maasina Rule was still going on—

ou,	iufala	no	lukat-em	haos	fo	silip (Maenuu)
EXCL	SRP(youPl)	NEG	search-TTS	house	for	sliip

hey, you wouldn't (have to) hunt for a house to sleep in.

lea-so	Masinga	Rul,	lea-so	usulia	ka	too
if	Maasina	Rule	if	as if	it	remain

Supposing that Maasina Rule still was going on

i	Malaita	lee-lea	ka	dao	si	kada	na
LOC	Malaita	go-go	it	reach	ART	time	DEM

on Malaita, up to the present time,

usulia	gomolu-gi	na	wane	kwao	lea-so	gomolu	dao	kou
as if	youPl	ART	man	white	if	youPl	arrive	DEI

and let's say that it was you Europeans who came to

Malaita	usulia	Masinga	Rul	e	too	'ua
Malaita	as if	Maasina	Rule	it	remain	still

Malaita—that is, if Maasina Rule was still going on—

ou,	gomolu	langi-si	nana-si	luma	ni	teola (Lau)
EXCL	youPl	NEG	search-TTS	house	for	sleep

hey, you wouldn't have to hunt for a house to sleep in.

Although Lau syntax follows a general Malaita pattern, it has some special twists. Obviously, at the level of morphology and lexical resources, Solomons Pidgin does not exactly parallel this or any other Southeast Solomonic language. But the syntactic use Maenuu makes of the resources available in Pidgin bears the unmistakable imprint of his native language. Not surprisingly, he learned Solomons Pidgin through Lau, as a young adult; and not surprisingly, when he speaks Solomons Pidgin he follows the channels and patterns of his native language.

My recordings of Pidgin as used by speakers of western Solomons languages suggest that they, too, calque extensively on their native languages, given the constraints under which they operate. That is, these western Solomons languages are Oceanic, but use syntactic patterns rather different from those of the Southeast Solomonic languages that, I argue, have given Solomons Pidgin its special cast, and more generally, from those of the EO languages. Within the limits of the code, western Solomons speakers appear to be bending syntactic patterns in the direction of the languages spoken natively by the men from whom I was able to record Pidgin accounts, although this must for the moment remain a working hypothesis.

A first fragment of suggestive evidence comes from Alik, the Simbo speaker mentioned in Chapter 12, who learned Pidgin in the 1920s as a policeman on Malaita:

taem—	kam	taem	bilong	taks	ia,	fo	raon		long	Malaita
time	come	time	POSS	tax	DEM	INF	go-round		LOC	Malaita

When the time for the tax came, to go around Malaita

oraete,	Mista	Belo	i		see	iufala	olketa	polis
then	Mr	Bell	SRP(3s)		say	FP(youPl)	PLU	police

then Mr. Bell said, "You police,

iufala	standbae	fo	tumora	iumi		go,	raon	long
SRP(youPl)	stand-by	INF	tomorrow	SRP(youPl)		go	around	LOC

you get ready to go tomorrow around

Malaita	fo	bei-em	taks,	olketa	pipol
Malaita	INF	pay-TTS	tax	PLU	people

Malaita. For the people to pay tax.

Here we have two constructions I have never heard from Malaita speakers of Pidgin. The first is the phrase "come time of tax, to circle Malaita." Southeast Solomonic speakers would here begin with a temporal phrase, but never a verb. The second sentence ("For pay the tax, the people"), with the subject NP in final position, again would be completely aberrant to a Malaita speaker.

On Simbo grammar we have little information, beyond Hocart's texts. However, Lanyon-Orgill (1969: 41) gives several alternative sentence patterns and notes: "The rules for word-order are ill-defined and there appears to be no problem in the native mind of accepting sentences like those quoted above, and again re-ordering the whole construction by placing the verb at the end." For the closely related Roviana language, Waterhouse (1949: 244) comments: "The subject may precede the verb, but more correctly follows the objective suffix [i.e., a direct object marked on the verb]."

Hocart's Pidgin sentences from Simbo include one in particular (1925: 234) that no Malaitan would produce: "Long-fellow he speak, he *vara-vara*; s'pose he short fellow, he *pito*." I analyze this as

long-fala	i	spik,	i	varavara
long-ADJ	SRP(it)	say	SRP(it)	varavara

If it's a long one he utters it's a varavara;

sapos	i	sot-fala,	i	pito
if	SRP(it)	short-ADJ	SRP(it)	pito

if it's a short one, it's a pito.

That is, *long-fala* appears to be the direct object of the first clause.

From two Ghanongga (Western Solomonic) speakers, Kazikana and Wiliamu, I recorded accounts similarly containing sentences that would be most unlikely for a Malaita speaker. Kazikana's account of his attachment to the Coast Watcher Donald Kennedy includes several syntactically interesting sentences, including:

hem-i	put-im	mifala	long	wan-fala	sipi,	Kenedi
SRP(he)	put-TRS	us(E)	LOC	one-NUM	ship	Kennedy

Kennedy put us on a ship.

lukat-em	sipi,	kip-im	sipi	ia	iufala,	hem-i	see
guard-TRS	ship	keep-TRS	ship	DEM	FP(youPl)	SRP(he)	say

"You guard that ship, keep that ship," he said.

taem	mifala	istap	long	Seghe
when	SRP(weE)	stay	LOC	Seghe

When we were staying at Seghe,

Kenedi	nao	mifala	istap	wet-em
Kennedy	TOP	SRP(weE)	stay	with-TRS

we stayed with Kennedy.

In the first sentence, the subject NP again comes in sentence-final position. In Kennedy's instruction to them, the *iufala* comes in clause-final position. In Southeast Solomonic languages (or equivalent Pidgin sentence patterns), the implied "you" of imperative constructions can optionally be made explicit; but if so, it precedes the verb.

From the other Ranongga speaker, Wiliamu, I recorded, in an account of his wartime work as a medical dresser:

oraete,	taem	i	ronowe	long	busi	olketa,	mi	go
OK	when	SRP(3p)	run away	LOC	bush	FP(them)	SRP(I)	AUX

So when they ran away into the bush, I went and

luk-im	olketa,	mi	wok-em	olketa	samting
see-TTS	them	SRP(I)	fix-TTS	PLU	thing

saw them, I fixed their things,

sam-fala	soa	bulong	olketa
some-NUM	sore	POSS	them

their sores.

Again, note in the first clause the syntactic pattern where the subject NP (here the FP "them") follows the VP. We have virtually no grammatical information on Ghanongga, but Ray comments that "the Ganonnga is evidently very near the Eddystone (Simbo) and Roviana" (1926: 565). We may guess that these speakers of Western Solomonic languages are producing Pidgin clauses with the subject NP in postverbal position following the syntactic patterns of their native languages. However, on these points of variation and calquing, much work obviously remains to be done.

The Solomons evidence, although unavoidably incomplete and inferential, very strongly suggests that, in inheriting from the Labor Trade a pidgin with a very strong Oceanic cast syntactically as well as semantically, speakers of different Solomon Islands languages bend the common code in the direction of their native languages. The evidence we have examined suggests that Oceanic speakers, and particularly Southeast Solomonic speakers, learn Solomonic Pidgin in terms of the syntactic patterns and semantic categories of their first languages; and use it following syntactic patterns and discourse strategies of these substrate languages. That they can do so so pervasively further reinforces a picture of a pidgin language with a remarkable history, and a remarkable linguistic nature: a language very different from those portrayed in general accounts of pidgins and creoles.

CHAPTER 14

 Conclusion

A NUMBER of questions are raised by the parallels and calquing patterns explored in Chapter 13.

1. How can a lingua franca that allows of such syntactic complexity, paralleling that of a natural language, be reconciled with the view linguistic theorists have consistently taken of pidgins as radically simplified and syntactically limited? Is Solomons Pidgin a pidgin? (We are dealing with Kwaio speakers who learned Solomons Pidgin in adulthood, and with a "bush" dialect that apparently reached its present form by the 1920s—not urban speakers who might have learned a creolized version).*

2. If Solomons Pidgin so closely follows the syntactic patterns of particular substrate languages, how can its speakers use it to communicate with one another?

3. How could a pidgin have evolved that, despite its almost total lexification from English as superstrate language, has a structure so close to that of Southeast Solomonic Oceanic languages?

The first question allows of no easy answer. As Bickerton (1981, 1984) argues, Melanesian Pidgin is anomalous, when seen against the background of the documented pidgins and creoles of the Northern Hemisphere, in the degree of its syntactic elaboration and stabilization. Some of the literature on Tok Pisin suggests that much of this elaboration has taken place in the past fifty years. The Solomons Pidgin data indicate that

---

*See Jourdan 1985 for a sustained argument that the further expansion and streamlining of Solomons Pidgin in the contemporary urban context is primarily a result of Pidgin becoming the primary language of a speech community, rather than of nativization by the first generation growing up in Honiara; her data show that the main innovators have been adults for whom Pidgin is a second, but primary, language.

that dialect, at least, had attained a degree of syntactic complexity and stabilization approaching those of a natural language more than half a century ago.

How do we account for such complexity and elaboration? Bickerton (1984) suggests that the long period of Melanesian Pidgin's use as a plantation language, hence its transmission over several generations, created the conditions for its expansion and stabilization. But earlier, in his 1977 correspondence with me, he had speculated whether an early pidgin had gone through a phase of nativization and had become repidginized after going through a phase of radical expansion. I have noted that Bickerton now places less stress on the possible role of nativization on nineteenth-century Pacific pidgin, arguing that it seems neither likely on sociolinguistic grounds nor necessary to account for the linguistic developments. But the data on the crucial time period—roughly the 1850s—and the crucial areas—the eastern Carolines, the Gilberts, Rotuma, the Loyalties, and particularly ships with mixed Island crews—are too fragmentary to allow us to do more than guess. Purely on linguistic grounds, the possibility cannot be ruled out that a generation of "nativizers" expanded a developing pidgin into a creolized form, which they then disseminated as a lingua franca of the Labor Trade. But it seems unlikely, on the basis of the evidence I have assessed, and on sociolinguistic grounds, that nativization in this early period had a strong formative influence *linguistically* on a developing Pacific pidgin. Those Islanders who acquired childhood fluency in this language of shipboard life and for whom it may have been the main language (although for most of them it would not have been a mother tongue) would have been relatively few in number, and scattered; they had neither the numbers nor the political position with which to exert a major formative linguistic influence on the developing language, although I believe they played a crucial part in its dissemination and, as its most fluent speakers, served as models for adult language learners, Islanders and Europeans.

A good deal of the evidence we would need to assess the possible influence on a developing Pacific pidgin of those who learned it in early childhood and used it as their main common language may well exist, in the form of linguistic fragments and accounts of shipboard and shore life in this decade; but if so, it remains to be excavated from archives and microfilms.

The question of how fluent Island speakers of Solomons Pidgin (or of Bislama) who calque so closely on their diverse native languages use it to communicate with one another has received little attention. Perhaps the political obstacles that have precluded my studying Solomons Pidgin discourse in plantation settings, in relation to patterns in substrate languages and strategies of communication, will be removed. Such research would be possible in Vanuatu as well, and it remains a fruitful direction for further research. For the Solomons, a partial answer is that the syntactic structures of Southeast Solomonic languages are quite similar, and those of the Malaita languages (whose speakers have been the dominant element in almost every setting where Pidgin has been the common linguistic medium) are virtually the same, requiring only minor adjustments to one another. In using Solomons Pidgin along the syntactic channels of their native languages, Malaitans have been producing essentially common linguistic coin. No doubt a To'aba'ita speaker interpreting a Kwaio speaker who is calquing Pidgin tense/aspect/mode markers directly onto those of his native language loses some of the finer shadings of semantic marking from, say, *bae hem-i das luk-im*. But there would be no obstacles to effective communication in such loss of semantic detail produced as speakers of different Malaita languages bent Pidgin to their own slightly different designs. How much bending there may be, and how much loss, remain to be determined.

I have sought, in the preceding chapters, to answer the last question. The answers are complex, since what we are dealing with is an interplay between the more-or-less-shared structures of Eastern Oceanic substrate languages, the structure of English (which parallels EO patterns in many respects), universal constraints and limited structural possibilities, the faculties humans call on in producing "foreigner talk," and paths of second-language learning. No simple answer is possible. But I find it inconceivable that Solomons Pidgin and Southeast Solomonic languages could share so many structural and semantic patterns unless the EO substrate had a much stronger and more pervasive impress on a developing pidgin, at the various stages in its history, than most Melanesian Pidgin specialists have recognized.

Deciphering the historical and linguistic processes that have produced dialects of Melanesian Pidgin so different from the pidgins characterized by syntactic theorists, and so like the Oceanic languages of the southwestern Pacific, is a continuing challenge. I have sought to lay out the evidence, including my own data on relationships between Solomons Pidgin and Kwaio, in a way that challenges accepted views and invites further examination by linguists better qualified than I, and by historians who may find—or have found—critical scraps of evidence in musty archives.

Appendix

On the pages that follow, I set out some extracts from narrative accounts in Kwaio and Solomons Pidgin that allow comparison of constructions in the two languages. In 1984, working with two middle-aged Kwaio speakers, Jonathan Fifi'i and Tome Kwalafane'ia, I recorded several stories from each, in Kwaio, about experiences in childhood or young adulthood. A week or more later, I asked each to give me an account of the same events in Pidgin. As we would expect, the same events are usually recounted in greater detail in one language or the other, so the accounts are not strictly parallel (as they might have been had one been recorded immediately after the other). Nonetheless, parallel segments from the Kwaio and Pidgin narratives that describe the same events, set out on pages facing one another, allow us to compare both details of morphology and syntax and patterns of discourse—narrative styles and rhetorical devices—in the two languages.

For points of Kwaio grammar, readers can refer to my *Kwaio Grammar* (1985). Constructions in the two languages that are of special interest are here explicated in footnotes. The phonology may require brief explication to make the English sources of Pidgin lexical usages transparent. Like most speakers of bush Pidgin, Fifi'i in fact uses phonological patterns with considerable variation. But his native language has no [p]; and [l] and [r] are in complementary distribution. Kwaio speakers of Pidgin often use [f] in place of [p] in "standard" Pidgin. The following equivalences may make others transparent:

kafusaet	'capsize'
safen	'sharpen'
laetafu	'right up'
fisi	'piece'
rif	'leave'
lelebeti	'little bit'

The first text comes from Fifi'i's story of how his father shot two pigs, belonging to a close relative, which were raiding his garden; and then deceived the owner. In this episode, Fifi'i's father, who did not have ammunition for his old shotgun, produced a homemade shotgun shell with which to kill one (or, as it turned out, both) of the marauding pigs. A second fragment, occurring shortly after the first in Fifi'i's narrative, tells how his father, armed with his shotgun and single homemade shell, goes with his young son to the taro garden where marauding pigs have been damaging the crop.

The third sequence of paired texts comes from Tome Kwalafane'ia, a Kwaio man in his sixties who had worked on plantations in the late 1930s, then had served with the Solomon Islands Labour Corps in World War II. He had just arrived in Honiara when I recorded these texts in 1984; before that, he had been largely cut off from contemporary Pidgin for many years. Unlike Fifi'i, he commands only the "bush" dialect of Pidgin represented here (Fifi'i also commands a repertoire of contemporary town Pidgin, and some English).

Kwalafane'ia's account deals with events at Stanmore Plantation in the western Solomons just before the Japanese invasion of the Solomons, and tells how, having finished his contract, he arrived with his Kwaio workmates at Gavutu Island, the Burns Philp headquarters, just as it came under Japanese air attack. The Malaita laborers, there to be paid off and returned to their "passages," were caught up in the bombing attacks and took refuge in the forest on the adjacent mainland. Two short segments, which are continuous in the Kwaio account and slightly separated in the Pidgin account, will serve to illustrate Kwalafane'ia's Pidgin. A salient contrast between Fifi'i's speech and Kwalafane'ia's is that, like many Kwaio speakers with long plantation experience, Kwalafane'ia uses Pidgin loanwords quite extensively. One reason Kwaio speakers acquire Pidgin so quickly is that Kwaio has a very substantial vocabulary of Pidgin loanwords, used in everyday Kwaio conversation as equivalents to vernacular terms or, in some cases, replacing them as a result of word-tabooing (Keesing and Fifi'i 1969).

me-e	sui	ma	ka	lau-nge'eni-a	mola	nga	fee*	'efu'efu
and-srp(it)	be finished	and	srp(he)	fashion-trs-it	just	ART	unit	'efu'efu

And so he made an internode of 'efu'efu (bamboo).

'efu'efu	nga	'augwa'i	lo'oo	'ola	ngaa	'ino'ona	la'u	nga	ka'o
'efu'efu	ART	'augwa'i	DEM	thing	ART	like	also	ART	ka'o

'Efu'efu—that's a (kind of) 'augwa'i (bamboo), something . . . like ka'o.

ma	'efe'efu	ne-'e	tegela'a
but	'efu'efu	TOP-srp(it)	be strong

But 'efu'efu is really strong.

ngai	e	lau-nge'eni-a	sui	e	aru-a	nuku	i	'ubula-i
FP(him)	srp(he)	fashion-trs-it	then	srp(he)	put-it	powder	LOC	inside-it

He made it, then he put gunpowder inside it.

e	firi-a	nuku	'ubula-i
srp(he)	pour-it	powder	inside-it

He poured gunpowder inside it.

firi-a	no'ona	e	sui	ma	ka	age-a	la'u
pour-it	DEI	srp(it)	be finished	and	srp(he)	do-it	also

Put it there and then he also put

ni	me'e	agalo	i	'ubula-i
PLU	piece	cord	LOC	inside-it

pieces of cord inside,

ma	ka	mudu	faa-fi-a	e	gama-ri-a	leeleka
and	srp(he)	hammer	on-trs-it	srp(he)	pound-trs-it	go-go

and hammered on it, pounded it until

kee†	tii	no'o.	kee	ngasi	no'o
AUX	be hard	PRF	AUX	be hard	PRF

it was hard. It was hard.

*Kwaio has a developed set of numerical classifiers, including *fe'e*, used for spherical or nodelike objects, and *me'e* for pieces.

†The auxiliary (or aspect marker?) *kee* often carries an implicit (zero-marked) third-person SRP, especially before stative verbs.

wandee   hem-i   waawak-em   wan-fala   samding;   hem-i   wak-em   karisi
one day   SRP(he)   fashion-TTS   one-ADJ   thing   SRP(he)   fashion-TTS   shell
One day he made a thing; he made a shotgun shell.

dis-fala   karisi   hem-i   katarisi,   ia?
DEM-ADJ   shell   SRP(it)   cartridge   RHET
This "karisi" was a cartridge, right?

bataa   Pijin   bulongo   mifala   hem-i   karisi,   ia? ;   nem   blong   hemu
but   Pidgin   POSS   us(E)   SRP(it)   karisi   RHET   name   POSS   it
But in our Pidgin, it was "karisi," understand? That's what it was called.

hem-i   tek-em   wan-fala   bambu   wane   kaeni   bambu   hem-i   strong   bambu
SRP(he)   take-TTS   one-ADJ   bamboo   one   kind   bamboo   SRP(it)   strong   bamboo
He took a bamboo, a kind of bamboo that was strong.

mifala   nem   bulong   hem   mifala   kol-em   'efu'efu
FP(weE)   name   POSS   it   SRP(weE)   call-TTS   'efu'efu
Our name for it is "'efu'efu."

dis-fala   nem   blong   hem   mifala   kol-em,   ia?   'efu'efu   nao   mifala   kol-em
DEM-ADJ   name   POSS   it   SRP(weE)   call-TTS   RHET   'efu'efu   TOP   SRP(weE)   call-TTS
That (stuff), that's our name for it. "'Efu'efu" is what we call it.

nao   hem-i   kat-emu   wan-fala   fisi   long   hemu.   kat-emu   googo*   finis
so   SRP(he)   cut-TTS   one-ADJ   piece   POSS   it   cut-TTS   AUX   be finished
So anyway, he cut one piece of it. He cut it and then

hem-i   safen-em   lelebeti   bodi   bulong   hem   mek-em   hem-i   fiti
SRP(he)   shave-TTS   slightly   body   POSS   it   CAUS-TTS   SRP(it)   fit
he shaved down the casing slightly, so that it would fit

insaeti   longo   baa   bulong   raefolo.   kaakat-em   googo   finis   oraet
inside   POSS   barrel   POSS   rifle   cut-TTS   AUX   be finished   then
inside the rifle barrel. (He) cut it and then

hem-i   kafusaet-em   baura.   baura   meke-tunem   mifala   save   long   hem   nuku
SRP(he)   pour-TTS   powder   powder   synonym   SRP(weE)   know   LOC   it   nuku
he poured powder (inside). Our other word for powder was "nuku."

kafusaet-em   insaet   nao.   kafusaet-em   insaet   hem-i   wak-em   finisi
pour-TTS   inside   PRF   pour-TTS   inside   SRP(he)   fashion-TTS   be complete
(He) poured it inside. (He) poured it in.

hem-i   mek-em   sam-fala   ropu   'anaa   hem-i   hamar-im.   hamar-im   hamar-im
SRP(he)   make-TTS   some-ADJ   cord   and   SRP(he)   pound-TTS   pound-TTS   pound-TTS
He made some cord and he pounded it in.

hamar-im   i   strong   insaet   long   dis-fala   bambu
pound-TTS   SRP(it)   be strong   inside   POSS   DEM-ADJ   bamboo
He pounded and pounded and pounded it until it was packed inside that bamboo.

*Fifi'i is using *googo finis* here and below as equivalent to Kwaio *kee sui*.

e   sui   ma   ka   aru   'ino'ona   te'e   ni   me'e   fou,
SRP(it)   be finished and   SRP(he)   put   thusly   only   PLU   piece   stone
When that was done, he added a bunch of pieces of stone,

te'e   ni   me'e   foubolo   siisika   'ubula-i
only   PLU   piece   foubolo   small   inside-it
just some piece of little foubolo pebbles inside there,

fe'e-ni-a   ni   me'e   bolete,   ni   me'e   bolete
with-TRS-it   PLU   piece   shot   PLU   piece   shot
with some pieces of shot—some pieces of shot.

sui   ma   ka   bi'i   du'uta-a   no'o   ma   ka   gama-ri-a   la'u
then   and   SRP(he)   ASP   plug-it   PRF   and   SRP(he)   pound-TRS-it   again
Then he plugged it up, and pounded it again.

ne-'e   gama-ri-a   la'u   'ubu-na   nga   fee   'efu'efu
TOP-SRP(he)   pound-TRS-it   again   inside-it ART   unit   'efu'efu
He pounded it again inside that length of 'efu'efu.

gama-ri-a   e   sui   me-e   bi'i   aru-a   leeleka*
pound-TRS-it   SRP(it)   be finished   and-SRP(he) ASP   put-it   go-go
Pounded it and then kept it until it

ma   kee   tii   no'o.   nga   'ola   e   fida'ana   kabi—   karisi,
and   AUX   be hard   PRF   ART   thing   SRP(it)   be like   cartridge   karisi
was solid. That thing was just like a shotgun shell—a "karisi,"

'imani   mi   fa'a-lata-a   mola   'ino'ona
FP(usE)   SRP(weE)   CAUS-be named-it   just   thusly
that's what we called it.

　　*The Kwaio idiom here for the passage of time is *leeleka*, a reduplication of the verb *leka* 'go,' repeated several times if need be to show the passing of a long time interval. This device, used in all Malaita languages, is manifest in the Pidgin *googo*.

oraeti   hem-i   put-um   sam-fala   sumol-fala   birake   siton
then   SRP(he)   put-TRS   some-ADJ   small-ADJ   black   stone
Then he put in some small black stones.

birake   siton   ia   hem-i   put-um   oloketa   sumol-fala
black   stone   DEM   SRP(he)   put-TRS   PLU   small-ADJ
Those black stones, he put lots of little—

sumol-fala   fisi   nomoa   'inisaet   long   dat-fala   bambu
small-ADJ   piece   only   inside   LOC   DEM-ADJ   bamboo
small pieces inside that bamboo.

finis   hem-i   put-um   moa   go   sam-fala   fisi   longo   bolete
then   SRP(he)   put-TRS   also   DEI   some-ADJ   piece   POSS   shot
Then he also put in some pieces of shot.

nao   dis-fala   bolet   hem-i   mek-em   hem-i   hamar-im   tuu
then   DEM-ADJ   shot   SRP(he)   make-TRS   SRP(he)   pound-TRS   too
Then he pounded these pieces of shot as well.

haahamar-im   hamar-imu   googo   hem-i   strongo   nao
pound-TRS   pound-TRS   until   SRP(it)   be strong   PRF
Pounded it, pounded it until it was firm.

furu   laetafu   hem-i   furu   laetafu   nao
be filled   completely   SRP(it)   be filled   completely   PRF
It completely filled up,

'inisaet   longo   dis-fala   bambu
inside   POSS   DEM-ADJ   bamboo
the inside of this bamboo.

maetwote   finis   hem-i—   hem-i   stop-em   go   long   sam-fala   pepa,
EXCL   then   SRP(he)   SRP(he)   plug-TRS   DEI   with   some-ADJ   fiber
Well, when that was done he plugged it up with some fiber,

sam-fala   fisi   long   basikete   bulong   mifala.   finis   hem-i   rif-im   nao
some-ADJ   piece   POSS   basket   POSS   us(E)   then   SRP(he)   keep-TRS   PRF
some pieces of the baskets we make. And then he put it aside.

bata   wan-fala   piles   hem-i   stafu   pilesi   fo
but   one-ADJ   place   SRP(it)   remain   place   for
But one place was left, a place where

baebae   i   save   put-um   samting   fo   mek-em   bosita
FUT   SRP(he)   MOD   put-TRS   thing   INF   CAUS-TRS   explode
he would be able to put something to make it fire.

no'ona   sui   ngai   e   —'ola   e   age-a   fa-i
DEI   then   FP(him) SRP(he)   —thing   SRP(he)   do-it   for-it
Then he—the thing he made for it—

late'e   masisi   lo'oo   masisi   ba'ita   maamaa-na   ka   mekumeku
kind of   match   DEM   match   big   top-its   SRP(it)   be red
was a kind of match, a big match with a red head;

ma   masisi,   late'e   masisi   bokisi   a-i   me-e   ba'ita   iki
and   match   kind of   matches   box   LOC-it   and-SRP(it)   be big   very
and (these) matches, this kind of matches came in a really big box.

'ola   e   nigi   no'ona   alata   i   na'o.   na'a-nga
thing   SRP(it)   arrive   DEI   time   LOC   before   so then
(It was) something that came in the old days. So then

ngai   e   furi-a   mola   nga   maai-'ola   a-i   i   maamaa-na   no'ona
FP(him)   SRP(he)   cut-it   only   ART   section-thing   POSS-it   LOC   top-its   DEM
he cut off a piece of it, at the top end

ma   masisi   no'ona   'ola   gwa'a   wane   ma   te-'e—
and   match   DEM   thing   even if   man   and   FUT-SRP(he)
And that was a kind of match you—

te-'e   ridi-fi-a   mola   naa   fou.   na'a-nga   maamaa-na   no'o   ngai   no'ona
FUT-SRP(he)   strike-TTS-it only   LOC   stone   so then   top-its   TOP   FP(it)   DEI
you could just strike it on a stone. And the head of one of those

ma   ngai   e   tegela'a   fida'ana   kabi
and   FP(him)   SRP(it)   be strong   like   cartridge
was as hard as a cartridge.

ngai   e—   sufu-tala-i   naa   fee   'efu'efu   la'akau
FP(him)   SRP(he)   drilling-of-it   LOC   piece   'efu'efu   DEM
He—once a hole was drilled in that length of 'efu'efu,

e   kee   sui   ma   ka   kuru-me'eni-a   kau   'ubula-i
SRP(it)   AUX   be finished   and   SRP(he)   insert-TTS-it   DEI   inside-it
then he inserted (the matchhead)

ma   ka   age-a   ka   tegela'a   la'u   tooto'o-la-na   nga   lefu   fa-na
and   SRP(he)   make-it   SRP(it)   be strong   also   matching-of-it   ART   place   for-it
and worked it until it was fast, in just the right place

nga   ladakabi   'a-ni   kee   to'o   a-i   ma   ngai   e   busu   no'o
ART   hammer   INF-it   AUX   hit   LOC-it   and   FP(it)   SRP(it)   burst   PRF
so the hammer would strike it, and it would fire.

nao	hem-i	rukuruku	longo	masisi	bulongo	mifala.	dis-fala	masisi	ia,
so	SRP(he)	search	LOC	match	POSS	us(E)	DEM-ADJ	match	DEM

So then he looked for the kind of matches we used. This kind of match,

dis-fala	masisi	i	kam	rongrongtaem,	samting	long	hem.*	rongrongtaem.
DEM-ADJ	match	SRP(it)	come	long ago	thing	LOC	it	long ago

one that we had long ago, had a special feature. In the old days.

hem-i	kamu	nao	biki	bokis,	ia?	bataa	'eni	bulong	dis-fala	masisi
SRP(it)	come	PRF	big	box	RHET	but	tip	POSS	DEM-ADJ	matches

They came in a big box, right? Anyway, the tip of one of these matches

hem-i	gar-em	red-fala	samting	long	hem.	hem	nao	bilesi	fo	laeti*
SRP(it)	have-TTS	red-ADJ	thing	LOC	it	FP(it)	TOP	place	for	ignite

had a red thing on it. That was the place that ignited.

dis-fala	masisi	ia	nomata	siton	safosi	thei	sikras-em	long	hemu
DEM-ADJ	match	DEM	even	stone	if	SRP(they)	strike-TTS	LOC	it

This kind of match was one where, even if you struck it on a stone,

baebae	hem-i	save	laeti	nomoa.	nao	hem-i	kat-em	nao
FUT	SRP(it)	MOD	ignite	only	so	SRP(he)	cut-TTS	PRF

it would ignite. So he cut (one).

kat-em	finis	hem-i	mek-em	sumolo-fala	holo
cut-TTS	be complete	SRP(he)	make-TTS	small-ADJ	hole

He cut it and then he made a small hole.

holo	hem-i	fo—	long	borom	bulong	dis-fala	bambu
hole	SRP(it)	for	LOC	bottom	POSS	DEM-ADJ	bamboo

This hole was for—it was on the base of this bamboo.

hem-i	mek-em	finis	stik-im	stik-im	googo	fit-im
SRP(he)	make-TTS	be complete	insert-TTS	insert-TTS	until	fit-TTS

He made it, drilled it, drilled it until (it) was the size of

dis-fala	masisi	ia.	taem	hem-i	finis	oraeti	hem-i	put-umu	long
DEM-ADJ	match	DEM	when	SRP(he)	be finished	then	SRP(he)	put-TTS	LOC

that match. When he finished then he put it (the match head)

insaet	long	sumol-fala	holo	ia
inside	LOC	small-ADJ	hole	DEM

into this little hole.

nao	hem-i	mek-em	i	strong	·	tuu	fo	i	strong	lelebeti
then	SRP(he)	CAUS-TTS	SRP(it)	be strong		too	INF	SRP(it)	be strong	slightly

Then he made it fast too, to be relatively fixed.

*Note the verbless clauses in these prepositional and equational sentences; the equational sentence uses the FP, not SRP.

SECOND EPISODE

sui	ma	ka	me'e	iri-a	a-gu,	ka	fa'a-nanau-nau
then	and	SRP(he)	AUX	tell-TTS	LOC-me	SRP(he)	CAUS-learn-me

Then he briefed me, intructed me

'oo	ula	lo'oo,	mo-o	sia	wawadiri
SRP(you)	stand	DEI	and-SRP(you)	NEG	move around

"You stand here, and don't move.

'oo	sia	wawadiri	la'u.	'oo	sia	de'e	la'u
SRP(you)	NEG	move around	more	SRP(you)	NEG	crash around	more

Don't move any more. Don't make any noise in the undergrowth.

ula,	'oo	to'oru	wado,	ma	maa-mu	ka	tooto'o	fa-mu
stand	SRP(you)	sit	ground	and	eye-you	SRP(it)	be fixed	on-you

Stand still, or sit down, and keep an eye on yourself."

nau	ku	to'oru	wado	ku	nagwa	no'o
FP(me)	SRP(I)	sit	ground	SRP(I)	be hidden	PRF

I sat down, concealed.

ku	'ame	'asu	no'o,	to'oru	aloalo	no'o.	ngaia	ka	ango	no'o
SRP(I)	NEG	move	PRF	sit	quietly	PRF	FP(him)	SRP(he)	crawl	PRF

I didn't move around, just sat quietly. He crawled off.

e	ango	no'o,	ango,	ma	ka	ango	ma	ka	baba	no'o
SRP(he)	crawl	PRF	crawl	and	SRP(he)	crawl	and	SRP(he)	duck down	PRF

He crawled, crawled, crawled, and then ducked down,

ma	ka	ango	no'o
and	SRP(he)	crawl	PRF

and then crawled on.

leeleka,	leeleka,	ma	ka	ria-si-a	rua	boo,	rua	boo	te'efou	lo'oo
go-go	go-go	and	SRP(he)	see-TTS-it	two	pig	two	pig	together	DEI

Went and went, and he saw two pigs, two pigs together there.

e	ria-si-a	sui,	ma	ngaia	ka	to'oru	no'o	i	wado
SRP(he)	see-TTS-it	be finished	and	FP(him)	SRP(he)	sit	PRF	LOC	ground

He saw them, and he sat down.

nao,	destaem	hem-i—	hem-i	toko	longo	mi	nao,	tis-im	mi	nao
then	then	SRP(he)	SRP(he)	talk	LOC	me	PRF	teach-TTS	me	PRF

Then he talked to me, instructed me:

iu	stapkwaeti,	iu	no	sekeseke,	iu	no	woowokabaot,
SRP(you)	stay quiet	SRP(you)	NEG	move	SRP(you)	NEG	wander around

"You stay quiet, and don't move around. Don't wander around,

iu	no	borok-em	sam-fala	tirii	i	dae
SRP(you)	NEG	break-TTS	any-ADJ	tree	SRP(it)	be dead

don't crash around in the dry branches.

'anda	iu	no	mekenois	long	'eni	samting.	mi	go,	ia
and	SRP(you)	NEG	make noise	LOC	any	thing	SRP(I)	go	RHET

and don't make any kind of noise. I'm going, OK?"

oraeti,	hem-i	go	nao.	hem-i	go,	hem-i	no	go	i	sitireti
then	SRP(he)	go	PRF	SRP(he)	go	SRP(he)	NEG	go	SRP(it)	be straight

So off he went. He went, but not in a direct way.

bataa	hem-i	go	sulou,	sulou,	sulou
but	SRP(he)	go	slowly	slowly	slowly

But he crept slowly, slowly, slowly.

taem	hem-i	go,	nao—	googo	hem-i	ruk-im	tu-fala	bikibiki
when	SRP(he)	go	then	go-go	SRP(he)	see-TTS	two-ADJ	pig

When he went—then he saw two pigs.

ou,	maewote,	tu-fala	bikibiki	nao.	finisi,	hem-i	sidaon*
oh	EXCL	two-ADJ	pig	PRF	then	SRP(he)	sit

"Hey, there are two pigs." Then he sat down.

*For these older speakers, *sidaon* is used as exactly equivalent to the Kwaio *to'oru*, which carries a range of meanings including 'sit,' 'live,' and 'wait,' a striking case of semantic equivalence.

ngai   e   ria-si-ga,   ma   gila   gila   fanga   no'o   mai
FP(him)   SRP(he)   see-TRS-them   and   FP(them)   SRP(they)   eat   PRF   DEI
He saw them eating, coming in his direction.

la   fanga   no'o   mai,   la   fanga   no'o   mai   naa   go'u
SRP(they)   eat   PRF   DEI   SRP(they)   eat   PRF   DEI   LOC   taro
They were eating, eating, in his direction in the taro (garden).

ngai   e   ria-si-ga   gala   fanga,   rua   boo   la'akau
FP(him)   SRP(he)   see-TRS-them   SRP(they2) eat   two   pig   DEM
He saw the two of them eating, those two pigs

gala   fanga,   gala   fanga,   gala   fanga,   ma   ngai   e
SRP(they2)   eat   SRP(they2) eat   SRP(they2) eat   and   FP(him)   SRP(he)
were eating, eating, eating, and he

to'oru   i   wado   ma   maa-na   ka   to'oto'o,   ka   bubu-ni-ga   mola
sit   LOC   ground   and   eye-him   SRP(it)   be fixed   SRP(he)   stare-TRS-them just
sat on the ground and kept his eye fixed, and just stared at them.

lefu   no'ona   ngai   e   manadai-a,   'a-gala-i   ula   tooto'o,
point   DEM   FP(him)   SRP(he)   think-it   for-SRP(they2) stand   even
What was in his mind was for them to stand in line,

gala   abula   no'o   gala   ula   tooto'o,   kee   sui*
SRP(they2) turn   PRF   SRP(they2) stand even   AUX   be finished
to turn and stand in line, and then

ma   ngai   te-'e   bi'i   'ui-ga
and   FP(him)   FUT-SRP(he) ASP   shoot-them
he would shoot them.

ngai   e   to'oru   aloalo   mola   fa-i
FP(him)   SRP(he)   stay   quietly   just   for-it
He just stayed still waiting for it (to happen).

'ola   e   irito'o-na   mola   'a-ni   'ui-ga   mola,   te'ete'efou,
thing   SRP(he)   try-it   just   INF-SRP(he)   shoot-them   just   together(RED)
What he was trying was to shoot them together,

'a-ni   gala-i   mae   te'ete'efou
INF-SRP(it)   SRP(they2)   die   together(RED)
so they'd die together.

*The common Kwaio *kee sui* in narrative is exactly equivalent to the *googo finis* used twice by Fifi'i in the earlier episode about making the shotgun shell.

taem   hem-i   sidaon,   hem-i   rukuruku   nao
when   srp(he) stay   srp(he) look(RED)   PRF
While he waited, he kept his eyes peeled.

rukuruku   raon-em*   tu-fala   biki,   rukuruku   raon-emu   tu-fala   biki   ia
look(RED)   around-TTS two-ADJ   pig   look(RED)   around-TTS two-ADJ   pig   DEM
Kept his eye on the two pigs, kept his eye on those two pigs.

rukuruku   rukuruku—   tu-fala   biki   ia   tufala   wokabaot,   kaikai,
look(RED)   look(RED)   two-ADJ   pig   DEM   srp(they2)   wander   eat
(He) looked and looked—while those two pigs drifted along, ate,

wokabaot,   kaikai,   wokabaot,   kaikai
wander   eat   wander   eat
drifted along, ate, drifted, ate.

samting   hem-i   raek-emu,   dis-fala   tu-fala   bikibiki   ia
thing   srp(he) want-TTS   DEM-ADJ   two-ADJ   pig   DEM
What he wanted was for those two pigs

fo   i   standap   wankaeni,   'anaa   nara-fala   bikibiki   fo   i   standafu
INF   srp(it) stand   even   and   one-ADJ   pig   INF   srp(it) stand
to stand in line, so one pig was standing

bihaen   long   nara-fala   bikibiki,   bifoa   baebae   hem-i   mek-em   samting
behind   LOC   one-ADJ   pig   before   FUT   srp(he) CAUS-TTS   thing
behind the other, before he made the thing

i   bosita.   sut-im—   sut-imu   dis-fala   bikibiki
srp(it) fire   shoot-TTS   shoot-TTS   DEM-ADJ   pig
fire. To shoot those pigs.

hem-i   wand-em   tu-fala   bikibiki   ia   fo   dae   wantaem,   ia?
srp(he) want-TTS   two-ADJ   pig   DEM   INF   die   at once   RHET
He wanted those two pigs to die at the same time, right?

*Here Fifi'i uses *rukuruku raon-em*, with an intransitive verb followed by a prepositional verb, as he would use the exactly corresponding Kwaio *agaaga (i) suri-a*.

rua   boo   la'akau   gala   riu   kwai-riu,   gala   faafanga   ma
two   pig   DEM   SRP(they2)   pass   back&forth   SRP(they2)   eat(RED)   and
Those two pigs went back and forth,

gala   riiriu   kwai-riu   gala   faafanga   ma   gala
SRP(they2)   pass(RED)   back&forth   SRP(they2)   eat(RED)   and   SRP(they2)
ate and wandered back and forth, ate and

riiriu   kwai-riu.   kee   sui   ma   gala   ula,   gala   kee
pass(RED)   back&forth   AUX   be finished   and   SRP(they2)   stand   SRP(they2)   AUX
wandered back and forth. And then the two of them stood, they

ula   tooto'o   no'o
stand   even   PRF
stood in line with one another.

gala   ula   gala   kee   tooto'o   no'o   ma   ngai   e   bi'i
SRP(they2)   stand   SRP(they2)   AUX   even   PRF   and   FP(him)   SRP(he)   ASP
The two of them stood in line, and then he

kwala-nge'e-ni-ga   'ani-a   kwanga   me-e   bi'i   fele   naa   fe'ekete   lofo'u
aim-TTS-them   with-it   gun   and-SRP(he)   ASP   squeeze   LOC   trigger   DEM
took aim at them with his gun, and squeezed the trigger,

ma   kwanga   ka   busu   no'o
and   gun   SRP(it)   fire   PRF
and the gun fired.

oraet,	hem-i	rukuruku,	rukuruku,	tu-fala	bikibiki	ia
then	SRP(he)	look(RED)	look(RED)	two-ADJ	pig	DEM

So then he watched and watched and watched, and these two pigs

wokabaot,	kaikai,	wokabaot,	kaikai,	wokabaot,	kaikai
wander	eat	wander	eat	wander	eat

wandered around, eating.

kaikai-em	taro	ia,	goo-go	hem-i	ruku	gut-fala	nao
eat-TTS	taro	DEM	go-go	SRP(he)	look	well-ADJ	PRF

Ate that taro—and then he watched carefully.

hem-i	sidaon.	hem-i	sidaon	nao	bata	hem-i	redi	longo	kwanga	nao
SRP(he)	stay	SRP(he)	wait	PRF	but	SRP(he)	be ready	LOC	gun	PRF

He waited. He waited, but with his gun ready.

mek-em	fo	suti	nao.	rukuruku,	rukuruku,	rukuruku,
CAUS-TTS	INF	shoot	PRF	look(RED)	look(RED)	look(RED)

Ready to shoot. Watched and watched and watched until

tu-fala	bikibiki	googo*	stane	wanekaen	nao
two-ADJ	pig	AUX	stand	in line	PRF

the two pigs were in line with one another.

tufala-i	stane	wankaen,	hem-i	ruku	gutu-fala	long	tufala	nao
SRP(they2)	stand	in line	SRP(he)	look	well-ADJ	LOC	them	PRF

The two stood in line, and he took careful aim at them.

taem	bulong	hem	hem-i	sut-im	tufala	nao
time	POSS	him	SRP(he)	shoot-TTS	them2	PRF

When the time came he shot them both.

dis-fala	kwanga	hem-i	bosita
DEM-ADJ	gun	SRP(it)	fire

That gun fired.

*The *googo* is used here as an auxiliary equivalent to Kwaio *kee*.

THIRD EPISODE: KWALAFANE'IA

Tomu Niuboo,   ma   inau,   ma   wane   la   fa'a-lata-a   la   'Eribe'u
Tomu Niuboo   and   FP(me) and   man   SRP(they) CAUS-be named-it   ART   'Eribe'u
Tomu Niuboo, I, and a man named 'Eribe'u

na'a   miru   leka,   miru   leka   fa-na   kwaikwailo-ngari
so   SRP(we3E) go   SRP(we3E) go   for-it   hunt-canarium nuts
went to gather canarium nuts.

kwaikailo-ngari   'ubu-na   nga   ano   loko'u   i   Gela
hunt-canarium nuts   inside-it   ART   forest   DEM   LOC   Gela
Hunt for canarium nuts in the bush there on Gela.

miru   kwaikwailo-ngari   sui   ma   miru   so'oso'o-fi-a   ngari   lo'oo,
SRP(we3E) hunt-nuts   then   and   SRP(we3E) pick up-TRS-it   nut   DEM
We hunted for canarium nuts and then we picked up those nuts

miru-a   age-a   karisi   fa-i,   miru   ngari-a,   me'e   nigi   'aa'ae-na
SRP(we3E)   make-it   leaf   for it   SRP(we3E) take-it   AUX   arrive base-it
and we made a leaf (container) for them, we took them, and got to the foot

fou   lo   'a-miru   bi'i   to'oru,   'a-meru-i   bi'i
rock   DEM   for-SRP(we3E)   ASP   sit   for-SRP(we3E)   ASP
of the rock there, in order to sit down and

bakabaka-a   ngari   la'akau.   miru   longo   kau,   ma   'erofileni   e
crack(RED)-it   nut   DEM   SRP(we3E) listen   DEI   and   airplane   SRP(it)
crack those nuts. We listened, and an airplane was

ruururuu   no'o   mai.   la   Niuboo   wane   ngai   ne-'e   su'a   la'a   a-i   i
hum   PRF   DEI   ART   Niuboo   man   FP(him)   TOP-SRP(he) know   also   LOC-it LOC
humming toward us. Niuboo, a man who knew

suri-a   ngaia   wane   e   nana'i   i   Gavutu   lo'oo,   ngai   e
around-it   FP(him)   man   SRP(he)   stay   LOC   Gavutu   DEM   FP(him)   SRP(he)
about it, he being a man who was staying at Gavutu there,

'ilaba'a: ou,   nga   'erofileni   e   ruuruu   mai,
say thus   oh   ART   airplane   SRP(it)   hum   DEI
said "Oh, the plane that's coming

nga   'enemii   lo'o   no'o,   suri-a   ruuruu-nga   e   ori   matari*
ART   enemy   DEM   TOP   because-it   hum-NOM   SRP(it)   return   differently
is the enemy, because the sound is different.

*"Return differently" (implying coming back by a different path) is a Kwaio metaphor
for 'be different.'

nao	mifala,	tiri-fala	nomoa,	go,	go	long	soa.	mifala		go	faend-em	nate,	ia?
then	FP(weE)	three-ADJ	only	go	go	LOC	shore	SRP(weE)		go	find-TRS	nut	RHET

So we, just us three, went to the shore. We went to hunt for canarium nuts.

googo	finis		nao	mifala	teke	nate	ia	kam*	nao,	mifala	sidaon
AUX	be finished		PRF	SRP(weE)	take	nut	DEM	DEI	PRF	SRP(weE)	sit

And then we took those nuts.

weit-em	olketa	siton	nao,	olketa	hamar-imu	nate	long	hem	ia,
with-TRS	PLU	stone	PRF	SRP(they)	pound-TRS	nut	with	it	DEI

We sat down with stones, the kind they pound nuts with,

mifala	wante	hamar-im	nate	ia,	bulek-em	fo	nate	nomoa
SRP(weE)	want	pound-TRS	nut	DEM	break-TRS	for	nut	only

so we could pound the nuts, to break them and get the meat.

mifala	seke	nao	ma	'erofilen	i	mekenois	kamu*	nao
SRP(weE)	check	PRF	and	airplane	SRP(it)	sound	DEI	PRF

We checked and a plane was making a noise in our direction.

mifala	see,	ee,	wanem?	ating	.bulong	Diapan	nao,	ia?†
SRP(weE)	say	EXCL	what	probably	POSS	Japan	TOP	RHET

We said, "Hey, what's that?" "It's probably Japanese."

nara-fala	mane	ia	hem-i	gogo	wet-em	mitufala	ia
other-ADJ	man	DEM	SRP(he)	go(RED)	with-TRS	us2(E)	DEM

That was another man who had gone with the two of us.

ou,	ating	i	mekenois	mifala	hir-em	olsemu	'erofileni
oh	probably	SRP(it)	sound	SRP(weE)	hear-TRS	like	airplane

"Oh, it seems to sound like the plane

hem-i	kam	iastade,	ia?	saond	bulong	hem	i	olsem	hem	nao
SRP(it)	come	yesterday	RHET	sound	POSS	it	SRP(it)	be like	it	PRF

that came yesterday. The sound is the same."

*For the common Oceanic directionals 'hither' and 'thither' (in Kwaio *mai* and *kau*), Pidgin uses *kam* and *go*. In Bislama and Tok Pisin, these directionals are rendered with serial clauses, *i kam* and *i go*.

†This clause is a verbless prepositional phrase, with an implied subject.

The next section immediately follows in Kwaio narrative and is slightly separated in Pidgin narrative.

nga	rua	'efofeleni	ngaa	lofo'u	i	Gavutu	loko'u,	rua	wasimani	lofo'u	a-i
ART	two	airplane	FP(it)	DEI	LOC	Gavutu	DEM	two	sentry	there	LOC-

The two planes that were there at Gavutu, the two patrol planes there—

ai	ngaai*	sikis	koloko	mone	ma	ka	'aoto
one	other	six	o'clock	morning	and	SRP(it)	out

one of them would take off at 6:00 in the morning.

leeleka	e	laalaone	'ubu-na	nga	gani	lo'oo,	tala'ina,	leeleka	sikis
then	SRP(it)	circle	inside-it	ART	day	DEM	today	until	six

Then it would circle around during the day, on a day—say today—until six

koloko	ma	ka	me'e	sifo,	te-'e†	me'e	sifo
o'clock	and	SRP(it)	AUX	descend	FUT-SRP(it)	AUX	descend

o'clock and then it would land, would go ahead and land.

ma	nga	ai	lofo'u	e	naana'i	e	du'a-a	no'o
and	ART	one	DEM	SRP(it)	stay	SRP(it)	replace-it	PRF

And the one that had stayed there would take its place.

e	eta	naa	sikis	koloko	laulafi	lo'oo,	e	leka	fa-na
SRP(it)	begin	LOC	six	o'clock	evening	DEM	SRP(it)	go	to-it

It would start at six in the evening, and would go until

nga	sikis	koloko	mone,	te-'e	me'e	sifo	la'u
ART	six	o'clock	morning	FUT-SRP(it)	AUX	descend	again

six in the morning, and then it would land again.

gala	sensi	'i-no'ona
SRP(they2)	swap	thusly

The two of them would change places like that.

*Note here that Kwalafane'ia uses in Kwaio a rhetorical style exactly the same as that used by Fifi'i in Pidgin in describing the two pigs in the garden; to describe the first of a pair of entities, one says "the other one" (Kwaio "one other" and Pidgin *nara-wan*).

†Here and in the next sentence the "future marker" clearly marks irrealis (or nonaccomplished) mode.

tu-fala   wasimane   long Gafutu   ia,   wan-fala   hem-i   go   nao, ia?
two-ADJ   sentry   LOC   Gavutu   DEM   one-ADJ   SRP(it) go   PRF   RHET
One of the two patrol planes from Gavutu was away, right?

hem-i   state   long sikis-kolok   mone   nao, hem-i   waka   raon   nao, longo
SRP(it) start   LOC   6:00   morning   PRF   SRP(it) work   around   PRF   LOC
It took off at 6:00 AM, and patrolled around at

Diafosi   nao.   googo   nara   sikesiki   i   go   moa   longo   'ifiningi
Diafosi   PRF   then   other "section"   SRP(it) go   again LOC   evening
Diafosi (?). Then the other crew went again in the evening,

baebae*   hem-i   kam   nao   na   nara-fala   hem-i   sensi   moa
FUT   SRP(it) come   PRF   and   other-ADJ   SRP(it) swap   again
then it would come back and the other would change with it again.

*Here, as in the Kwaio, the "future marker" indicates irrealis or nonaccomplished mode.

References Cited

References Cited

Abbott, J. H. M. 1908. *The South Seas (Melanesia)*. London: Adam and Charles Black.

Adams, R. 1984. *In the Land of Strangers: A Century of European Contact with Tanna, 1774–1874*. Pacific Research Monographs 9. Canberra: Australian National University.

Alexander, G. 1927. *From the Middle Temple to the South Seas*. London: John Murray.

Anderson, R. 1983. "A Language Acquisition Interpretation of Pidginization and Creolization," in R. Anderson, ed., *Pidginization and Creolization as Language Acquisition*. Rowley, Mass.: Newbury House.

Anderson, S. R., and S. Chung. 1977. "On Grammatical Relations and Clause Structure in Verb-Initial Languages," in P. Cole and J. M. Sadock, eds., *Syntax and Semantics*, Vol. 8: *Grammatical Relations*. New York: Academic Press.

Bailey, B. 1966. *Jamaican Creole Syntax*. Cambridge: Cambridge University Press.

Beaune, G. 1894. *La Terra australe inconnue: onze croisières aux Nouvelles-Hébrides*. Lyon: Delhomme and Briguet.

Bickerton, D. 1976. "Pidgin and Creole Studies," *Annual Review of Anthropology* 5: 169–93.

———. 1977. "Pidginization and Creolization: Language Acquisition and Language Universals," in A. Valdman, ed., *Pidgin and Creole Linguistics*, pp. 49–69. Bloomington: University of Indiana Press.

———. 1981. *Roots of Language*. Ann Arbor, Mich.: Karoma Press.

———. 1984. "The Language Bioprogram Hypothesis," *Brain and Behavior Sciences* 7: 173–221.

Bingham, H. 1866. *Story of the Morning Star, the Children's Missionary Vessel*. Boston: American Board of Commissioners for Foreign Missions.

Blust, R. 1984. "Malaita-Micronesian: An Eastern Oceanic Subgroup?," *Journal of the Polynesian Society* 93: 99–140.

Bradshaw, J. 1979. "Causative Serial Constructions and Word Order Changes in Papua New Guinea." Paper presented at the annual meeting of the Linguistic Society of America.

Brenchley, J. L. 1873. *Jottings during the Cruise of H.M.S. Curacoa among the South Sea Islands in 1865*. London: Longmans, Green.

Bridge, R. C. 1886. "Cruises in Melanesia, Micronesia and Western Polynesia in 1882, 1883 and 1884, and Visits to New Guinea and the Lousiades in 1884 and 1885," *Proceedings, Royal Geographical Society and Monthly Record of Geography*.

Burnett, F. 1910. *Through Polynesia and Papua: Wanderings with a Camera in Southern Seas*. London: G. Bell and Sons.

Camden, W. 1977. *A Descriptive Dictionary Bislama to English*. Vila, Vanuatu: Maropa Press.

———. 1979. "Parallels in Structure of Lexicon and Syntax Between New Hebrides Bislama and the South Santo Language as Spoken at Tangoa," in *Papers in Pidgin and Creole Linguistics* 2. Pacific Linguistics A-57. Canberra: Australian National University.

Cayley-Webster, H. 1898. *Through New Guinea and the Cannibal Countries*. London: T. Fisher Unwin.

Charpentier, J.-M. 1979. *Le Bislama: Pidgin des Nouvelles-Hébrides*. Paris: SELAF.

Churchill, W. 1911. *Beach-la-Mar: The Jargon or Trade Speech of the Western Pacific*. Washington, D.C.: Carnegie Institution.

Clark, R. 1977. *In Search of Beach-la-Mar: Historical Relations among Pacific Pidgins and Creoles*. Working Papers, in Anthropology, Archaeology, Linguistics, Maori Studies 48. Auckland: University of Auckland.

———. 1979. "In Search of Beach-la-Mar: Towards a History of Pacific Pidgin English," *Te Reo* 22/23: 3–66.

———. 1983. "Social Contexts of Early South Pacific Pidgins," in E. Woolford and W. Washabaugh, eds., *The Social Context of Creolization*. Ann Arbor, Mich.: Karoma Press.

Codrington, R. H. 1885. *The Melanesian Languages*. Oxford: Clarendon Press.

Collins, J. 1980. *Ambonese Malay and Creolization Theory*. Kuala Lumpur: Dewan Bahasa Dan Pustaka Kementerian Pelajaran Malaysia.

Collinson, C. 1926. *Life and Laughter 'Midst the Cannibals*. London: Hurst and Blackett.

Comrie, B. 1981. *Language Universals and Linguistic Typology: Syntax and Morphology*. Oxford: Basil Blackwell.

Coote, W. 1882. *Wanderings, South and East*. London: Sampson Low, Marston.

Corne, C. 1981. "A Re-Evaluation of the Predicate in Ile-de-France Creole," in P. Muysken, ed., *Generative Studies on Creole Languages*. Dordrecht: Foris.

Corris, P. 1970. "Kwaisulia of Adagege," in J. W. Davidson and D. Scarr, eds., *Pacific Islands Portraits*. Canberra: Australian National University Press.

———. 1973. *Passage, Port and Plantation: A History of Solomon Islands Labour Migration, 1870–1914*. Melbourne: University of Melbourne Press.

Cromar, J. 1935. *Jock of the Islands: Early Days in the South Seas*. London: Faber and Faber.

Crowley, T. 1984. "Serial Verbs in Paamese," paper presented at Fourth International Conference on Austronesian Linguistics, Suva.

Damon. 1861. *Morning Star Papers*. Honolulu: Hawaiian Missionary Society.

Dana, R. H. 1840. *Two Years Before the Mast*. New York: Harper.

Deck, Norman. 1934. *Grammar of the Language Spoken by the Kwara'ae People of Mala, British Solomon Islands*. Journal of the Polynesian Society reprint no. 5, from vols. 42–43.

Deck, Northcote. 1910. "Across Malaita," South Sea Evangelical Mission Pastoral Letter, March 1910.

Dutton, T. 1980. *Queensland Canefields English of the Late Nineteenth Century*. Pacific Linguistics D-29. Canberra: Australian National University.

Erskine, J. E. 1853. *Journal of a Cruise among the Islands of the Western Pacific*. London: J. Murray.

Fatnowna, O. N. n.d. *Malaita and Mackay: A Family and a People*. Sydney: Angus and Robertson, in press.

Fillmore, C. 1968. "The Case for Case," in E. Bach and R. Harms, eds., *Universals in Linguistic Theory*. New York: Holt, Rinehart, Winston.

Geraghty, P. 1983. *The History of the Fijian Languages*. Honolulu: University of Hawaii Press.

Giles, W. E. 1968. *A Cruize in a Queensland Labour Vessel to the South Seas*. Ed. D. Scarr. Pacific History Series 1. Canberra: Australian National University Press.

Givón, T. 1984. *Syntax: A Functional-Typological Introduction*. Vol. 1. Philadelphia: John Benjamins.

Goodman, M. 1985. Review of D. Bickerton, 'Roots of Language,' *International Journal of American Linguistics* 51/1: 109–37.

Grace, G. 1955. "Subgrouping of Malayo-Polynesian: A Report of Tentative Findings," *American Anthropologist* 57: 337–39.

———. 1971. "Languages of the New Hebrides and Solomon Islands," in T. E. Sebeok, ed., *Current Trends in Linguistics*, Vol. 8: *Linguistics in Oceania*. The Hague: Mouton.

———. 1976. Review of R. C. Green and M. Kelly, eds., 'Studies in Oceanic Culture History,' *Journal of the Polynesian Society* 85: 103–47.

———. 1981. "Indirect Inheritance and the Aberrant Melanesian Languages," in J. Hollyman and A. Pawley, eds., *Studies in Pacific Languages and Cultures in Honour of Bruce Biggs*. Auckland: Linguistic Society of New Zealand.

Guiart, J. 1956. *Un Siècle et demi de contacts culturels à Tanna, Nouvelles-Hébrides*. Publications de la Société des Océanistes 5. Paris.

Gulick, L. 1862. "Micronesia," *Nautical Magazine*, 3 parts, April: 169–82; May: 237–45; June: 298–308.

Guy, J. 1974. *Manual of Bichelamar—Manuel de Bichelamar*. Pacific Linguistics C-34. Canberra: Australian National University.

Hall, R. A., Jr. 1943. *Melanesian Pidgin English: Grammar, Texts, Vocabulary*. Baltimore: Linguistic Society of America.

———. 1955. *Hands Off Pidgin English!* Sydney: Pacific Publications.

———. 1966. *Pidgin and Creole Languages.* Ithaca, N.Y.: Cornell University Press.

Hanlon, D. n.d. "Upon a Stone Altar: A History of the Island of Pohnpei to 1890." Honolulu: University of Hawaii Press. Forthcoming.

Harrison, S. P. 1978. "Transitive Marking in Micronesian Languages," in S. A. Wurm and L. Carrington, eds., *Second International Conference on Austronesian Linguistics: Proceedings,* Fascicle 2: 1067–1127. Pacific Linguistics C-61. Canberra: Australian National University.

Hempenstall, P. 1978. *Pacific Islanders under German Rule.* Canberra: Australian National University Press.

Herr, R. A., and A. Rood, eds. 1978. *A Solomons Sojourn: J. E. Phillips' Log of the Makira, 1912–13.* Hobart: Tasmanian Historical Research Association.

Hezel, F. 1983. *The First Taint of Civilization: A History of the Caroline and Marshall Islands in Pre-Colonial Days, 1521–1885.* Center for Pacific and Asian Studies, Pacific Islands Monograph Series, No. 1. Honolulu: University of Hawaii Press.

Hocart, A. M. 1922. "The Cult of the Dead in Eddystone of the Solomons," *Journal of the Royal Anthropological Institute* 52: 71–112.

———. 1925. "Medicine and Witchcraft in Eddystone of the Solomons," *Journal of the Royal Anthropological Institute* 55: 229–70.

———. 1931. "Warfare in Eddystone of the Solomon Islands," *Journal of the Royal Anthropological Institute* 61: 301–24.

———. 1937. "Fishing in Eddystone Island," *Journal of the Royal Anthropological Institute* 67: 33–41.

Horrocks, C. C. 1878. Report on Polynesians at Mackay, 13 August 1878. Letter 3074. COL/A265, Queensland State Archives, Brisbane.

Howard, A. 1970. *Becoming a Rotuman.* New York: Teachers College Press, Columbia University.

Howe, K. R. 1977. *The Loyalty Islands: A History of Culture Contacts, 1840–1900.* Honolulu: University of Hawaii Press.

———. 1978. "Tourists, Sailors and Labourers: A Survey of Early Labour Recruiting in Southern Melanesia," *Journal of Pacific History* 13: 22–35.

Jacomb, E. 1914. *France and England in the New Hebrides.* Melbourne: George Robertson.

Janson, T. 1984. "Articles and Plural Formation in Creoles: Change and Universals," *Lingua* 64: 291–323.

Jarman, R. 1838. *Journal of a Voyage to the South Seas in the "Japan".* London: Longman and Tilt.

Jones, J. D. 1861. *Life and Adventure in the South Pacific, by a Roving Printer.* New York: Harper (orig. published anon.).

Jourdan, C. 1985. "Sapos Iumi Mitim Iumi: The Social Context of Creolization in the Solomon Islands," Ph.D. thesis. Australian National University.

———. 1986. "Creolization, Nativization or Substrate Influences: What Is Happening to Bae in Solomon Islands Pijin," in S. Romaine et al., *Papers in Pidgin and Creole Linguistics* 4. Pacific Linguistics A-72. Canberra: Australian National University.

Keesing, R. 1978. "Politico-Religious Movements and Anti-Colonialism on Malaita: Maasina Rule in Historical Perspective," *Oceania*, 2 parts, 48: 241–61; 49: 46–73.

———. 1985. *Kwaio Grammar*. Pacific Linguistics B-88. Canberra: Australian National University.

———. 1986. "Subject Pronouns and Tense-Marking in Southeast Solomonic Languages and Solomons Pijin: Grounds for Substratomania?," in S. Romaine et al., *Papers in Pidgin and Creole Linguistics* 4. Pacific Linguistics A-72. Canberra: Australian National University.

———. 1987. "Pijin Calquing on Kwaio: A Test Case," in D. Laycock and W. Winter, eds., *A World of Language: Festschrift for Prof. S. A. Wurm.* Pacific Linguistics C-100. Canberra: Australian National University.

———. n.d.1. "Solomons Pijin and the Malaita Languages: Kwaio Grammar and Pijin Grammar." Manuscript, Dept. of Anthropology, Australian National University, 1983.

———. n.d.2. "Solomons Pijin Pronouns and the Oceanic Substrate." Manuscript, Dept. of Anthropology, Australian National University, 1984.

———. n.d.3. "'Fella' in Nineteenth Century Pacific Pidgin." Unpublished manuscript, 1987.

Keesing, R., and P. Corris. 1980. *Lightning Meets the West Wind: The Malaita Massacre*. Melbourne: Oxford University Press.

Keesing, R. M., and J. Fifi'i. 1969. "Kwaio Word Tabooing in Its Cultural Context," *Journal of the Polynesian Society* 78: 154–77.

Lamont, E. H. 1867. *Wild Life Among the Pacific Islanders*. London: Hurst and Beckett.

Lanyon-Orgill, P. A. 1969. *The Language of Eddystone Island*. Stanley, Perthshire: Crichton Press.

Lee, I. 1920. *Captain Bligh's Second Voyage to the South Seas*. London: Longman's, Green.

Levy, R. 1980. "Languages of the Southeast Solomon Islands and the Reconstruction of Proto-Eastern-Oceanic," in P. B. Naylor, *Austronesian Studies: Papers of the Second Eastern Conference on Austronesian Linguistics*. Michigan Papers on South and Southeast Asia. Ann Arbor: University of Michigan. Paperback ed.

Lichtenberk, F. 1984. *To'aba'ita Language of Malaita*. Working Papers in Anthropology, Archaeology, Linguistics, Maori Studies 65. Auckland: University of Auckland.

London, J. 1909. "Beche de Mer English," *The Contemporary Review* 96 (Sept.): 359–64.

Lynch, J. 1973. "Verbal Aspects of Possession in Melanesian Languages," *Oceanic Linguistics* 12: 69–102.

———. 1981. "Melanesian Diversity and Polynesian Homogeneity: The Other Side of the Coin," *Oceanic Linguistics* 20: 95–130.

————. 1982. "South-west Tanna Grammar Outline and Vocabulary," in J. Lynch, ed., *Papers in the Linguistics of Melanesia* 4. Pacific Linguistics A-64. Canberra: Australian National University.

————. 1983. "Towards a Theory of the Origin of the Oceanic Possessive Constructions," in A. Halim, L. Carrington, and S. A. Wurm, eds., *Papers from the Third International Conference of Austronesian Linguistics*. Pacific Linguistics C-74. Canberra: Australian National University.

Lynch, J., and A. Capell. 1983. "Sie Grammar Outline," in J. Lynch, ed., *Studies in the Languages of Erromango*. Pacific Linguistics C-79. Canberra: Australian National University.

Lynch, J., and D. Tryon. 1985. "Central-Eastern Oceanic: A Subgrouping Hypothesis," in A. Pawley and L. Carrington, eds., *Austronesian Linguistics at the 15th Pacific Science Congress*. Pacific Linguistics C-88. Canberra: Australian National University.

MacCallum, T. M. 1934. *Adrift in the South Seas, Including Adventures with Robert Louis Stevenson*. Los Angeles: Wetzel.

MacDonald, B. 1982. *Cinderellas of the Empire: Towards a History of Kiribati and Tuvalu*. Canberra: Australian National University Press.

McFarlane, S. 1873. *The Story of the Lifu Mission*. London: James Nisbet.

McLaren, J. 1923. *My Odyssey: South Seas Adventures*. London: Ernest Benn. (2d ed. published 1946.

Mann, W. T. 1948. *Ant Hill Odyssey*. Boston: Little, Brown.

Markham, A. H. 1873. *The Cruise of the Rosario amongst the New Hebrides and Santa Cruz Islands*. London: Sampson Low, Marston.

Moore, C. 1986. *Kanaka: A History of Melanesian Mackay*. Port Moresby: Institute of Papua New Guinea Studies and University of Papua New Guinea Press.

Moresby, J. 1876. *Discoveries and Surveys in New Guinea and the d'Entrecasteaux Islands*. London: John Murray.

Mosel, U. 1980. *Tolai and Tok Pisin: The Influence of the Substratum on the Development of New Guinea Pidgin*. Pacific Linguistics B-73. Canberra: Australian National University.

Mosel, U., and P. Mühlhäusler. 1982. "New Evidence for a Samoan Origin of Tok Pisin," *Journal of Pacific History* 17/3–4: 166–75.

Moses, J. A. 1973. "The Coolie Labour Question and German Colonial Policy in Samoa, 1900–1914," *Journal of Pacific History* 8: 101–24.

Moss, F. J. 1889. *Through Atolls and Islands in the Great South Seas*. London: Sampson Low, Marston.

Mufwene, S. S. 1986. "The Universalist and Substrate Hypotheses Complement One Another," in P. Muysken and N. Smith, eds., *Substrate Versus Universals in Creole Genesis*. Amsterdam: John Benjamins.

Mühlhäusler, P. 1976. "Samoan Plantation Pidgin English and the Origin of New Guinea Pidgin: An Introduction," *Journal of Pacific History* 11/2: 122–25.

————. 1978a. "Samoan Plantation Pidgin English and the Origin of New

Guinea Pidgin," in *Papers in Pidgin and Creole Linguistics* 1. Pacific Linguistics A-54. Canberra: Australian National University.

———. 1978b. "Papuan Pidgin English Rediscovered," in S. Wurm and L. Carrington, eds., *Proceedings of the Second International Conference on Austronesian Linguistics*, Fascicle 2: 1377–1446. Pacific Linguistics C-61. Canberra: Australian National University.

———. 1980. "Structural Expansion and the Process of Creolization," in A. Valdman and A. Highfield, eds., *Theoretical Orientations in Creole Studies*. New York: Academic Press.

———. 1981. "The Development of the Category of Number in Tok Pisin," in P. Muysken, ed., *Generative Studies on Creole Languages*. Dordrecht: Foris.

———. 1985a. "External History of Tok Pisin," in S. Wurm and P. Mühlhäusler, eds., *Handbook of Tok Pisin (New Guinea Pidgin)*. Pacific Linguistics C-70. Canberra: Australian National University.

———. 1985b. "Internal Development of Tok Pisin," in S. Wurm and P. Mühlhäusler, eds., *Handbook of Tok Pisin (New Guinea Pidgin)*. Pacific Linguistics C-70. Canberra: Australian National University.

———. 1986. *Pidgin and Creole Linguistics*. Oxford: Basil Blackwell.

———. n.d.1. "Queensland Kanaka English and Its Place Among the Pidgin Englishes of the Southwestern Pacific." Unpublished manuscript.

———. n.d.2. "Nature and Nurture in the Development of Pidgin and Creole Languages." Paper presented at the Symposium on Pidgin and Creole Languages, University of Duisburg, March 1987.

———. n.d.3. Review of R. B. LePage and A. Tabouret-Keller, *Acts of Identity*, forthcoming in *Lingua*.

Muysken, P., and N. Smith, eds. 1986. *Substrate Versus Universals in Creole Genesis*. Amsterdam: John Benjamins.

Mytinger, C. 1942. *Headhunting in the Solomon Islands Around the Coral Sea*. New York: Macmillan.

O'Connell, J. F. 1972. *A Residence of Eleven Years in New Holland and the Caroline Islands*. Ed. Saul Riesenberg. Canberra: Australian National University Press.

O'Connor, D. S. 1968. "The Problem of Indentured Labour in Samoa Under the Military Administration," *Political Science* 20: 10–27.

Palmer, G. 1871. *Kidnapping in the South Seas*. London: Dawson's.

Paton, G. 1895. *Letters and Sketches from the New Hebrides*. London: Hodder and Stoughton.

Paulding, H. [1831] 1970. *Journal of a Cruise of the USS Dolphin among the Islands of the Pacific Ocean*. Honolulu: University of Hawaii Press.

Pawley, A. 1972. "On the Internal Relationships of Eastern Oceanic Languages," in R. C. Green and M. Kelly, eds., *Studies in Oceanic Culture History*, Vol. 3. *Pacific Anthropological Records* 13: 1–142. Honolulu: Bernice P. Bishop Museum.

———. 1973. "Some Problems in Proto-Oceanic Grammar," *Oceanic Linguistics* 12: 103–88.

———. 1977a. "On Redefining Eastern Oceanic." Unpublished manuscript.

————. 1977b. "The Verb Phrase in Proto-Oceanic." Unpublished manuscript.

————. 1981. "Melanesian Diversity and Polynesian Homogeneity: A Unified Explanation for Language," in J. Hollyman and A. Pawley, eds., *Studies in Pacific Languages and Cultures in Honour of Bruce Biggs*. Auckland: Linguistic Society of New Zealand.

Pawley, A., and L. A. Reid. 1979. "The Evolution of Transitive Constructions in Austronesian," in P. B. Naylor, ed., *Austronesian Studies: Papers of the Second Eastern Conference on Austronesian Languages*. Ann Arbor: University of Michigan.

Pionnier, J.-N. 1913. "Pigeon English ou Bichelamar," *Revue de Linguistique et Philologie Comparée*, 2 parts, 46: 109–17; 184–98.

Pisier, G. 1975. *Les Aventures du Capitaine Cheyne dans l'Archipel Calédonien*. Noumea: Publications de la Société d'Etudes Historiques de la Nouvelle-Caledonie 7.

Price, C. A., with E. Baker. 1976. "Origins of Pacific Island Labourers in Queensland, 1863–1904: A Research Note," *Journal of Pacific History* 11: 106–21.

Queensland. 1885. Report of Royal Commission on Recruiting Polynesian Labourers in New Guinea and Adjacent Islands.

————. 1896. Letter from Governor of Queensland to Commander in Chief, Royal Navy in Pacific, April 15, 1896, transmitting testimony from investigation of attack on boats of labor vessel "Rio Loge" off Malaita forwarded by Immigration Agent, Pacific Island Labour Branch, Queensland, in files of Pacific Manuscript Bureau.

Raabe, H. E. 1927. *Cannibal Nights: The Reminiscences of a Free-Lance Trader*. New York: Payson and Clarke.

Rannie, D. 1912. *My Adventures among South Sea Cannibals*. London: Seely, Service.

Ray, S. 1907. "The Jargon English of the Torres Straits," in *Reports of the Cambridge Anthropological Expedition to Torres Straits*. Cambridge: Cambridge University Press.

————. 1926. *A Comparative Study of the Melanesian Island Languages*. Cambridge: Cambridge University Press.

Rehg, K. L. 1981. *Ponapean Reference Grammar*. Honolulu: University of Hawaii Press.

Reinecke, J. E. 1937. "Marginal Languages: A Sociological Survey of the Creole Languages and Trade Jargons." Ph.D. dissertation, Yale University.

Riesenberg, S. 1972. "Introduction," in J. F. O'Connell, *A Residence of Eleven Years in New Holland and the Caroline Islands*. Ed. Saul Riesenberg. Canberra: Australian National University Press.

Romilly, H. H. 1893. *Letters from the Western Pacific and Mashonaland, 1878–1891*. London: David Nutt.

Ross, M. 1986. "A Genetic Grouping of Oceanic Languages in Bougainville and the Western Solomons," in P. Geraghty, L. Carrington, and S. A. Wurm, eds., *Proceedings of the Fourth International Conference on Austronesian Linguistics*. Pacific Linguistics C-94. Canberra: Australian National University.

Salisbury, R. 1967. "Pidgin's Respectable Past," *New Guinea* 2/2: 44–48.

Sankoff, G. 1977. "Variability and Explanation in Language and Culture: Cliticization in New Guinea Tok Pisin," in M. Saville-Troike, ed., *Linguistics and Anthropology*. Washington, D.C.: Georgetown University Press. [Reprinted in G. Sankoff, *The Social Life of Language*, Philadelphia: University of Pennsylvania Press, 1980.]

Sankoff, G., and P. Brown. 1976. "On the Origin of Syntax in Discourse: A Case Study of Tok Pisin Relatives," *Language* 52: 631–66. [Reprinted in G. Sankoff, ed., *The Social Life of Language*, Philadelphia: University of Pennsylvania Press, 1980.]

Sankoff, G., and S. Laberge. 1973. "On the Acquisition of Native Speakers by a Language," *Kivung* 6: 32–47. [Reprinted in G. Sankoff, *The Social Life of Language*, Philadelphia: University of Pennsylvania Press, 1980.]

Saunders, K. 1979. "Troublesome Servants," *Journal of Pacific History* 14: 168–83.

Scarr, D. 1973. *I the Very Bayonet*. Canberra: Australian National University Press.

Schuchardt, H. [1883] 1980. "Kreolishche Studien V: Uber das Melaneso-englishche," in H. Schuchardt, *Pidgin and Creole Languages*, ed. and tr. G. G. Gilbert. London: Cambridge University Press.

———. [1889] 1980. "Beiträge zür Kenntnis des englishe Kreolisch II: Melaneso-englishches," in H. Schuchardt, *Pidgin and Creole Languages*, ed. and tr. G. G. Gilbert. London: Cambridge University Press.

Seemann, B. [1862] 1973. *Viti: An Account of a Government Mission to the Vitian or Fijian Islands 1860–61*. London: Dawson's.

Shineberg, D. 1967. *They Came for Sandalwood*. Melbourne: University of Melbourne Press.

Siegel, J. 1986. "Pidgin English in Fiji: A Sociolinguistic History," *Pacific Studies* 9: 53–106.

———. 1987. *Language Contact in a Plantation Environment: A Sociolinguistic History of Fiji*. Cambridge: Cambridge University Press.

Silverstein, M. 1972. "Chinook Jargon: Language Contact and the Problem of Multi-level Generative Systems," *Language*, 2 parts, 48: 378–406; 596–625.

Simons, G. 1977. *The Ghaimuta Language of Interior Guadalcanal*. Working Papers for the Language Variation and Limits to Communication Project 8. Ithaca, N.Y.: Cornell University.

———. 1980. "The Verbal Sentence in Arosi: A Reinterpretation of Eastern Oceanic Sentence Structure," in P. B. Naylor, ed., *Austronesian Studies: Papers of the Second Eastern Conference on Austronesian Linguistics*. Ann Arbor: University of Michigan. Paperback ed.

———. 1982. "Word Taboo and Comparative Austronesian Linguistics," in A. Halim, L. Carrington, and S. A. Wurm, eds., *Papers from the Third International Conference on Austronesian Linguistics*, Fascicle 3: *Accent on Variety*. Pacific Linguistics C-76. Canberra: Australian National University.

Simons, L. 1986. "Malaitan Influence on Two Grammatical Particles in Solomon Islands Pijin," in S. Romaine et al., eds., *Papers in Pidgin and Creole Lin-*

guistics, No. 4. Pacific Linguistics A-72. Canberra: Australian National University.

Sohn, H.-M. 1975. *Woleaian Reference Grammar*. PALI Language Texts: Micronesia. Honolulu: University of Hawaii Press.

Steel, R. 1880. *The New Hebrides and Christian Missions*. London: James Nisbet.

Taylor, D. 1971. "Grammatical and Lexical Affinities of Creoles," in D. Hymes, ed., *Pidginization and Creolization of Languages*. Cambridge: Cambridge University Press.

Thomas, J. 1886. *Cannibals and Convicts: Notes of Personal Experience in the Western Pacific*. London: Cassell.

Tryon, D. 1967. *Nengone Grammar*. Pacific Linguistics D-6. Canberra: Australian National University

———. 1968. *Iai Grammar*. Pacific Linguistics D-8. Canberra: Australian National University.

Tryon, D., and B. Hackman. 1983. *Solomon Island Languages: An Internal Classification*. Pacific Linguistics C-72. Canberra: Australian National University.

Wallis, M. D. 1851. *Life in Feejee, or Five Years among the Cannibals, by a Lady*. Boston: William Heath.

Walsh, D. 1978. "Tok Pisin Syntax—the East Austronesian Factor," in *Papers in Pidgin and Creole Linguistics* 1. Pacific Linguistics A-54. Canberra: Australian National University.

Ward, R. G., ed. 1966. *American Activities in the Central Pacific, 1798–1870*. Ridgewood, N.J.: Gregg Press.

Waterhouse, J. H. L. 1949. *A Roviana and English Dictionary*. Rev. by L. M. Jones. Sydney: Epworth.

Watson-Gegeo, K. A. 1986. "The Study of Language Use in Oceania," *Annual Review of Anthropology* 15: 149–62.

Wawn, N. T. [1893] 1973. *The South Sea Islanders and the Queensland Labour Trade, 1875–91*. Ed. with introduction by P. Corris. Pacific History Series 5. Canberra: Australian National University Press.

Wolff, J. 1980. "Verbal Morphology and Verbal Senses in Proto-Austronesian," in P. B. Naylor, ed., *Austronesian Studies: Papers of the Second Eastern Conference on Austronesian Languages*. Ann Arbor: University of Michigan. Paperback ed.

Wood, C. F. 1875. *A Yachting Cruise in the South Seas*. London: H. S. King.

Woodford, C. M. 1890. *A Naturalist among the Headhunters*. London: George Philip and Son.

Young, F. 1926. *Pearls from the Pacific*. Edinburgh: Marshall Bros.

Index

Library of Congress Cataloging-in-Publication Data

Keesing, Roger M., 1935–
    Melanesian Pidgin and the oceanic substrate / Roger M. Keesing.
    p.   cm.
    Bibliography: p.
    Includes index.
    ISBN 0-8047-1450-9 (alk. paper)
    1. Tok Pisin language. 2. Oceanic languages. 3. Substratum
(Linguistics) 4. Languages in contact—Pacific Area. I. Title.
PM7891.Z9N447 1988
427'.9953—dc19   87-37604
                                                      CIP